Sweet Stuff

Sweet Stuff

Karen Barker's American Desserts

PHOTOGRAPHS BY ANN HAWTHORNE

The University of North Carolina Press CHAPEL HILL AND LONDON

Designed by Richard Hendel
Set in Mrs. Eaves and Emmascript
by Eric M. Brooks
Printed in the United Kingdom
by Butler & Tanner

The paper in this book meets the
guidelines for permanence and durability
of the Committee on Production Guidelines
for Book Longevity of the Council on
Library Resources.

Library of Congress
Cataloging-in-Publication Data
Barker, Karen.
Sweet stuff: Karen Barker's American desserts /
Karen Barker; photographs by Ann Hawthorne.
p. cm.
Includes bibliographical references and index.
ISBN 0-8078-2858-0 (cloth: alk. paper)
1. Desserts. 2. Cookery, American. I. Title.
TX773.B345   2004
641.8'6—dc22   2003019371

08 07 06 05 04   5 4 3 2 1

For My Sweeties

Contents

Acknowledgments

Many, many thanks to the following folks:

- My family, for their tremendous love and support and for instilling early on the notion that one of life's greatest joys is sharing food and good times.
- My wonderful staff at Magnolia Grill, past and present, particularly Phoebe Lawless.
- Tammy Carwane, for helping this techno-boob every step of the way with manuscript preparation, and PennySue McKenzie, for assisting in the finishing process.
- Everyone at the University of North Carolina Press, for again proving that smaller and local can be the best way to go. Special thanks to Ron Maner, Rich Hendel, and David Perry.
- Ann Hawthorne, photography genie and all-around fabulous gal.
- Greg Plachta for the great jacket photograph and John Bloedorn and Keith Wenger for the perfect place to take it.
- The many friends and customers at Magnolia Grill, who allow me to share a little sugar on a daily basis.
- All the bakers and food writers whose words I've devoured over the years — knowledge is nothing if it isn't shared. Special thanks to Maida Heatter, whose books always made me feel as if I were baking in the kitchen alongside her.
- My husband Ben, whose encouragement, understanding, inspiration, and love made this book possible and make my life grand. XX.

Sweet Stuff

Introduction

Like many people, I believe that one should always save room for dessert. It has been proven time after time that the appearance of a luscious dessert elicits delight at virtually any table. So what exactly is it about sweet stuff that people find so appealing?

Food in general, and dessert in particular, often seems to generate almost primal memories. Food memories can take you back in time, triggering a wide range of emotions and powerful recollections. From my childhood in Brooklyn, I remember "the box" being brought in the door from Ebinger's Bakery, with a wickedly delicious blackout cake inside. The Capri was the source of fancy Italian butter cookies and my dad's favorite napoleons. Junior's was the standard-bearer in the cheesecake department, and I still occasionally long for those Chock Full o' Nuts coffee shop whole-wheat donuts. For everyday snack consumption there were Ding-Dongs, Ring-Dings, Devil Dogs, Ho-Ho's, Sno-balls, and Twinkies. There was one grandmother's boiled plum dumplings and the other's Russian apple cake. My mother's chocolate pudding pie and my Aunt Eleanor's chocolate cake still rank high on my list of ultimate comfort foods. Summer in the Catskills meant plump cinnamon buns and danish from Katz's. Social activity revolved around the coffee klatch and group barbecues. I mastered the art of making the perfect s'more early on.

I concede that perhaps I have been more profoundly affected than most people by early dessert memories. I had an uncle who was a principal owner of a great old-fashioned Jewish deli in Miami Beach. Like the proverbial "kid in a candy shop," this "girl in a bakery" was allowed to peruse the counters that were positively heaped with an amazing selection of sweets and sample as many items as I wished. Is it possible that my fate was sealed at the age of ten? I knew then and there that I wanted to learn how to produce such wonderful treats myself.

Although I am now a restaurant pastry chef, I am convinced that the best desserts have a direct link to the home kitchen. The sights, aromas, and tastes of honest, simple baking evoke warm sensations of family and a distinct sense of place. Some baking is about appearances, and when done well these dramatic creations are truly an edible art form. My personal baking style is decidedly more down-home in nature. I like to categorize it as traditional American with a twist. American desserts go way beyond the symbolic patriotic notion of linking the proverbial pie with Mom and the "American experience." To some extent the designation as I use it transcends nationality. The culinary melting pot that is often referred to as "American cuisine" has tremendous regional variation and yet retains many common threads. Socially and historically, American dessert-making is based heavily on homemade dishes. Typically, they rely on pure, intense flavors. American desserts are sassy, never muted or shy, and conjure up images of lofty layer cakes, flaky pies, just-churned ice cream, and an array of cobblers, crisps, and cookies. They bring to mind holidays, birthday parties, picnics, and childhood. American desserts are not illusionary creations based on sugar and air. Frankly, I don't care if a cake is lopsided, a pie crust crumbles slightly, or cookies are a bit irregular in shape as long as the item in question tastes delicious. I find homey imperfections charming—they let the diner know that the items are handmade.

For some, baking is an innate, almost intuitive skill. My maternal grandmother turned out an incredible variety of Eastern European baked goods and never followed a written recipe or used a standardized measure. Somehow her half an egg shell of milk mixed with a touch of oil, an egg yolk, a handful of sugar, and a juice glass of flour materialized into delicious, flaky cookies. Her substantial repertoire was kept in her head, and she claimed that baking was something a girl just learned to do in her day. In reality what usually happened was that from a very early age children were trained, standing side by side next to an experienced baker (usually an elder member of the clan), to faithfully reproduce the family favorites. If you have not developed baking skills by osmosis, fear not: knowledge can be acquired and techniques can be learned. The most important factor in successful baking, for professional and home bakers alike, is working with a great recipe.

I would like to think that I follow in my grandmother's footsteps of being a natural baker, but I greatly value the ever expanding assemblage of recipes that I've developed and collected over the years. What I have gathered in these pages is a compilation of favorites that I go back to time and time again. Many of the basics are components that show up in any number of dessert variations. A few great recipes can become the backbone to a much broader repertoire of desserts. These desserts are not groundbreaking—they are new riffs on old themes—but they all have one thing in common: they're based on proven recipes that can easily be executed by the home cook. This is not a Magnolia Grill dessert book, although many of the recipes have appeared on Grill menus. Some recipes are adaptations of family favorites. The collection also includes variations of traditional American standards that are given my own personal stamp. These desserts are equally at home at VIP parties, informal barbecues, and bake-sale fundraisers. These American desserts are guaranteed to make people smile.

I bake professionally, but there is not an item I make in my restaurant kitchen that can't be fully rendered at home. Many people are skeptical of cookbooks written by chefs. In some cases the recipes are simplified to the point where they are not representative of the author's true cooking style. In others, the difficulty and length of the preparations make it unlikely that the average home cook will actually tackle the recipes. I have tried to create a grouping of recipes that is simultaneously inspiring and doable. My desserts do not rely on advanced techniques, specialized equipment, or hard-to-find ingredients. Within each recipe I offer visual clues (telling you how to judge consistency or doneness by appearance, for example) and provide professional tips. In some instances, when it seemed that information about procedures or ingredients beyond what was needed in a specific recipe might be helpful, I have provided such details in a sidebar.

Most of the recipes come with suggested serving accompaniments. A basic recipe can be enhanced with the preparation of a sauce, an ice cream, or a fruit garnish. If there's one significant difference between home desserts and restaurant desserts, it's the number of these "extras" that are often employed to compose complete plates. Each cake, tart, or crumble can certainly stand on its own, and there are occasions when the simplest presentation is the most appropriate approach. You are in complete control of how complicated you wish to make a dessert. Premium store-bought ice cream is a perfectly acceptable alternative to homemade. A basic bakery poundcake can be toasted and topped with a quickly made fruit compote and flavored whipped cream. Homemade cookie dough, made ahead and frozen, can give you a freshly baked batch in no time.

One of my goals is to encourage you to bake more at home. It is possible to fit dessert-making into the busiest of schedules with just a bit of planning. Many people don't realize how much professional baking is done in advance. Although many bakeries and restaurants don't actually bake items until the day they are needed (and in some cases this is essentially done "to order"), much of the preparation work is done ahead of time. A refrigerator and freezer can be a baker's best friends. Try to read recipes well in advance. If your pastry dough is made and rolled out and you have a garnishing sauce in the fridge, putting together a fabulous fresh-baked tart can take less than an hour. Whip some cream and you have a four-star dessert.

My general cooking background has taught me how to layer flavors and textures for a more interesting end result. On the sweet as well as the savory side of the kitchen, "seasoning" and achieving flavor balance is key to turning out memorable desserts. Taste is, of course, subjective and very personal; and I, for example, prefer desserts with forthright flavors and a lower sugar profile. Small changes in recipes can occur as a result of ingredients being altered even slightly. A chocolate cake will taste different depending on the brand of chocolate you use. The exact brand (and water content) of your butter might have an effect on pastry. The freshness and pungency of a spice can change its prominence in a given recipe. Differences are perhaps most apparent when dealing with fresh fruits. Acidity levels, water content, ripeness, sugar levels, etc., can all vary enormously—not all peaches are created equal! Accomplished cooks and bakers develop a sense of where and how to adjust for these variations. For example, I might find myself adding or deleting a bit of sugar or lemon juice to bring a fruit filling into balance. If the fruit is particularly juicy, you might need to add a bit more thickening agent to a pie filling. If your cherries are a bit "flat," a few grinds of black pepper, a splash of citrus, and a sprinkle of sugar will perk them up. This is not high-tech, hard-to-figure-out stuff. The more you bake, the easier it becomes to rely on your intuition. Common sense may well be the greatest asset for any cook or baker.

Achieving a comfort level with the actual process is key to accomplished baking. A wonderful recipe and the best ingredients are important elements, but ultimately the success of a recipe is in the baker's hands. The psyche of the baker definitely transfers through to the dessert itself. It's often said that the secret ingredient to a wonderful dish is love. To me this maxim is most apparent in dessert-making. I enjoy eating desserts, but feeding them to other people is a special joy. It's a simple fact that sweets make people happy. So, can we say sugar = love? It might be impossible to prove that equation, but in the South, the expression "give me a little sugar" means give me a little love (usually in the form of a hug and a kiss), and, amazingly, in New York, my Russian grandmother used virtually the same phrase (albeit in Yiddish).

I hope that within these pages you find information and recipes that will educate and stimulate, and will prompt you to spend time in the kitchen. A great dessert can leave an impression that lasts a lifetime, especially a great American dessert.

Before Getting Started

In a rush to try out a new cookbook, I find, people often plunge into preparing recipes without reading much of the introductory material. If you are an experienced baker, most of what this chapter says will probably strike you as common sense; however, a quick read through it might answer queries that could pop up down the line. I have always found it much easier to try to gain the answers to questions that I have concerning a particular recipe ahead of time rather than when I'm in the middle of actual preparation. The best way to achieve this is to prepare a basic *mise en place*.

Mise en place is a culinary term and one of the first and most important principles taught in cooking schools and professional kitchens. It is a wonderful concept for the home baker to employ because it will keep you organized. Simply put, *mise en place* translates to "everything in its place." It means that prior to starting the preparation and baking process you gather all of the necessary ingredients and equipment and arrange them where they are easily accessible, in the order to be used. The first step is to carefully read through the entire recipe—if something is not entirely clear, now is the time to do research or clarify the information. The rest of this section will delineate my personal preferences for ingredients and equipment, as well as discuss some basic general techniques.

INGREDIENTS

Great ingredients are the absolute foundation of successful dessert-making. The following general guidelines will provide you with a peek at what's in my fridge and pantry. You shouldn't have any problems finding the ingredients called for in the recipes that follow; but if items like vanilla beans, premium chocolate, or specialty spices are difficult for you to come by, you can consult the list of sources at the end of the book.

FRUITS. When dealing with fruit-based desserts or accompaniments, I always think about the natural season first and then determine an appropriate recipe or application for whatever is best and freshest in the market. A fabulous recipe for a peach and raspberry shortcake will do you absolutely no good in December. By following the inherent guidelines dictated by a fruit's growing season you will be best assured of a great-tasting final product. Farmers' markets are the best resource for peak-season, locally harvested fruits, but many supermarkets have also made more of an effort to respond to consumer demand for high-quality produce. Purchasing within season not only will furnish you with the ultimate in terms of taste and texture but will provide you with the best value as well.

There is a definite rhythm to the dessert year, although it can vary somewhat depending on your location. The winter season often centers around citrus, while rhubarb and early strawberries always herald the start of spring for me. Summer, with its tremendous and varied bounty, is my favorite time of year, bringing a profusion of berries, figs, melons, and stone fruits. Fall traditionally signals the arrival of apples, cranberries, and persimmons.

The growing period for some fruits can be quite extended. Following the harvest of blueberries up the East Coast of the United States and across to Michigan and the Northwest, one can enjoy fresh blueberries from May through September. The appearance of other fruits in the market can be quite fleeting. Apricots or cherries, for example, are generally around for only a few precious weeks.

In this age of globalization in the agricultural industry, fruit imported from Central and South America can stretch the traditional boundaries of availability into wintertime. Occasionally these products can be good, but more often than not they lack the juicy flavor intensity and, more important, the textural quality that native (particularly locally grown) fruit has.

When choosing fruit, look for ripe, fragrant specimens that are not overly soft or bruised. This is not to say that you should seek out only perfectly formed fruit—sometimes the prettiest is not necessarily the tastiest. Imperfections and irregularities don't necessarily affect flavor. When in doubt, try to sample the fruit (as you can often do at farmers' markets, for example).

Now that I've gotten on my soapbox about using in-season fresh fruit, let me admit to occasionally using what is sometimes called IQF fruit. This is fruit that has been picked at peak season and has been individually quick-frozen with no sugar added. I sometimes utilize such fruit in recipes for cooked sauces and sorbet bases. Blueberries, blackberries, raspberries, pitted cherries, and cranberries can all be frozen in a single layer on baking sheets and then repacked in tightly sealed freezer bags. If you're lucky enough to have a U-Pick-It berry farm near you or if you hit

the absolute optimum week of cherry season when the fruit is perfect and the price is right, you can stock your freezer. IQF fruit is also available at many supermarkets. Again, it's not the right choice when the natural texture of the fruit is key, but if you need to whip up a quick fruit sauce, it can be a lifesaver.

CHOCOLATE. I truly am not a brand name snob, but I've found that the type of chocolate you use makes a significant difference in your final product. An interesting exercise is to blind taste several types of chocolate side by side. Sample "off the shelf" supermarket varieties, mixed in with premium brands as well as some commercially made chocolate chips, and judge for yourself.

I often use Callebaut chocolate—Belgian chocolate that is widely available and fairly affordable. Callebaut makes unsweetened, milk, and white chocolate as well as semisweet. I am also a big fan of Valrhona, El Rey, and Scharffen Berger chocolates. Make sure to pay attention to the type of chocolate called for in a recipe. Bittersweet chocolate may be substituted for semisweet, but unsweetened, milk, and white chocolate are all recipe specific.

If you do a significant amount of dessert-making, it may pay for you to purchase chocolate in bulk. If you can't do this locally, see the ordering sources at the end of the book. You also might consider splitting commercial-sized bars with a few friends.

I like to store my chocolate in large, opaque, rectangular plastic containers with airtight snap-on lids. If you use chocolate only sporadically, you might want to wrap it tightly in foil first. Keep it in a cool (65–70°), dry place, such as a closed pantry. I use a large heavy-duty knife with a curved blade that is shaped like a scythe to chop chocolate. I always do this on a butcher-block counter or on a sturdy cutting board set on a damp kitchen towel to keep the board from sliding. Using a rocking, lever-like motion and applying downward pressure at the same time, you can reduce an 11-pound commercial block of chocolate into manageable pieces in no time. It is important to chop these pieces into even smaller shards for melting purposes. Finely chopped chocolate melts more quickly and evenly than chocolate left in large chunks.

While there are those who advocate using a microwave to melt chocolate, I prefer a standard double boiler setup. I do not own an "official" double boiler—I just use a stainless bowl set on top of a partially filled saucepan of water. This saucepan and bowl combo can be used anytime a double boiler is called for. It is extremely important to avoid scorching your chocolate while melting it. Make sure that the water does not actually touch the bottom of the bowl and that it is kept at a bare

simmer. You also want to take care to avoid getting any moisture in the chocolate both as it melts and when removing the top of the double boiler.

COCOA. When listed as an ingredient, cocoa refers to unsweetened cocoa powder. The recipes in this book were tested with a Dutch-process cocoa from Holland. This type of alkalized cocoa is lower in acidity than American-style natural cocoa and has a mellower flavor. It is also darker in color. Each type has its fans, and the choice is often one of personal preference. For most recipes (including all of the ones in this book) the two different types of cocoa can be used interchangeably. In some cakes, however, where baking soda is the primary leavening ingredient and there is no other acidic ingredient such as sour cream, buttermilk, or lemon juice, natural cocoa should be employed. The Dutch-process variety does not, on its own, provide enough of an acidic balance for proper chemical activation. As a result, it often produces a strange, not entirely pleasant aftertaste, and it can also inhibit proper rising and affect texture.

VANILLA. If you see vanilla beans listed as an ingredient, I mean the pod-shaped bean itself. Aromatic and intense, these beans are almost literally worth their weight in gold, but when you want more flavor bang for your buck, using fresh vanilla beans is the way to go. I prefer Bourbon Madagascar vanilla beans, but there are several other varieties available. Look for plump, moist, fragrant beans, wrap them tightly in plastic, and store them in a covered glass or plastic container in a cool dark place. Don't refrigerate. Most recipes will call for splitting the beans, incorporating the scraped seeds and perhaps steeping the remaining pod. Once the bean has been used, you can rinse the scraped pods, dry them, and bury them in a canister of granulated sugar to make your own vanilla sugar.

If you see the word "vanilla" indicated in a recipe, it refers to vanilla extract. Vanilla extract is a liquid flavoring made from a vanilla bean–infused alcohol base. Please use a pure vanilla extract in your dessert-making. Imitation or vanilla "flavored" extracts do not impart the proper flavor profile. Store vanilla extract tightly sealed in a cool, dark place.

NUTS. Nuts are characteristically high in oil content and have a tendency to go rancid if not stored properly. It is best to purchase nuts from a supplier that is known to have a steady turnover of stock. Busy natural food stores are generally an excellent source. For short-term usage, you can keep nuts in a cool pantry area. For storing over longer periods, I would advise freezing them in airtight plastic containers.

To intensify nuts' natural flavor I almost always lightly toast them before using them in a given recipe. This is very important if using nuts that have been frozen since frozen nuts seem to turn a bit "flabby" in both taste and texture. A light toasting will restore their character.

SPICES, HERBS, AND EXTRACTS. All flavoring extracts should be natural, and all dried spices and herbs should be fresh (meaning not ancient). It's an excellent idea to go through your herb and spice collection at least once a year and restock any items that are faded, lack aroma, or are just plain old. I often buy small quantities of bulk spices and replenish them as needed rather than purchase an entire jar of something that would realistically take several months to use. I have found that different manufacturers' herbs and spices may vary in intensity. As a result, just as in savory cooking, when you use herbs and spices in preparing desserts, occasional adjustments need to be made to suit your taste. When black pepper is called for in a recipe, I always use medium coarse freshly ground pepper. Occasionally fresh herbs are called for; when that is the case, please do not substitute dried herbs.

SALT. Salt is an integral dessert ingredient. As an all-around flavor enhancer, a tiny amount of added salt will highlight and intensify the finished flavor of a dessert. With rare exceptions, you should not taste salt as a component of a dessert, but its presence will provide a certain level of complexity and balance. For years I baked with iodized table salt but cooked with coarse kosher salt. After finally realizing that I preferred the unadulterated, purer flavor of the kosher variety, I've developed these recipes using kosher salt. If you choose to substitute iodized, you will want to cut back on the called-for quantity by about 40 percent, as a measured teaspoon of iodized salt weighs more and is saltier than a measured teaspoon of kosher salt.

FLOUR. Unless otherwise specified, all references to flour mean all-purpose flour. There are a few recipes that call for cake flour or whole-wheat flour. I generally prefer unbleached flour, although for shortcakes and biscuits I often use Southern-style soft wheat flour (not self-rising) because I think it makes lighter, fluffier biscuits.

CORNMEAL. I like the texture and color of coarsely ground yellow cornmeal. White or finely ground meal can be used, but the resulting products will be different in texture.

SUGAR. When a recipe says "sugar," it means standard granulated cane sugar. Confectioners' sugar and brown sugar are also frequently used. I always use light brown sugar. When measuring brown sugar, I lightly pack it into dry measures—tamp it down without exerting great pressure.

MAPLE SYRUP. I like the darker and, I think, more flavorful B-grade maple syrup. Be sure that your syrup is pure syrup and not a maple-flavored pancake syrup.

HONEY. There is an amazing number of honeys available these days, ranging from generic supermarket clover honey to rare terrain-specific varietals. Sourwood honey is a favorite of mine, but I suggest you try tasting different types and choose one that suits your preference and the particular recipe in which its being used. For example, chestnut and buckwheat honeys are incredibly interesting but strong honeys and are not suitable if a delicate flavor is desired. Local farmers' markets are the best source of interesting regionally produced honeys.

CORN SYRUP. I always use light corn syrup.

SORGHUM. A cereal grain–based syrup, sorghum is a delicious sweetening agent often found in the rural South. It has a delicate balanced flavor, and I often use it interchangeably with maple syrup or molasses. It also lends itself to being drizzled over ice creams or poached fruits.

MOLASSES. I use dark molasses in my desserts. Lighter molasses (generally more amber in color) can be substituted, but its taste is not as rich. Do not, however, use blackstrap molasses, which is quite powerful and can be overwhelming in flavor.

BUTTER. OK, here is a very important rule—always use unsalted butter for these recipes and do not substitute margarine. There are advantages to the higher-butterfat, lower-moisture European-style premium butters. They taste great and are wonderful for sauces and certain types of doughs, such as puff pastry or butter cookie dough. For others, such as pie dough, I find they make a product that is almost too delicate and flaky and definitely harder to roll. For consistency's sake and because it's the most widely available product, standard Land O Lakes unsalted butter has been used in testing all of the recipes presented here. Make sure your butter is stored well wrapped, as it can pick up refrigerator odors quite easily.

Many recipes call for room-temperature butter. This means that the butter should be malleable—softened, but not at all oily or melted. Ideally, this should be about 68 to 72°. Depending on the temperature of both your kitchen and your refrigerator, butter can take anywhere from 20 minutes to several hours to come to proper consistency. If you are in a rush to "temp up" your butter, cut it into small pieces.

VEGETABLE OILS AND SHORTENINGS. When vegetable oil is called for, I tend to use canola oil, but safflower oil, corn oil, or a blended vegetable oil can be used.

There are baking recipes that make good use of strongly flavored nut and olive oils, but unless they are specifically called for, I would not freely substitute them. When vegetable shortening is designated, I use plain Crisco. Do not substitute the butter-flavored variety.

LARD. Lard must be addressed as an ingredient because some folks feel it makes for the best pie crusts and biscuits. I like both the flavor and exceptionally flaky texture lard produces, and I sometimes use it with savory fillings. A lard-based crust is also delicious paired with apples, pears, dried fruit, and nuts. It can, however, overpower delicately textured summer fruits and is not the best choice for chocolate or custard pies. Lard can be substituted for shortening in my basic pie crust or used in a 50:50 ratio with butter for savory biscuit recipes.

CREAM AND OTHER DAIRY PRODUCTS. If at all possible, use cream that is plain pasteurized as opposed to ultrapasteurized. I think it has better flavor and whips to greater volume. It is, however, often difficult to find. There seems to be little standardization of what is considered heavy cream vs. whipping cream. You should always look for the cream with the highest butterfat content. Heavy cream (sometimes labeled heavy whipping cream) is usually at least 36 percent butterfat, but products containing only up to 30 percent butterfat can be called whipping cream as well.

Ideally, when a recipe calls for buttermilk, you should try to find whole-milk buttermilk. It is richer and lends a better flavor to your desserts. For the same reasons, I always use whole milk (as opposed to 2 percent or skim milk) in my recipes.

If you have access to artisanal dairy products in your area, I urge you to try them. Often found in old-fashioned glass bottles, these healthier, tastier products harken back to another era, when food was not mass-produced as it is today.

EGGS. All of the recipes in this book were developed using large eggs. Eggs are easier to separate when cold, but in many recipes, room-temperature eggs are called for. Room-temperature eggs whip to greater volume and incorporate more easily into doughs and batters. When gathering your *mise en place*, remove the number of eggs needed from your refrigerator and allow them to come to room temperature. You can hasten this process by placing the eggs in a bowl and covering them with warm water. Allow them to sit for several minutes, drain, and proceed with the recipe.

EQUIPMENT

The recipes presented in this book have been tested in a home kitchen, using standard, commonly found baking equipment. The following is a fairly complete guide to a very well stocked kitchen based on my personal preferences. Having the proper tool can make a baker's job easier; however, it's amazing what can be accomplished with ingenuity and common sense. I have rolled out pastry with wine bottles and baked quick breads in coffee cans, and I spent a year that felt like a lifetime baking in an apartment where the oven had no thermostat. While the preparation of most recipes can easily be accomplished with the basics, I've also included some information on a few professional tools and specialized items.

Major Powered Items and Smaller Appliances

OVENS. I have found there to be little difference in the performance of gas versus electric ovens. What is critical, regardless of how your oven is powered, is that the thermostat be relatively accurate. If your oven is off by more than 15°, you should see about getting it recalibrated. Many ovens have hot spots, and the more you bake the more you will understand your oven's individual personality. It's always a good idea to rotate baking sheets and pans to compensate for any minor heating irregularities. I have a gas oven and always set my oven racks in the bottom and middle positions. I tend to do most of my baking on the bottom rack; if, however, you have an electric oven with bottom elements, you should probably use the middle rack. I try to avoid baking in the top third of the oven because it tends to be hotter and items overbrown. Convection ovens with built-in circulating fans are wonderful for baking certain items (meringues, some cookies, individual pastries, and some cakes) but should not be used for custards, cheesecakes, and cakes made in Bundt or tube pans. If used, convection ovens should be set 25° lower than the baking temperature given in a recipe and the baking time should be slightly reduced. Note that all of the recipes presented here were tested in conventional, not convection, ovens.

MIXERS. If you do a lot of baking, I think a freestanding heavy-duty electric mixer is a necessity. It is the real workhorse of a baker's kitchen. If you purchase one of good quality, you should have it for a lifetime. Look for models with a powerful motor. After years of intensive use, the Kitchen Aid K5A I received as a wedding gift is still going strong. I use the same model at the restaurant as well. Mixers should come with both paddle and whip attachments. I would suggest purchasing an additional mixing bowl and whip—it will make the preparation of recipes calling for beaten egg whites easier and more efficient. If you don't own a freestanding mixer, a handheld portable model is a reasonable alternative. In theory, all recipes can be made entirely by hand, but a little electric power goes a long way and will make the baking process more enjoyable.

FOOD PROCESSORS. I use my food processor to make cookie and pastry doughs, chop nuts, purée fruits, and grind breadcrumbs. Of course, it has many applications for savory cooking as well. It is a wonderful timesaving device and a worthwhile investment if you spend even a modest amount of time in the kitchen. Ideally, you should purchase a sturdy, reputable model with at least a 6-cup bowl capacity. If you do not own a processor, remember that everything this machine does can be accomplished by hand using a knife, food mill, or pastry cutter.

BLENDERS. Handheld wand-style blenders are great for liquefying and puréeing. Cleanup is a snap, and your end result is always very smooth and well emulsified. Standard bar-type blenders are also handy for making flavored oils and syrups, batters, and milkshakes. A processor can generally be substituted in doing most of these tasks as well.

COFFEE GRINDERS. Freshly toasted and ground spices will give your cooking a real flavor boost. If you choose to fresh grind spices, be sure to use a grinder that is specifically reserved for that purpose.

ICE CREAM MAKERS. My preference is for electric machines with self-contained motors, but these models come with hefty price tags. Old-fashioned hand-cranked salt and ice bucket units and their updated electric counterparts or inexpensive chamber models where you prefreeze the freezer insert will also produce delicious homemade frozen desserts.

ELECTRIC FRY PANS OR DEEP FRYERS. These are useful because you can set and consistently control the temperature of your frying medium. I often use an elderly fry pan that my husband has had since college, but frying in a deep saucepan with an accurate deep fat frying thermometer will also result in tasty fritters, donuts, and beignets.

WAFFLE IRONS. Yes, this is a highly specialized appliance—there's not much you can do with a waffle iron other than make waffles. However, the possibilities within this genre are limitless. It's worth owning one just to turn out memorable breakfasts for family and friends. Check out Dorie Greenspan's *Waffles from Morning to Midnight* for a multitude of great ideas for brunch, snack, main dish, and—of course—dessert waffles. I find a traditional nonstick 6½- to 7-inch round waffle iron to be the most versatile, but recipes can also be made in deep Belgian wafflers as well as shallow five-of-hearts-style irons. Even though I use a nonstick iron, I still spray it lightly with cooking oil between making each waffle to ensure easy removal. Particularly when dealing with sweet dessert waffles, there is a tendency for even the nonsticks to stick.

Pots, Pans, Baking Sheets, and Assorted Bakeware

I advocate buying the best quality cookware that you can. I look for heavy-bottomed nonreactive pots and saucepans. For bakeware, I prefer stainless or heavy-gauge aluminum pans. One exception to this rule is my preference for clear Pyrex pie plates—I like the way they conduct heat, and I like being able to see the bottom crust. I love half-size sheet pans for baking cookies and making jelly rolls. I do not use nonstick bakeware. I find that these pans affect the exterior finishes on cakes and can alter the baking time significantly.

Try to use the pan size that a recipe calls for, but realize that you can usually be somewhat flexible about this. Consult the equivalent pan size chart in Appendix 1 if you wish to substitute a different size. If sizing is not exact to the recipe, make sure not to overfill your pans and realize that baking times can vary according to pan size.

Be realistic about the types of pans you need. If you don't care for angel food or chiffon cakes, you may not really need a removable-bottom tube pan. There are a few key "extra" pieces of equipment I like to have on hand, though. For certain recipes I prefer the look of a small individual dessert. I often use 8-ounce straight-sided ovenproof ramekins to bake single-portion cakes, crisps, custards, etc. Similarly, I think that 3-inch flan rings are wonderful for making individual tarts.

Miscellaneous Tools of the Trade

BLOWTORCH. Yes, the kind you find in the plumbing aisle of the hardware store! These are butane fueled and are terrific for making crème brûlée, caramelizing fruit, toasting marshmallow or meringue toppings, and loosening delicate cakes from their pans. Forgo the mini versions featured in many cookware catalogues—for the same price you can get a stronger hardware version that is much more efficient.

JUICER. The electric ones are great, but I've always used an old-fashioned citrus "reamer" with a base that collects the juice.

ROLLING PIN. I prefer an American-style ball bearing pin with handles, but many people prefer a tapered French-style pin. Use the one you feel most comfortable with.

FOOD MILL. While I often use a food processor to purée, I sometimes like a food mill because it purées and strains at the same time. An old-fashioned Foley Food Mill is a versatile piece of equipment—great for making dessert sauces and mashed potatoes!

MEASURING EQUIPMENT. It is imperative to measure all ingredients accurately using the proper tools. Liquid (pourable) ingredients should be measured in see-through, well-marked liquid measures with a pouring spout. Dry ingredients should be scooped and leveled into dry cup measures. You should also have a complete set of measuring spoons. Make sure your measuring equipment is sturdy and not dented.

SCALE. Most American home cooks have not converted to weighing ingredients, although this methodology is quite common in the professional kitchen. I find an ounce scale very accurate and easier for measuring things like chocolate, butter, and shortening than trying to pack these ingredients into dry measures. Weighing ingredients also has its advantages when you are multiplying recipes.

THERMOMETER. Good quality oven and freezer thermometers are necessary to check the accuracy of your appliances. In addition, a sturdy deep-fat-frying/candy thermometer is needed for certain recipes.

TIMER. Busy bakers are adept at multitasking, and one of the easiest ways to keep track of multiple batches of cookies or a panful of toasting nuts is to set a timer. Better safe than sorry (and burnt).

WIRE STRAINER. Look for sturdy, fine-mesh stainless strainers. They are invaluable for straining sauces, removing seeds from purées, sifting dry ingredients, and sprinkling desserts with powdered sugar.

SQUEEZE AND SPRAY BOTTLES. While some bakers and cooks have taken the cult of the squeeze bottle a bit too far (not every plate needs to be dripped and squiggled), plastic squeeze bottles do give you a great deal of control over placement and sauce quantity when garnishing individually plated desserts. These can be purchased through kitchenware shops or catalogues. Hair supply shops also often carry them.

I use a spray bottle in the pastry-making process. Spray bottles are also terrific for misting bread doughs. Check the garden department of your local hardware shop for these.

PASTRY BRUSHES. Good quality pastry brushes are the best way to apply glazes, soaking syrups, and egg washes. I have a separate set of dessert-only brushes and keep them separate from my barbecue tools.

PASTRY BAG AND TIPS. Employing some very basic piping skills is an easy way to dress up a dessert. I like to keep 2 or 3 large (14-inch) pastry bags and a basic assortment of tips on hand. Large and small open round and star tips should meet most decorating needs. If possible, it's useful to reserve one bag solely for meringue and egg white use.

PARCHMENT PAPER. I hate it when I find myself without parchment paper! Parchment is silicone-treated paper that can be used to line baking sheets and cake pans, providing a virtually guaranteed nonstick surface. Your cookies will bake more evenly and your cakes will be much easier to remove from their pans if you utilize a parchment liner. It can now be found in roll form in many supermarkets and can be bought in bulk sheet packages through restaurant supply houses—try splitting a box with several baking friends.

SILPAT SHEETS. These are silicone-coated baking mats—fabulous because they can be washed and reused. They come in full-sheet-pan and half-sheet-pan sizes and *nothing* sticks to them. As wonderful as parchment paper is, silpats are the better choice for certain recipes, such as brown edge wafer cookies and Huguenot parfait crumbles. They also make a great surface on which to knead even the stickiest dough.

CARDBOARD CAKE CIRCLES. Professional bakers use these as a base for many cakes. They make depanning and icing cakes much easier, and they allow you to transport cake layers with ease as well as transfer tarts off their removable bottoms. You can find these in restaurant supply and specialty paper goods shops, or you can make your own by cutting out appropriately sized rounds from a clean cardboard box. I usually buy 12-inch circles and trim them if necessary.

Small Wares

This category includes small utensils and tools. It is easy to accumulate several drawers of small wares, but these items all have their individual, specialized uses.

WHISKS. I suggest having a stiffer whisk to facilitate the mixing of batter as well as a thin, flexible-wired balloon whisk for incorporating air into egg whites and cream. A selection of sizes to match the volume of ingredients you're dealing with is helpful.

PLASTIC SPATULAS. These handled scrapers are like an extension of your hands. When working with heated items, I tend to stir with wooden spoons, but spatulas are necessary for transferring mixtures, folding in ingredients, and bowl scraping. The newer silicone-coated spatulas and spoons are in fact heat resistant, but even they can begin to disintegrate if exposed to high temperatures for long periods. A spatula with a slightly more flexible blade tends to work better for folding.

METAL SPATULAS. These range from small offset spatulas that are perfect for little icing jobs and loosening delicate cookies to larger, flatter "burger flippers" that are just the right tool for turning pancakes. I would stock a minimum of a small offset spatula and a larger straight-sided spatula for frosting cakes.

SPOONS. Thick-handled, oversized wooden spoons are one of my favorite kitchen tools. They do not get hot and are a must for making a caramel and stirring custards.

BENCH SCRAPER. A heavy, stainless blade set into a wooden handle, a bench scraper is the best tool for cleaning work surfaces, facilitating work with sticky doughs, and portioning pastry.

KNIVES. Yes, bakers need a few good-quality multipurpose knives. My overall basics would be a small paring knife, an 8- or 10-inch chef's knife, an offset serrated bread knife, and a long, thin-bladed flexible slicing knife. I also like to use a heavy, curved-bladed knife for chopping chocolate.

SCISSORS. I use scissors to cut parchment paper and cardboard cake circles. They're also useful for snipping dried fruits, trimming waffles, and removing excess unbaked pastry.

VEGETABLE PEELER. A sharp, efficient vegetable peeler is a necessity. My preference is for an Oxo swivel-bladed peeler but any variety with a sharp blade will work.

ZESTERS AND GRATERS. The zester of choice these days seems to be a rasp-style Microplane tool that is wonderful for zesting citrus. There are special models that are meant to be used on nutmeg, ginger, and hard cheeses as well, but I find that the original Microplane will work on all of these items. I like using the large, open holes on a box grater for grating cheddar and other semifirm cheeses.

CUTTERS. It's useful to have a sharp, graduated set of round cutters for making cookies and biscuits. Cutters in specialty shapes—stars, hearts, and a variety of holiday symbols—can help customize your baking.

ICE CREAM SCOOPS. I keep a variety of sizes on hand. Beyond scooping ice cream, spring-loaded scoops are great for placing batter into ramekins or muffin tins. Small scoops scaled to teaspoon and tablespoon sizes are very handy for portioning cookie dough.

A Note on Ice Baths and Water Baths

Many of my recipes call for an ice or water bath. These are not really pieces of equipment but general procedures. An ice bath is used to quick-chill ingredients. To make an ice bath, place the item you wish to chill in a bowl and place that in a larger bowl that is partially filled with ice and a bit of water. If you're chilling a liquid, such as an ice cream base, periodically stir the liquid to equalize the temperature. Poached fruits are often chilled over an ice bath to inhibit carry-over heat and prevent overcooking.

A hot water bath, or bain-marie, is often used for baking custard-type desserts. Place the item to be baked in a shallow-sided pan and fill with warm water to the depth of about ½ to 1 inch. It is best to fill the pan while it is placed on your oven rack. The water bath allows for heat dispersal and a gentler baking process. Be sure that the water never boils.

The Basics A Baker's Building Blocks

Basic Pie Crust
Basic Tart Dough
My Favorite Dough
  for Individual Tarts
Flaky Puff-Style Pastry
Cream Cheese Pastry
Cinnamon Graham Pastry
Newton Tart Dough
Walnut Pastry Dough

The Caramelization
  Chronicles
Caramel Sauce
Cocoa Fudge Sauce
Chocolate Pudding Sauce
Creamy Peanut Butter &
  Honey Sauce
Hot Buttered Rum Raisin
  Sauce
Gingered Maple Walnut
  Sauce
Lynchburg Lemonade Sauce
Cinnamon Spiced
  Blueberry Sauce
Pineapple Caramel—&
  Variations on the Theme

A Couple of Apple Sauces
Raspberry Red Wine Sauce
Strawberry Crush
Concord Grape Syrup
Mint Syrup
Coffee Syrup

Chocolate Ganache
Homemade Chocolate Chips
Honeyed Almonds
Pecan Praline
Peanut Frangipane
Candied Chestnut Purée
Lemon or Lime Curd/
  Custard
Candied Orange Zest
Candied Orange Peel
Whipped Cream
Custard Sauce (Crème
  Anglaise)—A Basic
  Recipe & Variations
White Chocolate Cream
Crème Fraîche
Marshmallow Fluff

Within this chapter you will find recipes that are meant to be used as components of other recipes. I often refer to doughs, sauces, and garnishes as building blocks—pieces that will fit together in any number of combinations to form a variety of end results.

Every baker tends to have a core collection of basics that she or he turns to over and over again. For example, there are any number of delicious chocolate sauce recipes out there, but cocoa fudge sauce (page 37) is my all-time favorite. I might vary the flavor to match a specific dessert by adding a bit of liqueur or instant coffee, infusing the cream with fresh mint, or combining the cocoa sauce with some caramel sauce; but the rudimentary recipe is one I never change. My basic pie crust (page 26) is the one I use for all my pies and have relied on for years.

The best thing about all of these basics is that they can be made ahead of time. Some (as indicated) even freeze successfully. One of the ways professional bakers manage their days is by doing significant elements of preparation work in advance. I might make a menu cycle's worth of tart dough in one session, refrigerate what I will require for the next 2 to 3 days, and freeze the remainder. A large batch of raspberry sauce will be divided in half, with one part meant for immediate use and the other fresh-frozen for later in the week. Home bakers can do this on a smaller scale. It really is no more work to do a double recipe of pastry and save what you don't immediately need for the next time you have an occasion to use it. With a well-stocked freezer, putting together a complete dessert on short notice becomes a snap. The following are a few general tips that pertain to the advance preparation of basics:

- Label and date everything!
- Dough should be double wrapped for extended storage. I generally don't like to hold doughs for longer than 3 days in the refrigerator. They can be kept frozen for up to 3 months.
- Always stir sauces that have been made ahead thoroughly—they sometimes have a tendency to separate a bit.
- The best way to thaw pastry, cookie doughs, and sauces is gradually, overnight in your refrigerator. I confess that when time is of the essence I have relied on quickie countertop defrosting. A brief rechilling of doughs before rolling might be necessary if you do this.

- You can freeze your own prerolled pie shells (with or without accompanying "tops") in disposable aluminum tins. These are infinitely preferable to the commercially produced kind.
- While perhaps not ideal, it certainly doesn't hurt to have an "insta-dessert" on hand at all times. Get creative. A frozen poundcake, defrosted and lightly toasted before serving, can be delicious (especially if topped with ice cream). Frozen crisp topping can be defrosted in just a few hours and sprinkled on seasonal fruit, allowing you to serve a freshly baked dessert. Sundaes are a great way to end both family meals and VIP dinners—and all the components (with the exception of the whipped cream) can be frozen.

Basic Pie Crust

MAKES ENOUGH PASTRY FOR 2 SINGLE-CRUSTED PIES
OR 1 DOUBLE-CRUSTED PIE

I like to use a combination of butter and vegetable shortening in my pie crust. The butter contributes wonderful flavor, and the vegetable shortening gives the crust just the right amount of flakiness. I also thoroughly endorse the substitution of lard for the vegetable shortening. This recipe gives you a generous amount of pastry to allow for easier rolling.

INGREDIENTS

2⅔ cups flour
¾ teaspoon kosher salt
¾ tablespoon sugar
4 ounces (8 tablespoons) chilled butter, cut into pieces
4 ounces (½ cup + 1 tablespoon + 2 teaspoons) chilled vegetable shortening, cut into pieces
approximately ¼–½ cup cold water, as needed

PREPARATION

1 Place the flour, salt, and sugar in the bowl of a food processor with a steel blade. Pulse to combine.
2 Add the chilled butter and shortening; pulse until the fat is evenly cut in and the mixture resembles coarse cornmeal. Remove to a mixing bowl.

3 Working quickly, gradually add enough cold water, while tossing and stirring with a fork, until the dough just begins to come together. Divide the dough into 2 even portions, flatten into rounds, wrap in plastic, and chill for several hours or overnight.

Baker's Note: I always use regular Crisco shortening and Land O Lakes unsalted butter for my pie crusts. You can also substitute chilled lard for the vegetable shortening—this produces a distinctive, flavorful, and ultraflaky crust.

Basic Tart Dough

MAKES ENOUGH PASTRY FOR 1 10- TO 11-INCH TART

This dough is very easy to put together and makes a great all-purpose rich pastry crust. It can be done by hand or with a mixer, but as with most doughs, I find that using a food processor is quicker.

INGREDIENTS

1 ¼ cups + 2 tablespoons flour
2 tablespoons sugar
¼ teaspoon kosher salt
4 ounces (8 tablespoons) chilled butter, cut into pieces
1 egg yolk
2 tablespoons cream

PREPARATION

1 Place the flour, sugar, and salt in a food processor with a steel blade. Pulse to blend. Add the butter and pulse until the mixture resembles coarse meal.
2 In a small bowl, mix the egg yolk with the cream. Add the mixture to the processor and pulse until the dough comes together.
3 Remove the dough from the processor, knead several times, and pat into a flattened disc. Wrap in plastic and chill for at least 1 hour or up to 2 days before using. The dough can also be frozen.

Baker's Note: You can substitute milk or half-and-half for the cream if you wish. This recipe also doubles very easily, so consider freezing an extra shell for future use.

My Favorite Dough for Individual Tarts

MAKES ENOUGH PASTRY FOR 8 TO 10 4-INCH TARTS

Let me give credit where credit is due. This dough is based on one used by Maury Rubin in his *Book of Tarts*, a goldmine of information and inspiration. As the pastry chef at Magnolia Grill, Phoebe Lawless was instrumental in tinkering with the original recipe. We've changed it slightly and formatted it to be made in a food processor. What I love most about this recipe is that it's the only one I know of that produces a dough that doesn't need to be weighted when prebaked. Even my husband—who, although a great chef, considers himself pastry challenged—thinks this is an easy recipe to master.

INGREDIENTS

1½ cups flour
⅓ cup confectioners' sugar
¼ teaspoon kosher salt
10 tablespoons (5 ounces) butter, chilled and cut into pieces
1 egg yolk
1 tablespoon cream

PREPARATION

1 Place the flour, confectioners' sugar, and salt in a food processor with a steel blade. Pulse to blend. Add the butter and pulse till finely cut in. Add the egg yolk and cream and mix till the dough just comes together. Remove the dough from the processor, knead several times, and form into a log; wrap in plastic and chill for 1 hour.

2 Remove the dough from the refrigerator and cut into small pieces. Using the heel of your hand, just smear the dough sections across a lightly floured work surface. Gather the dough back together—this is best done with a bench scraper. Re-form the dough into a log shape, cut it into 8 1¾-ounce portions, flatten each, and wrap each in plastic. Chill thoroughly before rolling.

Baker's Note: After rolling out the initial 8 tarts, you can gather the dough scraps, chill them, and reroll the dough, generating 2 additional shells.

A great feature of this dough is that it can be made ahead and frozen unrolled (defrost in the refrigerator overnight before rolling), frozen rolled and unbaked, or frozen partially baked. If a recipe doesn't call for additional baking time, refresh frozen partially baked shells in a 350° oven for about 10 minutes before filling.

It's always a good idea to bake one or two extra shells in case you have some breakage, as these shells can be a bit delicate.

Flaky Puff-Style Pastry

MAKES ABOUT 1½ POUNDS OF DOUGH

Making classic, traditional puff pastry can be a daunting task for most bakers. Many supermarkets carry prerolled frozen pastry sheets that can be used instead. In my opinion, though, this quick and easy version of puff-style pastry is superior to the frozen product, and it is virtually foolproof.

INGREDIENTS

    2 cups flour
    1 teaspoon kosher salt
    3¼ sticks (26 tablespoons) butter, chilled and cut into small pieces
    1 teaspoon lemon juice
    scant ½ cup cold water

PREPARATION

1 Combine the flour, salt, and butter in a mixer bowl and mix on low speed, using a paddle, until the butter breaks up slightly (about 1 minute). Add the lemon juice and water and mix until the dough just barely comes together; sprinkle it with a bit of additional water if the dough seems dry. Mix for another second or two. Gather the dough mass into a rectangular shape and place on a lightly floured surface.

2 Using a lightly floured rolling pin, roll the dough into a 12 × 7-inch rectangle, with the long edge of the dough running vertically. Fold the dough into thirds, as if you were folding a business letter. Give the dough a quarter (90°) turn to the right. The open seam of the dough should now be on the right. Lightly reflour the work surface under the dough, the top of the dough, and the rolling

pin and repeat this same rolling/folding 3 more times, for a total of 4 quarter turns. Wrap the dough in plastic, place it in the refrigerator, and allow it to chill for about 30 minutes. This will also allow the dough to relax enough to complete the rolling process.

3 Remove the dough from the refrigerator, give it 2 more quarter turns, rewrap it in plastic, and allow it to chill for at least 30 minutes or up to 2 days before using. The dough can also be frozen for up to 2 months. If you choose to freeze it, wrap it in an extra layer of aluminum foil and defrost it overnight in the refrigerator before using.

Cream Cheese Pastry

MAKES ENOUGH PASTRY FOR 1 DOUBLE-CRUSTED PIE,
2 SINGLE-CRUSTED PIES, 12 SMALL TURNOVERS, OR
1 LARGE FRUIT COBBLER

This pastry was inspired by my grandmother's rugelach dough. For readers who have not had them, rugelach are a deliciously flaky traditional Eastern European cookie. It is a very easy dough to work with and rolls like a dream. In addition to making an excellent pie or turnover crust, it's a good choice for topping large-format or individual deep-dish fruit cobblers.

INGREDIENTS
    2¼ cups flour
    1 tablespoon sugar
    ½ teaspoon kosher salt
    12 tablespoons (6 ounces) butter, chilled and cut into pieces
    12 tablespoons (6 ounces) cream cheese, chilled and cut into pieces
    ¼ cup cream

PREPARATION
1 Place the flour, sugar, and salt in the bowl of a food processor fitted with a steel blade. Pulse to combine. Add the butter and cream cheese and pulse till they are cut in and the mixture resembles coarse meal. Add the cream and pulse briefly, just until the dough starts to come together.
2 If using for pies, divide the dough in half. If using for turnovers, divide into

12 small rounds (each will be about 2 ounces). If using to top a large fruit cobbler, pat into the approximate shape of your baking dish (i.e., 1 large oval or rectangle). Wrap the pastry in plastic and chill several hours before rolling out. It can be made 3 days ahead if refrigerated or several months ahead if frozen.

Cinnamon Graham Pastry

MAKES ENOUGH PASTRY FOR 1 LARGE TART

Whole-wheat pastries are often very crunchy, granola-like in personality—virtuous and healthy but a bit leaden. This dough bakes up to be exceptionally crisp and flaky and is best suited for informal, rustic-style tarts. I like making this dough in a food processor, but you can do it with a standing mixer or by hand as well.

INGREDIENTS

    1 cup flour
    ½ cup whole-wheat flour
    3 tablespoons sugar
    ¼ teaspoon kosher salt
    ¾ teaspoon cinnamon
    12 tablespoons (6 ounces) butter, chilled and cut into pieces
    2½ tablespoons cold water

PREPARATION

1 Combine the flours, sugar, salt, and cinnamon in a food processor with a steel blade. Pulse to blend. Add the cold butter and cut in, by pulsing, until the mixture resembles coarse meal. Add the water and pulse briefly to blend. The dough should just start to come together. Do not overprocess.
2 Remove the dough from the processor, gather into a flat round, and wrap well in plastic. Chill for several hours or overnight. Allow to sit at room temperature for about 5 minutes before rolling. This dough can be frozen for several months if well wrapped.

Baker's Note: You can make any size rustic tart you want using this dough—even small individual ones. This recipe will yield 2 medium-sized or 6 individual tarts.

Newton Tart Dough

MAKES ENOUGH PASTRY FOR 1 10½-INCH DOUBLE-CRUSTED TART

This pastry is halfway between a cookie and a tart dough. I particularly like using it with dried fruit and nut fillings, and it works very well in tarts that call for a double crust.

INGREDIENTS
    2½ cups flour
    ⅓ cup + 2 tablespoons sugar
    ½ teaspoon baking powder
    ½ teaspoon kosher salt
    ¼ teaspoon cinnamon
    10 tablespoons (5 ounces) butter, chilled and cut into pieces
    2 eggs
    1 egg yolk

PREPARATION
1 Combine the flour, sugar, baking powder, salt, and cinnamon in a food processor with a steel blade.
2 Add the butter and pulse until it is evenly cut in and the mixture resembles coarse meal.
3 Add the eggs and the yolk and pulse until the dough just starts to come together.
4 Remove the dough from the processor, gather it into a log, and place it on a lightly floured work surface. Cut the dough into pieces and, using the heel of your hand, smear the dough sections across the work surface. Gather the dough back together (this is best done with a bench scraper) and divide the dough into two pieces, one slightly larger than the other. The larger piece will be the bottom crust, and the smaller piece will be the top crust. Flatten the dough into rounds, wrap in plastic, and chill several hours or overnight.

Walnut Pastry Dough

MAKES ENOUGH PASTRY FOR 1 10½-INCH LATTICE TART

I most often use this pastry for a rustic lattice-style tart with a fruit-based filling. It is a rich, softer dough and, in all honesty, a bit difficult to work with, particularly in warm weather; but it's so delicious I think it's worth the extra effort.

INGREDIENTS

1¾ cups flour

½ cup lightly toasted, skinned, chopped walnuts

2 tablespoons sugar

¼ teaspoon kosher salt

½ teaspoon cinnamon

¼ teaspoon nutmeg

¼ teaspoon cloves

10 tablespoons (5 ounces) butter, chilled and cut into pieces

1 egg

2 tablespoons cream

PREPARATION

1 Combine the flour, walnuts, sugar, salt, cinnamon, nutmeg, and cloves in a food processor with a steel blade. Process until the nuts are finely ground.

2 Add the butter and pulse until it is cut in and the mixture resembles coarse meal.

3 Add the egg and the cream to the processor and, using quick pulses, process until just before the dough starts to come together. You may have to stop after the first few pulses and scrape the top of the bowl down before pulsing a few more times. Do not overprocess this dough—it is by nature soft.

4 Divide the dough into two portions—one about 11 ounces, the other about 7 ounces. Pat the larger piece into a flat round and the smaller piece into a flat rectangle. Wrap each in plastic and chill completely.

Baker's Note: I like to work with this dough chilled. Although it has a tendency to tear and crack, it's also an easy dough to patch and repair. This recipe will give you just enough dough to form a 10½-inch tart shell with a top lattice crust. Rather than weaving a formal lattice, I roll the dough out, cut it into

¾-inch-wide strips and then lay out 5 strips running in one direction and 5 strips on top of them running in the opposite direction. Save all your scraps when rolling this dough. You will have to reroll the pastry once or twice to form all the strips—if you have to, you can even piece two partial strips together to form one of proper length.

Serving Suggestion: This dough also makes a great crust for topping fruit cobblers.

The Caramelization Chronicles

Caramelizing is the act of cooking sugar to the point where it melts and starts to turn color. The flavor of sugar undergoes a magical transformation as a result of this process. Plain granulated sugar is characterized as merely tasting sweet. Caramel on the other hand is described as nutty, deep dark, and delicious. Sugar is fairly one-dimensional, whereas caramel is far more complex in nature.

There are two basic methods used to caramelize sugar. I often use the dry method, where plain sugar is evenly sprinkled over the bottom of a large-surfaced, heavy-bottomed unlined pot. It is imperative that you vigilantly tend to the sugar, gently moving it around the pan as it starts to brown. Vigorous stirring should be avoided. The caramelization is stopped by the addition of whatever liquid is called for in a particular recipe. This method works well when you are caramelizing sugar for something like a butterscotch sauce or an ice cream base—when the intense flavor of a medium to dark caramel is what you're after. Its main advantages are that it's fast and you rarely have crystallization problems. It is, however, almost impossible to produce a lighter caramel using the dry method. Some novices also find it intimidating because it can be a bit tricky achieving an even caramelization without any spot burning. Using a heavy-bottomed saucepan is mandatory with this method! An alternative tack is to use the wet method of caramelization.

For a wet caramel, sugar is combined with water and then cooked to the desired color. The sugar colors as the water gradually evaporates, making this process slower but easier to control. While burning is less of an issue in wet caramelization, crystallization is often a problem. Many recipes instruct you to wash down the sides of your pan with a wet pastry brush or to cook the sugar and water in a covered pot until the sugar dissolves. I actually prefer to put the sugar in the pot in an even layer and then slowly add just enough water to moisten the sugar, avoiding any splashing. Gently draw your finger through the sugar to disperse the water. At this point the addition of a few drops of lemon juice will aid in the prevention of crystallization. As an alternative you can add a teaspoon of corn syrup. Cook the sugar without stirring over low heat until it dissolves. Continue to cook the mixture until it just starts to pick up color. You can now tilt or swirl the pan to promote even caramelization. Once the desired color is reached, stop the caramelization with the additional liquid that is called for.

For most recipes I prefer a dark, rich caramel flavor. To me, the hardest part of caramelizing is determining the exact moment at which to stop the process. As caramel reaches its finishing point, the color deepens to amber. You should see an actual hint of smoke produced. The caramel will also give off a distinct aroma—it starts to "smell dark." There is a very small window between dark and burnt, though, so split-second timing is essential. If you don't take a caramel far enough, it will taste wimpy; and if you cook it too much, it can taste acrid. Practice does make perfect, and the more you do this the better you will get at deciding where the caramelization should be stopped.

For an excellent scientific but easy-to-digest explanation of the chemistry behind caramelization, see Shirley Corriher's book *Cookwise*. It is particularly useful for gaining an understanding of why sugar behaves the way it does and how you can control its idiosyncrasies.

There are a few important points to remember when caramelizing that apply to either the wet or dry method.

- Exercise extreme caution when caramelizing sugar. You are dealing with a molten substance, and sugar burns are very painful.
- Make sure your sugar is free of impurities and your equipment is very clean.
- Use a large, heavy-bottomed, unlined, preferably stainless steel pot or pan to cook caramel. Nonstick surfaces are unacceptable, and it is

difficult to judge a caramel's color accurately in a dark cast iron or Calphalon pan.

- Use a large, heavy-grade wooden spoon to stir caramel. It does not conduct heat and will not melt. I have found that supposedly heat-resistant spoons and spatulas are often not as resistant as they are advertised to be.
- When liquid is added to bubbling caramel to stop the caramelization, a large amount of heat and steam are given off. The caramel has a tendency to spatter, so stand back a bit and add your liquid at a controlled, steady pace.
- To prevent seizing, heat any ingredient used to stop caramelization before you add it. If the caramel clumps and hardens once the liquid is added, return it to medium heat and stir until the caramel bits are dissolved.
- To clean up stubborn sticky, hard caramel, fill the pot with water and bring it to a boil. You can place your spoon in the pot as well. Allow the water to simmer until the caramel dissolves.
- Any recipe that calls for dry caramelization can be made with a wet caramel if you feel more comfortable with that alternative.

Caramel Sauce

MAKES ABOUT 2 CUPS

Like "chocolate," "caramel" is a magic word on a dessert menu. This is a simple, unadulterated creamy caramel sauce that improves just about everything you spoon it onto—liquid gold!

INGREDIENTS

1½ cups cream
1½ cups sugar
5 tablespoons (2½ ounces) butter
1 teaspoon vanilla

½ teaspoon lemon juice
¼ teaspoon kosher salt

PREPARATION

1 Heat the cream to just under a boil. Meanwhile caramelize the sugar in a heavy saucepan until medium amber in color. Once the sugar has properly caramelized, carefully and slowly add the hot cream to the caramel. The mixture will spatter and steam. Cook for 1 minute, stirring to dissolve any caramel bits. Remove from heat.

2 Stir in the butter. Add the vanilla, lemon juice, and salt.

3 Cool the sauce to room temperature and strain through a fine-mesh strainer. This sauce can be made up to 4 days ahead if stored refrigerated. It can also be frozen. Bring back to room temperature before serving.

Baker's Note: You can add 2½ tablespoons of brandy, bourbon, or rum to this sauce. The flavor can also be varied by adding 1½ tablespoons of instant coffee (dissolve it in the hot cream) or stirring in 3 ounces of chopped semisweet chocolate along with the butter.

Serving Suggestions: This is delicious layered with not-just-plain-vanilla ice cream (page 261) and bourbon poached peaches (page 149). It's also great as an accent against banana pudding cream puffs (page 168) or coconut rum raisin bread pudding (page 180). Try it as a flavoring agent for milkshakes too!

Cocoa Fudge Sauce

MAKES 2 CUPS

A great chocolate sauce is like the perfect simple black dress—appropriate for almost every occasion. I love the deep dark finish that cocoa-based sauces have. This one is deluxe for using as a plate sauce, drizzling over ice cream, or eating by the spoonful all on its own.

INGREDIENTS
8 tablespoons (4 ounces) butter
½ cup brown sugar

⅓ cup sifted unsweetened cocoa

1 cup cream

a few grains kosher salt

½ teaspoon vanilla

PREPARATION

Melt the butter in a medium-sized saucepan. Whisk in the sugar and cocoa.
Whisk in the cream and salt. Bring to a simmer over medium low heat, whisking
often. Allow to simmer for 8 to 10 minutes until the sauce has thickened
somewhat. Remove from heat, add the vanilla, and strain through a fine sieve.
Cool and serve at room temperature. This can be made up to 1 week ahead of
time. It can also be frozen.

Baker's Note: These proportions give you a fairly bittersweet sauce. Feel free to
add a bit more sugar or vary the sweetening agent if you like. A honey-flavored
sauce is particularly delicious. You can modify this sauce in any number of
ways. Try adding a few tablespoons of liquor (bourbon, Grand Marnier, or
cognac), a bit of raspberry purée or some dissolved instant coffee to the sauce.
You can also infuse the cream with a handful of fresh mint and/or add a very
small amount of pure mint extract.

Serving Suggestions: This is my all-purpose chocolate sauce. It has a great consistency
and lends itself to being both an undersauce for something like chocolate
strawberry shortcakes (page 135) or an oversauce—try it over devil's food cake
with whipped ganache (page 203).

Chocolate Pudding Sauce

MAKES 2 CUPS

This sauce really does taste like liquid chocolate pudding. It's a natural paired with
desserts based on vanilla, peanut, or banana flavors.

INGREDIENTS

1½ cups milk, divided

¼ cup sugar

1 tablespoon + ½ teaspoon cornstarch

7 ounces semisweet chocolate, chopped into small pieces

½ teaspoon vanilla

PREPARATION

1 Heat 1¼ cups of the milk with the sugar in a medium-sized saucepan over low heat. Combine the cornstarch with the remaining ¼ cup of milk and reserve.

2 Add the chopped chocolate to the hot milk and whisk till the chocolate is completely melted. Whisk in the cornstarch-milk mixture and whisk gently over medium heat till the sauce thickens and just comes to a boil. Turn the heat down and simmer for 1 minute. Remove from heat and add the vanilla.

3 Strain the sauce through a fine-mesh strainer, cool over an ice bath, and refrigerate until ready to serve. This can be made up to 3 days in advance.

Baker's Note: You can substitute bittersweet, milk, or white chocolate for the semisweet if you wish. If the sauce seems overly thick, adjust the consistency with additional milk.

Serving Suggestions: Serve as an undersauce with peanut butter blondies (page 274) topped with a scoop of not-just-plain-vanilla ice cream (page 261). Chocolate pudding sauce is also a great complement to banana and peanut frangipane tarts (page 100).

Creamy Peanut Butter & Honey Sauce

MAKES 2 CUPS

My mother never stocked peanut butter in the house (because she didn't care for it), and as a result I don't think I ate it until I went away to college. As an adult, I find it has become one of my favorite dessert ingredients when I'm in the mood for something rich and indulgent. While natural organic health food varieties of peanut butter are, well, healthier, I like the addition of sugar and salt that super-market brands provide.

INGREDIENTS

¼ cup + 2 tablespoons corn syrup

¼ cup honey

2 tablespoons orange juice

¼ cup water

½ cup peanut butter

½ cup cream

1 egg

1 egg yolk

1 teaspoon vanilla

PREPARATION

1 Combine the corn syrup, honey, orange juice, and water in a heavy-bottomed saucepan. Cook over medium heat, whisking until the mixture starts to simmer. Add the peanut butter and whisk until smooth. Add the cream and allow to simmer for 2 to 3 minutes.

2 Combine the egg and egg yolk in a small mixing bowl. Whisk in a small quantity of the hot peanut butter mixture to temper. Place the egg mixture back in the saucepan and whisk for about 1 minute, till the eggs have cooked through and the mixture has thickened. Remove from heat.

3 Add the vanilla and strain the sauce through a fine-mesh strainer. Cool to room temperature and refrigerate if not serving immediately. This can be made up to 3 days ahead of time. It can also be frozen.

Baker's Note: You can add a generous couple of tablespoons of dark rum or bourbon to this sauce if you wish.

Serving Suggestions: Serve with chocolate-, banana-, or peanut-flavored desserts such as chocolate chip cookie tarts (page 102), banana upside down cakes (page 224), or peanut butter blondie and milk chocolate malt ice cream cake (page 274). For a grown-up kid's sundae, drizzle this sauce in tandem with Concord grape syrup (page 50) over not-just-plain-vanilla-ice cream (page 261)—marshmallow fluff (page 68) is optional.

Hot Buttered Rum Raisin Sauce

MAKES 1 CUP

This is a delicious cool-weather sauce that can warm up a number of fall and winter desserts.

INGREDIENTS

¼ cup + 2 teaspoons Myers dark rum, divided

½ cup + 2 tablespoons orange juice

¼ cup + 2 tablespoons raisins (I like to use a mix of dark and golden raisins)

¼ cup brown sugar

2 tablespoons ruby port

a few grains kosher salt

a few grains freshly ground black pepper

1 teaspoon cornstarch

½ teaspoon vanilla

1 tablespoon (½ ounce) butter

PREPARATION

1 Combine 2 tablespoons of rum and 2 tablespoons of orange juice with the raisins in a small saucepan. Heat until the mixture simmers. Turn the heat off and allow the raisins to plump for 30 minutes.

2 Add the brown sugar, ½ cup orange juice, 2 tablespoons of rum, the ruby port, and the salt and pepper to the plumped raisins. Bring back to a simmer over medium heat. Heat till the sugar dissolves.

3 Combine the cornstarch with the remaining 2 teaspoons of rum and stir into the simmering sauce. Heat till just thickened. Remove from the heat and stir in the vanilla. The sauce can be made up to this point as many as 3 days ahead of time. Store in the refrigerator.

4 To finish the sauce, reheat just to a simmer. Remove from heat and swirl in the butter. Serve immediately.

Baker's Note: You can vary this sauce by substituting apple cider for the orange juice. Depending on what you're serving it with, the addition of some cinnamon and/or nutmeg might be nice. Make sure to use a good-quality, preferably dark or golden rum for this sauce. Brandy or cognac may be substituted for the rum.

Serving Suggestions: This is fabulous served with chocolate chestnut tarts (page 104) and some whipped cream. It also pairs well with not-afraid-of-flavor gingerbread (page 222). You should also try it drizzled over not-just-plain-vanilla ice cream (page 261) or burnt orange caramel ice cream (page 262).

Gingered Maple Walnut Sauce

MAKES 1½ CUPS

In Northeastern ice cream parlor lingo these were called "wet nuts" and were integral to extravagant sundaes and splits. I've punched up the flavor with the addition of some fresh ginger, which gives this rich sauce just the right amount of zing.

INGREDIENTS

¾ cup corn syrup
½ cup maple syrup
¼ cup water
¼ cup sugar
¼ teaspoon ground ginger
¼ cup peeled and finely chopped fresh ginger
½ teaspoon lemon juice
1¼ cups toasted, skinned, coarsely chopped walnuts

PREPARATION

1 Combine the corn syrup, maple syrup, water, sugar, and ground and fresh ginger in a nonreactive saucepan. Bring to a simmer over medium heat, stirring once or twice. Allow to cook for 2 to 3 minutes and remove from heat. Let the mixture cool to room temperature.

2 Strain the mixture through a fine-mesh strainer pressing on the ginger to extract as much liquid as possible. Discard the ginger. Add the lemon juice to the sauce. Stir in the walnuts. This can be made up to 2 days in advance.

Baker's Note: Other nuts may be substituted for the walnuts—macadamias and pecans work well.

Serving Suggestions: Serve as an ice cream topper, with maple bourbon sweet potato pie (page 87), or with pumpkin cognac cheesecake brûlée (page 247).

Lynchburg Lemonade Sauce

MAKES 2 CUPS

Refreshingly tart and containing a large splash of Tennessee's finest, this dessert sauce was inspired by the classic Lynchburg lemonade cocktail.

INGREDIENTS

3 eggs
1 cup + 1 tablespoon sugar
grated zest of 1 lemon
¾ cup water
¼ cup Jack Daniels or bourbon whiskey
½ cup lemon juice

PREPARATION

1 Combine all the ingredients in the top of a double boiler and whisk together to combine. Place over barely simmering water and cook, whisking until thick and hot to the touch.
2 Remove from heat, strain through a fine-mesh strainer, and chill over an ice bath. Whisk lightly before serving. This can be made up to 3 days in advance.

Baker's Note: Try substituting lime juice for the lemon zest and juice and rum for the bourbon. If you want to omit the liquor, you can replace it with an additional 3 tablespoons of water and 1 tablespoon of lemon juice.

Serving Suggestions: I like this as an accent to lemon pecan tart (page 95). It's also a tasty addition to a piece of toasted not-afraid-of-flavor gingerbread (page 222).

Cinnamon Spiced Blueberry Sauce

MAKES ABOUT 2½ CUPS

My grandmother used to take me wild blueberry picking in the Catskill Mountains. If we were lucky, hours of labor would yield us several buckets of tiny, amazingly intense huckleberries. We used to lightly stew a portion of these, mix them with an equal portion of raw ones, and eat big bowls of them topped with sour cream and a bit of brown sugar. While there's nothing quite like the wild variety, cultivated and even individually quick-frozen berries make a darned good sauce.

INGREDIENTS

4 cups blueberries, divided
⅜ cup sugar
½ teaspoon cinnamon
⅛ teaspoon ground cloves
⅛ teaspoon nutmeg
a few grains kosher salt
2 tablespoons + 2 teaspoons orange juice
1½ tablespoons crème de cassis (or Grand Marnier
    or additional orange juice if you prefer)
1 teaspoon cornstarch

PREPARATION

1 Combine 2 cups of the blueberries with the sugar, cinnamon, cloves, nutmeg, salt, 2 tablespoons of the orange juice, and the cassis in a nonreactive saucepan. Bring to a simmer over medium heat, stirring occasionally, until the berries pop and release their juices.

2 Combine the cornstarch with the remaining 2 teaspoons of orange juice and stir this mixture into the simmering blueberries. Cook 1 to 2 minutes, until lightly thickened. Remove from heat and stir in the remaining 2 cups of blueberries. Taste and season with additional sugar or orange juice if necessary.

3 Chill the sauce over an ice bath and then refrigerate, covered, until ready to serve. This can be made up to 3 days in advance. It can also be frozen.

Baker's Note: I usually use Vietnamese cassia cinnamon, which is fairly strong in flavor. You may wish to adjust the amount of spice called for according to your taste.

Serving Suggestions: Try this with buttermilk panna cotta (page 188), not-afraid-of-flavor gingerbread (page 222), or brown sugar sour cream cheesecake (page 243).

Pineapple Caramel— & Variations on the Theme

MAKES 1 CUP

This recipe can be varied simply by substituting a different fruit juice, cider, nectar, or purée for the pineapple. These sauces are fairly intense and should be used primarily as an accent on the plate.

INGREDIENTS

1 cup sugar
½ cup pineapple juice
a few drops lemon juice
an additional ¼–½ cup pineapple juice

PREPARATION

1 In a medium-sized heavy-bottomed saucepan or sauté pan, heat the sugar till it starts to caramelize. While the sugar is cooking, place ½ cup of pineapple juice in a small saucepan and heat to just under a boil.

2 Once the caramel has turned a deep amber color, carefully and slowly add the hot pineapple juice to stop the caramelization. Continue to cook over medium heat, stirring until any bits of hardened caramel are dissolved.

3 Remove the caramel from heat and pour through a fine-mesh strainer into a stainless bowl. Add the lemon juice and ¼ cup of additional pineapple juice. Allow the caramel to come to room temperature and adjust the consistency with additional pineapple juice if necessary—it should have the viscosity of a thick but pourable syrup.

Baker's Note: You can substitute a couple of tablespoons of liquor for part of the juice used to thin the initial caramel if you wish. For example, you can make a pineapple rum caramel or a tequila lime caramel. You can also stir some chopped, toasted, skinned nuts into the caramel for a fruit-flavored version of "sundae nuts."

Serving Suggestions: Serve pineapple caramel with pineapple fritters (page 350) and orange coconut sorbet (page 284). A cider version is great dripped around ice cream–topped cinnamon apple date babycakes (page 234), and a brandied apricot caramel would accentuate the flavor of the giant apricot popover pancake (page 340).

A Couple of Apple Sauces

EACH RECIPE MAKES 1¾ CUPS

As American as Mom and applesauce — it doesn't have quite the same cachet as pie, but my Mom didn't make pies. She did, however, occasionally fix this quick and easy applesauce. I've also included the ingredients for a cranberry variation that results in a beautiful magenta-colored sauce. The procedure is exactly the same for both.

INGREDIENTS FOR SAUCE NO. 1
  1½ pounds peeled, cored, and sliced Granny Smith apples
    (about 4 cups sliced)
  ¾ cup apple juice or cider
  ¼ teaspoon cinnamon
  ¼ cup sugar
  a few grains kosher salt
  1 500 mg. vitamin C tab

INGREDIENTS FOR SAUCE NO. 2
  1¼ pounds unpeeled, cored and sliced, Cortland apples
    (about 3½ cups sliced)
  ¾ cup apple juice or cider
  ½ cup cranberries
  a few grains kosher salt

PREPARATION FOR EITHER SAUCE

1 Combine all the ingredients in a medium-sized nonreactive saucepan and cook at a low simmer, stirring often, until the apples are soft and fall apart (usually about 15 minutes). You may have to add a bit more apple juice if the mixture seems dry and in danger of sticking.

2 Put the mixture through a food mill, or purée it and strain through a fine-mesh strainer. Taste and add additional sugar if you wish. Cool and refrigerate till serving. This can be made up to 3 days ahead. If you are using this as a true sauce, you may want to thin it with additional apple juice or cider.

Baker's Note: You can really play around with this recipe by adding some fresh ginger or a bit of brandy, sweetening it with maple syrup, substituting pears or quince for some of the apples, etc., etc.

Serving Suggestions: Try layering the two types of sauce in a dessert glass and topping them with some cinnamon-flavored whipped cream. Serve with pecan shortbreads (page 302). Applesauce is also delicious with not-afraid-of-flavor gingerbread (page 222).

Raspberry Red Wine Sauce

MAKES ABOUT 1 ½ CUPS

The addition of red wine to a standard raspberry purée deepens both the flavor and color of this sauce.

INGREDIENTS

¾ cup red wine
3 cups raspberries, fresh or individually quick-frozen (not in syrup)
¼ cup sugar
a few grains kosher salt

PREPARATION

1 Place the red wine in a nonreactive saucepan and reduce by half over medium heat. Reduce heat to low.

2 Add the raspberries, sugar, and salt and cook, stirring occasionally, until the berries soften and the sugar dissolves. Simmer for 1 minute. Remove from heat and cool slightly.

3 Purée the mixture and strain it through a fine-mesh strainer. Discard the seeds. Taste and season if necessary. Depending on your berries, you may need to add a touch of citrus juice or a bit more sugar. Cool thoroughly over an ice bath. Refrigerate if not using immediately. This can be kept refrigerated for up to 3 days or frozen for several months.

Baker's Note: Any decent-quality red wine can be used for this sauce—if you'll drink it on its own, you can use it in the sauce. A fruity Zinfandel or Pinot Noir would be perfect.

Serving Suggestions: This sauce works wonderfully as an all-purpose accompaniment to goat cheese cheesecake in a hazelnut crust (page 252) or served on top of not-just-plain-vanilla ice cream (page 261) or frozen sourwood honey parfait (page 289). It would also be delicious with a traditional buttermilk custard pie and fresh berries or simply spooned over fresh sliced peaches with a dollop of crème fraîche (page 67).

Strawberry Crush

MAKES APPROXIMATELY 2 CUPS

The difference between height-of-season, locally grown strawberries and their commercially produced counterparts, tasted side by side, is striking. This simple sauce is a great vehicle for showing off this luscious, fragrant fruit. Hand-mashing the berries releases just the right amount of delicate juice while maintaining a rustic texture.

INGREDIENTS

3 cups hulled, sliced strawberries
2 tablespoons sugar

PREPARATION

1 Place the berries in a stainless mixing bowl. Sprinkle with the sugar. Using a potato masher or a large, sturdy fork, crush the berries so that they break up into a thick juicy sauce with visible chunks of berries.
2 Taste the sauce. You may have to add a bit of additional sugar or a few drops of lemon juice to adjust the flavor balance.

Baker's Note: You can vary the flavor profile of this sauce by adding some finely chopped fresh ginger, a small amount of Grand Marnier, or a bit of freshly ground black pepper. Honey or brown sugar can also be substituted for the sugar.

Serving Suggestions: This sauce is marvelous with goat cheese cheesecake in a hazelnut crust (page 252), buttermilk vanilla bean custard pie (page 85), or key lime soufflé pudding (page 185). It's also delicious as a topping for not-just-plain-vanilla ice cream (page 261), cream cheese strawberry swirl ice cream (page 265), or lemon chiffon ice cream (page 271).

Concord Grape Syrup

MAKES 1½ CUPS

Native American grapes, such as Concords or Muscadines, have a fabulously spicy, intensely fruity quality. But—while commercially produced grape juice and jelly are American mainstays—these late summer beauties are often overlooked as a dessert ingredient. They can be difficult to seed, so I tend to use them in applications where they are puréed and strained, such as grape sorbet or this versatile grape syrup.

INGREDIENTS

1 pound Concord or Purple Muscat grapes
¼ cup prepared Concord grape juice
2 tablespoons honey
1 tablespoon sugar
a few grains kosher salt

PREPARATION

1 Stem the grapes and place them in a heavy-bottomed saucepan with the grape juice, honey, sugar, and salt. Bring to a boil over medium heat, reduce heat, and simmer for about 15 minutes, stirring and mashing the grapes occasionally.

2 Purée the mixture with a food mill or a handheld mixer and then pass it through a fine-mesh strainer. Cool and adjust the seasonings with a bit of lemon juice or sugar if necessary. Store refrigerated for up to 5 days. It can also be frozen.

Baker's Note: These grapes are high in pectin, and as a result this syrup can thicken to sauce consistency. Depending on what you're using it for, you may wish to leave it thickened or dilute it slightly with additional grape juice.

Serving Suggestions: This would be great served with banana and peanut frangipane tarts (page 100) or drizzled over peanut butter blondies (page 274) topped with not-just-plain-vanilla ice cream (page 261). I've also served this as part of a dessert cheese plate with a wedge of creamy blue cheese and some walnut shortbreads (page 302).

Mint Syrup

MAKES ABOUT 1¼ CUPS

Squeeze-bottle cuisine—the application of drips and drops "artfully" administered to plates via highly controllable plastic tubes—has even filtered down to the home kitchen. As something of a traditionalist, I've never been much of a fan of some of the more outrageous permutations of flavored oils, vinegars, and purées that find their way onto dessert plates, but this vibrant, intensely fresh mint syrup is an exception.

INGREDIENTS

1¼ cups sugar
¾ cup water
2 cups packed fresh mint leaves

PREPARATION

1 Combine the sugar and water in a small saucepan and bring to a boil over medium heat. Turn the heat down and simmer several minutes, until the sugar is completely dissolved. Remove from heat and cool completely. Reserve.

2 Bring a small saucepan of water to a boil. Have a strainer and a bowl of ice water at the ready. Working quickly, place the mint leaves in the boiling water and blanch till just wilted (about 10 seconds). Immediately strain the mint and place the leaves directly in the ice water to set their color. Strain the mint again, pressing to remove excess liquid.

3 Place the mint leaves and half of the reserved syrup in a blender. Purée the mint, stopping several times to scrape down the blender bowl. Add the

remaining syrup and blend for 2 minutes. Transfer the mixture to a clean storage container and allow to sit overnight, covered, at room temperature.

4   Strain the syrup through a fine-mesh strainer and discard the solid mint purée. Store the syrup refrigerated for up to 2 weeks. Shake or stir lightly before using.

Baker's Note: For another interesting herbal syrup that can have dessert applications, try substituting fresh basil (cinnamon basil or chocolate basil is particularly good) for the mint.

Serving Suggestions: Serve a drizzle on the plate with dark chocolate Peppermint Pattie cake (page 210), spoon over bourbon vanilla ice cream (page 261) and bourbon poached peaches (page 149), or toss with fresh berries and top with crème fraîche (page 67). This is also wonderful for sweetening ice tea!

Coffee Syrup

MAKES 1 CUP

This intense syrup is ideal for creating coffee-based drinks, drizzling over ice cream, or using as a plate garnish on mocha-flavored desserts.

INGREDIENTS

1 cup hot brewed coffee
1 tablespoon instant coffee
½ cup brown sugar
½ cup corn syrup
½ cup cream
1 tablespoon coffee liqueur

PREPARATION

1   In a medium-sized saucepan dissolve the instant coffee in the brewed coffee. Add the sugar, corn syrup, and cream and place over medium heat. Bring to a simmer, lower the heat, and reduce the mixture until thickened, stirring periodically—the syrup should "sheet" from a spoon and will register 220° on a candy thermometer. Remove from heat and stir in the coffee liqueur.

2 Cool the syrup and check its consistency. If it seems a bit too thick, gradually stir in a small amount of additional brewed coffee. Store covered in the refrigerator for up to 1 week. Bring back to room temperature before using. This syrup can be frozen if desired.

Baker's Note: This syrup has a tendency to go nuclear and bubble up quite a bit during the reduction process. Make sure you use an adequately sized pot, reduce the syrup over low heat, and check it often.

Serving Suggestions: This is a key ingredient in making beat-the-heat frozen mocha velvet (page 270). Coffee syrup is also delicious drizzled on a plate with a slice of mocha molasses shoofly pie (page 89). An unusual combination is to serve this spooned over peppered Bartlett pears in sherry syrup (page 160) with a dollop of crème fraîche (page 67).

Chocolate Ganache

MAKES ABOUT 3 CUPS

Chocolate Ganache is an incredibly versatile basic building block that needs to be in every baker's repertoire. An uncommonly rich amalgamation of cream and chocolate, in its solid form ganache can be formed into truffles or used as a tart filling. At spreadable room-temperature consistency it makes an excellent fudge-like cake filling or icing. In its pourable liquid state it can do double duty as both a finishing glaze or a sauce. Be sure to use a premium brand of chocolate—your ganache will be as good as the chocolate used to make it.

INGREDIENTS
    2 cups cream
    16 ounces semisweet chocolate, chopped into small pieces

PREPARATION
1 Heat the cream in a heavy-bottomed medium-sized saucepan until it is just under a boil. Remove the pan from the heat and add the chopped chocolate. Replace the pan over very low heat and continue to cook, stirring constantly, until the chocolate is completely melted.
2 Remove from heat and strain through a fine-mesh strainer.

3 If the ganache is to be used as a sauce or glaze, allow it to cool to the point where it no longer feels warm to the touch but is still fluid and pourable. If it is to be used to make truffles, allow it to cool and then refrigerate it for several hours before forming the truffle centers. If the ganache is to be used as a filling or icing, it is best to allow it to cool to room temperature. It should reach thickened, spreadable consistency after sitting for several hours or overnight. Alternatively, you can make the ganache up to 1 week ahead of time, keep it refrigerated, and allow it to sit at room temperature for several hours before using. Quick-chilling liquid ganache over an ice bath is also possible, but be sure to stir often and monitor the change in consistency closely.

Baker's Note: You can change the flavor profile of ganache by infusing the cream base with crushed espresso beans, fresh herbs, or toasted spices. Cool (but not chilled to the point where it's solid) ganache can also be lightly whipped and turned into a lighter mousse-like cake filling—be careful not to overwhip, though, as the ganache can separate and curdle.

Homemade Chocolate Chips

MAKES 3 GENEROUS CUPS

You can always make your own chocolate chips or chunks by cutting up a large block of chocolate by hand, but I find the method below much easier, particularly if I need to make a large quantity. The results are more uniform, and the mess is minimal. Using homemade chips made from superior chocolate will take your cakes, cookies, and ice creams to a new level of chocoliciousness.

INGREDIENT
  16 ounces semisweet chocolate (you may substitute milk chocolate
    or white chocolate if you wish)

PREPARATION
1 Chop the chocolate into small pieces and melt in the top of a double boiler over low heat.
2 Line a jellyroll pan or half-size sheet pan with parchment paper and pour the melted chocolate down the center of the pan. The chocolate should be approximately ¼ inch thick.

3 Place the pan in the refrigerator until the chocolate is just set and loses its sheen—check it every few minutes. With the tip of a knife (I like to use a standard table knife with a pointed tip, as opposed to a paring knife), score the chocolate into ¼- to ⅓-inch squares. Place the pan back in the refrigerator or freezer to rechill for 5 to 10 minutes.

4 Remove the chilled pan and, grasping the edges of the parchment paper, flip the sheet over so that the chocolate is on the bottom and the parchment is on the top. Peel off the parchment and discard. Break the scored chocolate into individual chips and store in a closed plastic bag or covered airtight container for up to several days if refrigerated or several weeks if frozen.

Honeyed Almonds

MAKES 1 CUP

Giving almonds a quick dip in a honey-flavored syrup before toasting them makes them extra crispy and addictively delicious. Sprinkling the just-roasted nuts with salt, pepper, and spices turns a dessert garnish into a cocktail nibble.

INGREDIENTS

¾ cup sugar

1 cup water

¼ cup honey

1 cup skinned, sliced almonds

PREPARATION

1 Preheat oven to 350°.

2 Combine the sugar, water, and honey in a saucepan and bring to a boil. Reduce heat and simmer till the sugar is dissolved. Add the almonds and simmer for 3 minutes. Place the almonds in a fine-mesh strainer and drain off the sugar syrup.

3 Spread the almonds in a single layer on a silpat or parchment paper–lined baking sheet. Bake at 350° approximately 10 to 12 minutes, turning occasionally with a metal spatula, until golden brown.

4 Remove from oven, cool for a minute or two, and loosen the almonds from the baking sheet.

5   Once the almonds are completely cool, place them in an airtight container until ready to use.

Baker's Note: Once the nuts start to pick up color, check them often and do not allow them to become too toasted. Due to the sticky nature of these nuts, you really must bake them on a lined baking sheet. A silpat sheet makes cleanup a snap.

Serving Suggestions: These candied nuts are great sprinkled over any honey- or almond-flavored dessert. They also work well as a garnish for many poached fruits or as part of a cheese plate. Try serving peppered Bartlett pears in sherry syrup (page 160) with a dollop of crème fraîche (page 67) or a scoop of frozen sourwood honey parfait (page 289) and a scattering of almonds.

Pecan Praline

MAKES 1½ CUPS OF CHOPPED PRALINE

Combining caramelized sugar with lightly toasted nuts results in a crunchy praline. Frozen into ice creams, folded into buttercreams, or used as a sprinkled garnish, praline can add both texture and flavor to any number of desserts. If you do not have much experience caramelizing sugar, please read the note on caramelization (page 34) before proceeding.

INGREDIENTS

1 cup sugar
3 tablespoons water + a few drops of lemon juice (optional)
⅔ cup lightly toasted medium-sized pecan pieces

PREPARATION

1   I usually caramelize my sugar dry for praline. If, however, you feel more comfortable with wet caramelization, place the sugar in a medium-sized heavy-bottomed saucepan and add the optional water and lemon juice to moisten the sugar. This will allow the sugar to caramelize more evenly, but the process will take longer. Cook until the sugar caramelizes to a medium amber. Immediately add the toasted nuts and stir briefly to coat them with the caramel. Pour the mixture onto a lightly oiled baking sheet or a silpat sheet. Allow the praline to cool completely.

2 Once cooled, the praline can be broken into large shards (be careful with sharp edges—it really is somewhat glass-like), chopped or hammered into medium-sized to small pieces, or processor ground into praline "dust."

3 Store the praline airtight for up to 1 week before using. It will become sticky if exposed to humidity.

Baker's Note: Any type of skinned, lightly toasted nut can be substituted for the pecans.

Serving Suggestions: Try sprinkling walnut praline on winter fruits poached in red wine syrup (page 157) topped with crème fraîche (page 67), folding peanut praline into peanut butter ice cream (page 266), or using macadamia nut praline to garnish key lime coconut pie (page 90).

Peanut Frangipane

MAKES 2 CUPS

Frangipane, an almond-based pastry filling, is a basic in the world of French sweets. I've substituted peanuts to give it a distinctly American flavor.

INGREDIENTS

1½ tablespoons flour
⅓ cup sugar
1½ cups roasted, lightly salted peanuts
1 egg
1 teaspoon vanilla
1 tablespoon dark rum
8 tablespoons (4 ounces) butter, at room temperature

PREPARATION

Place the flour, sugar, and peanuts in a food processor with a steel blade. Process until the nuts are finely ground. Add the egg, vanilla, and rum and pulse until just combined. Add the butter and pulse, scraping the bowl down once or twice, until just blended. This can be refrigerated for up to 3 days, but bring it back to room temperature before using.

Baker's Note: If you don't have a food processor, you can chop the nuts very finely by hand or grind them along with the sugar and flour with a mortar and pestle. Combine with the other ingredients till well mixed. You may substitute any lightly toasted nut for the peanuts and any liqueur for the rum.

Serving Suggestions: This makes an excellent tart base (see banana and peanut frangipane tarts, page 100). Frangipane also makes a terrific crepe filling. If you have leftover frangipane, try spreading it on toast and then retoasting it to set the frangipane: eat it plain or embellish it with fresh fruit or preserves for a lovely breakfast treat. The combination of hazelnut frangipane and sliced strawberries or almond frangipane and apricots is especially delicious.

Candied Chestnut Purée

MAKES 2 CUPS

Candied chestnut purée is a delicious confection that can be used to flavor many different types of desserts. Several varieties of French-produced sweetened canned chestnut spread (Clément Faugier is a particularly good brand) are available in specialty stores, but it's not difficult to make your own.

INGREDIENTS
  12 ounces fresh chestnuts, shelled (see note on shelling chestnuts, page 105)
  1 cup milk
  3½ tablespoons sugar
  ½ cup corn syrup
  1½ tablespoons dark rum
  1 teaspoon vanilla

PREPARATION
1 Combine the chestnuts, milk, and sugar in a heavy-bottomed saucepan. The chestnuts should be just covered by the milk. Bring to a simmer and cook over low heat, stirring often, until the chestnuts are very soft and the milk has thickened. The cooking time can vary depending on the variety and age of the chestnuts. You may need to add additional milk during the cooking process.
2 Once they are tender, place the chestnuts and the remaining liquid in a food processor with a steel blade. Add the corn syrup, rum, and vanilla and process

till very smooth. You can alternatively rice the chestnuts in a food mill and then add the corn syrup, rum, and vanilla. The texture should be creamy, like that of peanut butter. Thin with a bit of additional milk if the consistency seems too stiff.

3 Cool completely and store refrigerated for up to 1 week.

Baker's Note: Already-peeled chestnuts that have either been frozen or vacuum packed can be used in place of fresh ones. Canned nuts are also available, but their flavor is usually not as intense and their texture is often compromised. In a pinch, they can be used for purées.

Serving Suggestions: Chestnut cream can be used as a tart filling (see chocolate chestnut tarts, page 104) or to flavor whipped cream (see chocolate chestnut cream roll, page 212). You can also use it to fill crepes, add flavor to ice cream bases or custard sauces, and enrich puddings, pastry creams, or buttercreams.

Lemon or Lime Curd/Custard

MAKES ABOUT 1 CUP

In old Southern cookbooks, this confection is often called a cheese or a jelly. While the British "curd" is probably its more familiar name, I personally prefer the term "custard." This version is a bit lighter than that in many recipes but no less delicious.

INGREDIENTS

    3 eggs
    1 egg yolk
    ½ cup sugar
    ¼ cup + 2 tablespoons lemon or lime juice
    4 tablespoons (2 ounces) butter

PREPARATION

1 Combine the eggs, egg yolk, sugar, and citrus juice in the top of a double boiler and whisk to combine. Place over just simmering water and cook, whisking often, till the mixture has thickened. This will take about 15 minutes. Remove from heat and whisk in the butter.

2   Strain the mixture through a fine-mesh strainer and cool over an ice bath. Store covered in the refrigerator for up to 2 weeks.

Baker's Note: About 1 cup of strained fruit purée that has been cooked with a minimum of liquid can be substituted for the citrus juice. Apricots, peaches, and blackberries make particularly good fruit curds/custards.

Serving Suggestions: At its simplest, this concoction is wonderful slathered on toasted bread or cake. You can also use it as a tart or cookie filling. For a delicious mousse-like cream, whip some lightly sweetened cream or crème fraîche to medium peaks and fold into an equal quantity of curd/custard.

Candied Orange Zest

MAKES ABOUT 1 CUP

Pretty as well as tasty, candied orange zest is a nice finishing touch that is easily made and keeps for weeks.

INGREDIENTS

3 navel oranges (preferably with deep-colored, unblemished skins)
2 cups sugar syrup (page 281)

PREPARATION

1   With a vegetable peeler, remove the zest from the oranges in long pieces. Try to avoid the white pith. With a sharp knife, cut the zest into thin julienne strips. Place the cut zest in a small saucepan and cover with cold water. Cook over medium heat until the water comes to a boil. Remove from heat and strain. Place the zest back in the saucepan and cover with fresh cold water. Repeat the blanching and straining process 2 more times.
2   After the zest is strained for the third time, cover it in the saucepan with the prepared sugar syrup. Bring to a boil, turn down the heat, and allow to simmer for about 20 minutes or until the peel is translucent and tender. Remove from heat and allow to cool in the syrup. Place in a storage container, making sure to completely cover the peel with sugar syrup. Store refrigerated up to 1 month.

Baker's Note: This recipe works equally well with lemon zest. I'm less enamored of candied lime zest because it tends to be tougher. Whenever possible, try to use organic citrus for candied zest. Try to avoid fruit whose skins have been sprayed and dyed—a condition that is not uncommon.

Serving Suggestions: I use the wispy strands of candied zest primarily for garnishing. It adds a spark of color and flavor to any dessert that has even a hint of citrus or in which citrus would be a complementary flavor. If drained and finely chopped, it's also a delicious addition to Cousin Steve's cheesecake (page 241) or cranberry crumb cake (page 229).

Candied Orange Peel

MAKES ABOUT 1 CUP

At first glance, this recipe appears to be similar to that for candied zest, but because the entire peel is employed, the cooking process and resulting product are markedly different.

INGREDIENTS
- 2½ cups sugar
- 1½ cups water
- 3 navel oranges (preferably with deep-colored, unblemished skins)

PREPARATION

1 Make a heavy sugar syrup by combining the sugar and water in a saucepan: bring to a boil, reduce heat, and simmer until the sugar dissolves. Reserve.

2 Remove the skin, including the white pith, from the oranges in thick strips. Scrape to remove any pulp clinging to the pith. Cut the peel into ¼-inch strips. Reserve the fruit for orange segments or fresh-squeezed juice.

3 Place the cut peel in a medium-sized saucepan. Cover with cold water and bring to a boil. Allow the peel to boil for 3 minutes. Drain, place the peel back in the pot, and cover with fresh cold water. Repeat the blanching and draining process 3 times. After the third blanching, place the peel back in the saucepan and cover with the reserved sugar syrup. Cook, stirring occasionally, over low heat for about 1 to 1½ hours until the peel is tender and translucent and most

of the syrup has been absorbed. Drain the peel and lay it out on a wire rack to dry slightly.

4 If I am using the candied peel for fruitcake, cookies etc., I allow the peel to dry on racks for several hours until just barely tacky to the touch. The peel itself, coupled with the given humidity, can affect the timing of this; you might even have to leave it overnight. Pack the peel in an airtight storage container, separating layers with parchment paper, and store in a cool, dry place until needed, for up to 2 weeks. If I plan to serve the candied peel as an after-dinner confection, I allow it to dry out on racks for a few hours until barely tacky and

then roll the strips in sugar until well coated and place them back on the racks to dry out overnight. Store the dried sugared peel airtight, separating layers with parchment paper. These too will keep for 2 weeks.

Baker's Note: Grapefruits and thick-skinned lemons can be substituted for the oranges. If you wish to make chocolate-dipped peel, allow the candied peel to dry on racks for several hours until no longer sticky, dip the ends in melted semisweet chocolate, and place on parchment paper until the chocolate is set.

Serving Suggestions: Try making Big Island fruitcake (page 232) using your own homemade orange peel. Chopped candied peel is also delicious added to muffins, shortcakes, and chocolate chip cookies. The resulting orange cooking syrup is terrific drizzled over morning pancakes. Pair sugarcoated candied zest with bourbon balls (page 318) and cornmeal vanilla bean shortbreads (page 300) for a very satisfying collection of dessert nibbles—perfect with after-dinner coffee.

Whipped Cream

MAKES 2 CUPS

You might be asking yourself, do I really need a recipe for whipped cream? Making whipped cream is not difficult, but in the world of desserts it's of key importance, because great whipped cream can accessorize a dessert perfectly while improperly whipped cream is a major detraction. Here is a very simple recipe followed by a detailed baker's note.

INGREDIENTS
    1 cup cream
    1 tablespoon sugar

PREPARATION
Place the cream in a large, chilled stainless bowl. Using a large, flexible, chilled balloon whip, hand-beat the cream until it is barely thickened. Whisk in the sugar. Taste the cream and adjust the sweetness with a bit more sugar if necessary. If flavoring the cream, whisk in any additions at this point. Continue to whip just until soft peaks form. The whipped cream should be billowy, not stiff. Use immediately or cover and refrigerate for several hours.

Baker's Note:

- Seek out a cream that is at least 36 percent butterfat. If at all possible, use cream that is not ultrapasteurized.
- It does take a bit of work, but I think best whipped cream is always hand-whipped. If necessary, whip a large quantity of cream in 2 batches.
- I like to lightly sweeten whipped cream with plain granulated sugar. I find that the flavor of cream can vary tremendously—much of this has to do with dairy cows' diet. It is necessary to regulate the exact amount of sugar added by taste rather than by a strict measure. By adding the sugar, pausing to taste the cream, and then making necessary adjustments, you will wind up with perfectly sweetened whipped cream.
- Properly whipped cream should barely hold its shape and plop gracefully when dolloped from a spoon. Do not overbeat your cream; but, if you do, try gently stirring in a bit of extra cream with a spatula to return cream that is too stiff to a proper consistency.
- It is possible to whip cream several hours ahead of time, but it will probably have to be rewhipped slightly just before serving.
- Keep whipped cream well covered and chilled if you are not using it right away—it picks up refrigerator odors quite easily.
- Cream will approximately double in volume when properly whipped.
- You can flavor whipped cream if you wish. Some people automatically add vanilla extract to whipped cream. I don't—although there are times when a distinct vanilla component might be desirable. A few tablespoons of good quality alcohol (bourbon, Grand Marnier, Kirsch, etc.) can also be beaten into lightly thickened cream. For coffee cream, add instant coffee or espresso that is dissolved in just enough hot water to make it fluid. I do this to taste and add some extra sugar to make up for the strong acidity of the coffee. You can also add small pinches of spices such as cinnamon or nutmeg to lightly thickened cream, whipping to distribute evenly. Sweetened nut pastes—made by processing toasted nuts with a small quantity of corn syrup till the mixture is smooth and has the consistency of tahini—can be beaten into whipped cream, as can ground praline (page 56). Another possibility is flavoring whipped cream with thick fruit purées. Otherwise known as "fools," the resulting mousse-like desserts are prepared by lightly folding the purées into sweetened cream beaten to medium peaks. Layered with additional fresh fruit in a parfait glass, these are deliciously refreshing light desserts that can be put together easily.

Custard Sauce (Crème Anglaise) — A Basic Recipe & Variations

MAKES 2⅔ CUPS

My father-in-law often talks nostalgically about the marvelous boiled or stirred custards of his youth. Bowls of the elixir were most often served on their own as a restorative home remedy after minor illnesses. It took me a while to realize that what he was referring to was a slightly thicker version of crème anglaise. The following basic formula is meant to be flavored to complement whatever it is being served with. Several suggested variations follow the basic recipe, but I encourage you to let your imagination run wild.

INGREDIENTS

1½ cups half-and-half
½ cup cream
6 egg yolks
⅔ cup sugar
⅛ teaspoon kosher salt
1½ teaspoons vanilla

PREPARATION

1 Heat the half-and-half and cream to just under a boil in a heavy-bottomed nonreactive saucepan.

2 Whisk the egg yolks, sugar, and salt together in a bowl. Gradually whisk in a portion of the hot cream. Transfer the tempered mixture back to the saucepan and cook over medium low heat, stirring constantly, until the custard thickens and coats the back of a spoon and feels very hot to the touch. This should take 8 to 10 minutes. Be careful not to allow the custard to overheat and scramble!

3 Once the custard has thickened, immediately strain it through a fine-mesh strainer, add the vanilla, and chill over an ice bath. This can be made up to 3 days in advance.

- Vanilla bean: Omit the vanilla extract. Split a vanilla bean in half. Whisk the seeds together with the egg yolks, sugar, and salt. Place the pod in the saucepan with the half-and-half and allow it to infuse the half-and-half as it heats.
- Tangerine: Combine the grated zest of 2 tangerines with the half-and-half. Place 1 cup of tangerine juice in a small saucepan and reduce to ⅓ cup over medium heat. Once the custard has thickened, add the reduced tangerine juice to it.
- Grand Marnier, brandy, bourbon, rum, etc.: Add 3 tablespoons of the desired liqueur or liquor to the thickened custard.
- Mint, basil, rose geranium, or other fresh herbs: Infuse the half-and-half mixture with about ¼ cup of fresh herb leaves, allowing them to sit in the heated half-and-half, covered, for 30 minutes prior to proceeding with the recipe. Reheat the half-and-half to temper the eggs.
- Nuts: Toast and finely chop 1 cup of almonds, pecans, hazelnuts, or walnuts. Allow them to sit in the heated half-and-half, covered, for 30 minutes. Strain this mixture, pressing down on the nuts to extract their oil. Discard the nuts and reheat the flavored half-and-half to temper the eggs.
- Chocolate: Finely chop 3 ounces of semisweet chocolate and place it in a bowl. Gradually whisk the hot, thickened custard into the chocolate and stir just until the chocolate is melted. Strain the finished sauce prior to chilling.
- Cinnamon: Infuse the half-and half-mixture with 2 broken-up cinnamon sticks and add ¾ teaspoon of ground cinnamon to the egg yolk, sugar, and salt mixture prior to tempering.
- Fruits: Add strained fruit purée to taste to the finished, thickened custard sauce.

Baker's Note: I prefer a thick, rich custard sauce, especially if I am going to thin it slightly by adding additional liquid flavoring at the end. You can control the richness and texture by using a portion of milk for the dairy base. This will give you a lighter consistency. Slightly reducing the number of egg yolks used does the same thing.

Serving Suggestions: Coconut rum raisin bread pudding (page 180) served with a tangerine anglaise is a terrific combination. A custard sauce is also fabulous poured over oven roasted fruits (page 151).

White Chocolate Cream

MAKES ABOUT 3 CUPS

Adding white chocolate to whipped cream produces a rich cream with an almost mousse-like consistency and an elusive vanilla-like flavor.

INGREDIENTS

1½ cups heavy cream
4 ounces white chocolate, chopped into very small pieces

PREPARATION

1 Bring ½ cup of the cream to just under a simmer in a medium-sized saucepan. Add the white chocolate, turn the heat down to very low, and continue to heat, stirring, until the chocolate is completely melted.
2 Remove from heat and gradually stir in the remaining 1 cup of cream. Strain the mixture through a fine-mesh strainer and chill several hours.
3 Whip the cream to soft peaks being careful not to overwhip. Use immediately or refrigerate for several hours.

Baker's Note: Always work with excellent-quality white chocolate (I like Valrhona or Callebaut) and be careful not to overheat it, as it has a tendency to scorch.

Serving Suggestions: This recipe was created to be a component of chocolate strawberry shortcakes (page 135). It can also be used as an accompaniment to rich chocolate desserts, as a filling for cream puff shells, or as part of a decadent ice cream sundae.

Crème Fraîche

MAKES ABOUT 1 CUP

Traditional French crème fraîche is a wondrous, tangy, thick, naturally cultured cream. It's obviously a great garnish for fruit-based desserts but also provides a rich, slightly acidic counterpoint to intense chocolate-, caramel-, and nut-flavored sweets. Delicious American-made crème fraîche is produced by Vermont Butter and Cheese, Cow Girl Creamery, and several other regional artisanal dairies. Unless you have access to raw milk, you cannot make true crème fraîche at home, but the following method will result in a reasonable facsimile.

INGREDIENTS

  2 tablespoons buttermilk (preferably whole-milk buttermilk)
  1 cup cream (not ultrapasteurized)

PREPARATION

Combine the buttermilk and cream in a small saucepan and heat, stirring over low heat, until just warm to the touch (85°). Be careful not to overheat. Pour into a nonreactive storage container, cover, and allow to culture in a warm place—I usually use a shelf near the range—until thickened. This can vary from batch to batch, but it usually takes about 24 hours. Stir lightly and store refrigerated for up to 1 week.

Baker's Note: You can flavor thickened crème fraîche by gently folding in vanilla bean seeds, ground cinnamon, a bit of butterscotch sauce, or a thick fruit purée.

Serving Suggestions: You can't go wrong serving a big plop of crème fraîche over just about any fresh fruit, fruit compote, or fruit-based pastry. You could also serve it with Fig Newton Zinfandel tart (page 97), mocha molasses shoofly pie (page 89), or chocolate Grand Marnier truffle tart (page 106). And try substituting crème fraîche for the cream component in not-just-plain-vanilla ice cream (page 261).

Marshmallow Fluff

MAKES 6 CUPS

At one time, peanut butter and fluff sandwiches were considered standard children's lunch fare. Alas, these days few kids seem to have encountered fluff. Delicious in a retro kind of way, this homemade version is an improvement, I think, over the commercial kind—it's quite tasty, particularly if you lightly toast it.

INGREDIENTS
    ½ cup water
    1 cup corn syrup
    1 cup sugar
    ⅓ cup egg whites
    ⅛ teaspoon kosher salt
    1 teaspoon vanilla

PREPARATION

1 Combine the water, corn syrup, and sugar in a saucepan and cook over
   medium heat until the syrup registers 230° on a candy thermometer. While
   the syrup is cooking, place the egg whites in the bowl of a mixer with a whip
   attachment and beat them together with the salt until they are foamy and
   just start to form soft peaks.

2 Once the syrup has reached the proper temperature, immediately remove it
   from the heat, place the mixer speed on low, and slowly add the syrup to the
   egg whites.

3 Add the vanilla and continue beating the egg whites on high speed until they
   are thick, glossy, and no longer warm to the touch. This should take several
   minutes, and the volume of the egg whites will increase significantly.

4 Once the fluff is cool, use immediately or refrigerate for up to 3 days. Stir
   lightly before using.

Baker's Note: This recipe yields quite a bit of fluff, but it's difficult to work with a
   smaller volume of egg whites. I suggest you share the results with some fluff-
   loving friends. The best way to toast the fluff is to lightly apply a butane torch.

Serving Suggestions: Fluff is a natural topping for milk chocolate malt ice cream
   (page 274). It can also be dolloped over maple bourbon sweet potato pie
   (page 87) or banana and peanut frangipane tarts (page 100).

A Pie Primer

Blueberry Blackberry Pie

Apple Rhubarb Cardamom Crumb Pie

Meyer Lemon Shaker Pie

Buttermilk Vanilla Bean Custard Pie

Maple Bourbon Sweet Potato Pie

Mocha Molasses Shoofly Pie

Key Lime Coconut Pie with Rum Cream

Chocolate Raspberry Fudge Pie

Lemon Pecan Tart

Fig Newton Zinfandel Tart

Banana & Peanut Frangipane Tarts

Browned Butter Date Nut Tart

Chocolate Chip Cookie Tarts

Chocolate Chestnut Tarts

Chocolate Grand Marnier Truffle Tart

Cranberry Linzer Tart

Lime Meringue Tart

Rustic Raspberry Tart

Pink Grapefruit Soufflé Tarts

Cherry Vanilla Turnovers

Rhubarb Cream Cheese Dumplings

The perfect pie or tart always involves something of a symbiosis between pastry crust and filling, but one can argue about which takes precedence, the crust or the filling. I'm of the mind that if the filling ingredients are top-notch, the success of a well-crafted pie lies primarily in the crust. This generalization applies to any dessert, for that matter, where pastry plays a prominent role.

Of all desserts, humble pies have always impressed me as being the most genuine and honest. People most often associate the best pie they ever ate with a specific individual. Baking pie is highly personal, and great pie-makers generally take a lot of pride in their skills. They might tell you that it's no big deal, that you just sort of put it all together; but I can tell you that achieving the perfect crust is really something of an art. I have consistently found dough-making to be the hardest thing to teach fledgling bakers. This is primarily because making dough is a very tactile process—you can't really begin to understand it until you actually begin to do it. Ideally, one learns to make pie at the side of an accomplished pie-maker—a recipe is key, but a visual picture is indeed worth a thousand words. And, as long as I'm spouting old adages, might I also say that practice does make perfect!

Some people have innate pastry-making skills—they tend to be relaxed about baking, to have a light touch and cold hands. For those of you who don't put yourselves in this category, here are a few tips to put you on the perfect pie trail.

- I prefer a mixture of vegetable shortening (for flakiness) and butter (for flavor) in pie crusts. Lard or a combination of lard and butter can also make an exceptionally tasty, flaky crust. For shorter tart crusts, I usually use all-butter formulas. No matter what type of fat you choose to use (you may have your own favorite recipe), work with well-chilled ingredients. I cut my fat into small pieces and freeze it briefly before putting the dough together.
- I use a food processor to cut the fat in to the dry ingredients. Multiple quick, short pulses using the steel blade is the quickest, most effective way to accomplish this task without overworking or overheating the dough.
- Once the cold fat is cut in to the dry ingredients, I transfer the mixture to a large, chilled stainless bowl to stir in the water by hand. This gives you a greater degree of control and will help prevent overprocessing.

- The easiest way to add water to form the dough is with a squeeze bottle (like the kind that mustard or ketchup comes in). Again, this gives you better control so that you will be less likely to overwet the dough. I often employ a fine-mist spray bottle as well, using it at the very end of the dough-making process to disperse just a bit of water over the dough if it seems a touch dry.
- Gradually "stir" water into the flour mixture, using a fork in a quick "scrambling" motion. Try to evenly distribute the water around the bowl, as opposed to adding it all in one spot. Continue to add water and toss the flour mixture until the dough is evenly moistened and comes together cleanly when lightly squeezed. It should have the consistency of play-dough—moist, not crumbly but not wet or sticky.
- Shape the dough into a flattened disc before wrapping and chilling. It is much easier to roll the dough into a round shape if you start with a round shape. Chill the dough thoroughly before rolling and remove it from the refrigerator 5 to 10 minutes before rolling.
- In addition to having a light touch when putting the dough together, it is also important to work quickly and deftly when rolling out the dough. Many people have a tendency to "worry" the dough too much in the rolling process. I advocate pounding the dough with a rolling pin to flatten it: lift and flour lightly under the dough frequently, giving it quarter turns. Once the dough is fairly thin, complete by actually rolling, working from the center to the edge.
- To ensure that your dough is not sticking, periodically pick it up from the work surface with the aid of a metal pizza peel, the thin metal bottom of a 10-inch removable-bottom tart pan, a thin, rimless cookie sheet, or a tool known as a giant pie spatula (which can be ordered from the King Arthur Flour Co.; see the list of sources at the end of the book). You can easily slide a lightly floured, thin piece of metal under the most delicate of thinly rolled crusts to maneuver it about without any risk of tearing the dough. A metal sheet or spatula is particularly useful for transferring rolled dough to a pie pan or picking up a top crust and placing it over a prepared filling.
- Save any dough scraps you have left over after forming your pie shells in case you need to repair a crack that develops in the blind baking process (see below).
- Place fruit-filled pies on a lined baking sheet to catch any bubbling juice drips. I usually use parchment liners, as they are nonstick, but foil can be used as well.

- Pie-making should be fun! Maintain a positive attitude, and, again, remember that your skill level will increase dramatically if you bake lots of pies.

A Note on Blind Baking

When making single-crusted pies and tarts, I always partially bake my crusts prior to filling them. This process promotes a crispier bottom crust and is commonly known as "baking blind." It is an extra step that many recipes may not stipulate, but I find that it is worth the effort. Roll out the crust and fit it into the pan. Chill, or preferably freeze, the dough until it is firm. Place a generous sheet of parchment paper or aluminum foil over the crust (there should be overhang on all sides to facilitate easy removal), fit it into the shell, and fill it with rice, dried beans, or reusable pie weights. Place the weighted crust in a 375° oven and bake it for approximately 20 minutes, until the edges just start to pick up some color and the bottom no longer looks raw. Carefully remove the liner and weights and return the shell to the oven for an additional 8 minutes or so. The pastry may puff up once the weights are removed. If this occurs, gently prick any air bubbles with a fork. Check the shell several times, repricking it as needed. Remove the partially baked shell from the oven when the bottom is set and dry to the touch. Do not overbake or cracks may develop. The shell should still be light in color. Occasionally a fully baked shell is called for, in which case it should be baked until it is evenly light golden brown in color. I seal my pastry shells as soon as they come out of the oven by brushing them with a bit of egg white. This helps keep the bottom crisp and usually fills in any small holes that might have been made when you pricked the pastry. Any large cracks or tears can be repaired with reserved dough scraps: this is especially important when using a very liquid filling. If you've forgotten to save your scraps, an emergency patching kit can be made by mixing a bit of flour with some water to form a paste that can be lightly spread on the shell as needed. It is best to try and time the blind baking process so that the partially baked shell is filled immediately upon being removed from the oven and then placed back in the oven to complete the baking process.

Blueberry Blackberry Pie

SERVES 8

Pie is definitely my favorite dessert; and if I have to choose just one, this is definitely my favorite pie. I've always surmised that pies could smooth the bumps of any even vaguely uncomfortable social situation. As a very nervous newlywed, I took this particular pie to my husband's oh so Southern family reunion—what an icebreaker for a Brooklyn girl!

INGREDIENTS FOR THE PIE

    1 9-inch basic pie crust (page 26)
    5 tablespoons flour
    1 cup sugar
    ¼ teaspoon kosher salt
    ½ teaspoon cinnamon
    2 pints blueberries
    1 pint blackberries
    grated zest and juice of 1 orange
    1 tablespoon (½ ounce) cold butter, cut into small pieces

INGREDIENTS FOR THE EGG GLAZE

    1 egg yolk
    1 teaspoon water

PREPARATION

1 Preheat oven to 400°.
2 Combine the egg yolk and water to make a glaze for the top crust. Reserve.
3 Working quickly, roll out the bottom crust to approximately ¼ inch thick and fit into a 9-inch Pyrex pie pan.
4 Combine the flour, sugar, salt, and cinnamon in a stainless mixing bowl. Mix well. Add the blueberries, blackberries, and orange zest and juice. Toss gently with your hands just to mix ingredients.
5 Place the fruit in the crust, mounding slightly in the center. Dot the filling with the cold butter.
6 Roll out the top crust. Trim the excess overhang from the bottom crust and brush the remaining edges lightly with the egg wash glaze. Cover the filling

with the top crust. Fold the edges of the top crust under the pie, pressing well to seal. Scallop the edges of the crust. Brush the top crust with the egg wash glaze. Cut steam vents in the top crust.

7   Place the pie on a lined baking sheet to catch possible juice spills.

8   Bake at 400° for 30 minutes. Reduce the oven setting to 375° and bake for an additional 40 to 50 minutes, until the juices have thickened and are bubbling and the crust is golden brown.

9   Cool completely before serving.

Baker's Note: You can easily vary this recipe by using all blueberries or by substituting 2 cups of sliced peeled peaches for the blackberries. Raspberries or regional berry types, such as loganberries or marionberries, can also be substituted.

Serving Suggestions: If having this pie for breakfast, I'd just serve coffee to go along with it. If it's meant to be a dessert, I can't overstate my opinion that the perfect accompaniment to pie is a scoop of homemade ice cream. In this case, not-just-plain-vanilla (page 261), lemon chiffon (page 271), or cream cheese blackberry swirl (page 265) would all be suitable ice creams for serving the pie à la mode.

Apple Rhubarb Cardamom Crumb Pie

SERVES 8 TO 10

My mother's favorite dessert has always been warm apple crumb pie, while my dad has always been partial to things that are made with rhubarb. So, Stan and Es, this one's for y'all.

INGREDIENTS FOR THE CRUMB TOPPING
   ½ cup sugar
   ½ cup brown sugar
   1 cup flour
   ⅛ teaspoon kosher salt
   ½ teaspoon cardamom
   8 tablespoons (4 ounces) butter, chilled and cut into pieces

INGREDIENTS FOR THE PIE

1 9-inch basic pie crust (page 26)

12 ounces rhubarb (scant 3 cups)

1¾ pounds Granny Smith apples (about 4 medium-sized apples)

2 tablespoons flour

¼ cup + 1 tablespoon brown sugar

¼ cup + 1 tablespoon sugar

½ teaspoon cardamom

¼ teaspoon kosher salt

grated zest of 1 small orange

juice of 1 small orange

½ teaspoon vanilla

PREPARATION FOR THE CRUMB TOPPING

Place the sugar, brown sugar, flour, salt, and cardamom in a processor with a steel blade. Pulse to blend. Add the butter and pulse just until the butter is cut in and distinct crumbs form. Do not overprocess. Alternatively, this can be done using a mixer with a paddle, or you can just rub all the ingredients together with your fingers. If you choose the last option, do not use ice-cold butter. Reserve the topping. It can be made several days ahead and refrigerated. Bring to cool room temperature before using.

PREPARATION FOR THE PIE

1 Preheat oven to 375°. Roll out the pie crust and fit it into a 9-inch pie pan. Chill until ready to use.

2 Slice the rhubarb ¾ inch thick. Peel, core, and slice the apples ½ to ¾ inch thick. Combine the rhubarb and apples in a mixing bowl with the flour, brown sugar, sugar, cardamom, salt, grated orange zest, orange juice, and vanilla. Toss the mixture to combine well.

3 Place the filling in the reserved shell, mounding the fruit slightly in the center. Press down and make sure the filling is fairly well packed.

4 Distribute the reserved crumb topping over the fruit, pressing to make it adhere.

5 Place the pie on a lined baking sheet. Bake at 375° for approximately 1½ hours, until the crumb topping is golden brown, the juices are bubbling and thickened, and the fruit tests done if pierced with a knife. Cool before

serving. Serve barely warm or at room temperature. This pie is best served the day it's made.

Baker's Note: You have quite a bit of flexibility in changing the fruit used for this pie. Pears would be a good substitute for the apples, and in lieu of rhubarb you could use cranberries, raspberries, or sour cherries.

Serving Suggestions: Fruit pies without ice cream are a bit forlorn. Serve this one with a scoop of not-just-plain-vanilla ice cream (page 261). I also occasionally add some ground cardamom to the vanilla base for the ice cream to provide an extra added dose of this fragrant spice.

Rhubarb

Technically a vegetable, rhubarb, or "pie plant," grows with abandon in many parts of the United States. Stalky and celery-like in appearance, its color can range from deep red to light green. Rhubarb is quite tart, and it is always sweetened and cooked when used in dessert preparations. Hothouse-grown rhubarb tends to be slender and pinker in color than its field-grown counterpart. The flavor of wild rhubarb is more intense, while the milder hothouse variety is prettier in appearance. Rhubarb should be firm when you purchase it. Look for unblemished thinner stalks—some hardier field-grown rhubarbs grow as big as baseball bats, and while they are fine for purées, they tend to be tough and stringy. Store rhubarb chilled and use it promptly after purchasing, and *never* use the green rhubarb leaves, as they contain poisonous oxalic acid.

Cardamom

Cardamom is a distinctive spice that adds great complexity (and wonderful aroma) to baked goods. Found in wildly divergent cuisines (Finnish and Indian come to mind), cardamom complements a wide range of flavors. It pairs well with dairy products, vanilla, oranges, apples, stone fruits, and dates. I first become enthralled with it when I was researching the Scandinavian baking tradition in this country. Although available ground, cardamom is best

purchased in its whole-pod form. It's quite pricey, but a little of this powerful spice goes a long way. Cardamom's papery shells can easily be split or cracked by hand. Grind the tiny interior black seeds with a mortar and pestle or a spice grinder. Once ground, cardamom loses both flavoring strength and its characteristic aroma, so grind "as needed." The ground spice can be added directly to baked goods or infused into liquids. Try to buy cardamom someplace where there's a high turnover on bulk spices. If you have an Indian or Middle Eastern market near you, it can be a wonderful resource for harder-to-find spices as can Whole Foods Markets or other quasi—health food stores. Mail order (see the sources listing at the end of the book) is also a possibility.

Meyer Lemon Shaker Pie

SERVES 8

Shaker lemon pie falls into the realm of dessert classics. No-nonsense and stream-lined like everything Shaker, it is stunning in its simplicity. This pie is made with whole, skin-on lemons and has a sweet tart characteristic that marmalade lovers will adore. If Meyer lemons are available, they would be my first choice in this pie, but any juicy, thinner-skinned lemon can be used. Please note that you must start the filling 1 day in advance of baking the pie.

INGREDIENTS
   3 medium-sized lemons (preferably Meyer lemons)
   2 cups sugar
   ¼ teaspoon kosher salt
   4 eggs, lightly beaten
   1 egg yolk + 1 teaspoon of water for glazing
   1 recipe basic pie crust (page 26) for a double-crusted pie

PREPARATION
1 Cut the lemons into paper-thin slices, removing any seeds. Cut the slices into quarters.

2 Combine the sliced lemons and any juices that may have collected with the sugar in a nonreactive bowl. Stir to distribute the sugar. Cover the bowl and place the mixture in the refrigerator for 24 hours. Stir the mixture 2 or 3 times during this maceration process.

3 Preheat oven to 350°. Remove the lemon mixture from the refrigerator. Add the salt and the lightly beaten eggs. Stir to mix well.

4 Combine the egg yolk with 1 teaspoon of water and mix to blend. Roll out the bottom pastry crust approximately ¼ inch thick and fit into a 9-inch pie pan (preferably Pyrex). Pour the filling into the shell, making sure that the lemon pieces are evenly distributed. Trim the excess overhang from the bottom crust and brush the edges with the egg glaze. Roll out the top crust and cover the filling. Fold the edges of the top crust under the pie, pressing well to seal. Flute the edges of the crust. Brush the top crust with the egg wash glaze. Cut steam vents in the top crust.

5 Bake the pie at 350° till evenly golden brown. The filling will set and puff somewhat. This should take about 45 minutes. Cool completely before serving.

Baker's Note: I find it easier to slice the lemons for this pie with a serrated knife.

Serving Suggestions: This pie should be served with a dollop of lightly sweetened whipped cream. Fresh berries or a berry sauce would not be inappropriate. Try it with strawberry crush (page 49) or cinnamon spiced blueberry sauce (page 45).

Meyer Lemons

Meyer lemons are a distinct varietal that have only recently begun to appear in markets outside of California. Popularized by Alice Waters at Chez Panisse, these lemons are amazing. Thought to be a hybrid of lemons and mandarin oranges, they are sweet, fruity and beautifully fragrant. Meyers tend to be softer and juicier than common lemons, with tender, flavorful skins. I first encountered Meyers when my husband and I visited our friends Doug and Marie Hamilton in Sausalito, California. They are lucky enough to have a well-established specimen growing in their backyard. In exchange for a few recipes, they sent us on our way with a huge sack of Meyers. If you do not have your own personal Meyer lemon source, check your local market—they are being commercially grown in several states now and can be found mostly in the fall and winter months. Some trees give off two crops a year, so occasionally Meyers are available during the summer as well.

If you cannot find the often elusive Meyer, substitute thin-skinned lower-acid lemons that yield when gently pressed in any recipe that calls for Meyer lemons. If at all possible, buy organic, unwaxed fruit.

Buttermilk Vanilla Bean Custard Pie

SERVES 8

Even if you are one of those people who thinks he absolutely can't abide buttermilk, please don't pass up this pie. It's a luxurious, updated version of an old Southern standard that plays an ultracreamy filling against a traditional crisp, flaky crust.

INGREDIENTS

1 9-inch basic pie crust (page 26), baked blind
1 cup sugar
seeds of 1 vanilla bean
4 egg yolks
¼ cup cornstarch
⅛ teaspoon kosher salt
1½ cups buttermilk (preferably whole-milk buttermilk)
½ cup cream
1 ounce (2 tablespoons) butter, melted

PREPARATION
1 Preheat oven to 350°.
2 Combine the sugar, vanilla bean seeds, and egg yolks in a mixing bowl; add the cornstarch and whisk until well combined. The mixture will be very thick. Add the salt. Gradually whisk in the buttermilk and cream and mix to blend. Whisk in the melted butter.

3 Place the partially baked shell on the bottom oven rack and carefully pour the filling into the shell. Bake at 350° for 15 minutes. Turn oven to 325° until the filling puffs slightly and is just set. This should take an additional 30 to 35 minutes. Remove, place on a rack, and cool completely.

4 Serve the pie at room temperature or lightly chilled. It is best eaten the day that it is made.

Baker's Note: It's important to form a nice high crust rim on this pie to accommodate all of the filling. As for most custards, the baking time for this pie can be somewhat variable. Make sure to check it often after the filling starts to set up and take care not to overbake it.

For a different, elegant presentation, bake the filling in individual tart shells (see my favorite dough for individual tarts, page 28). This recipe will fill 8 to 10 individual tarts. The baking time should be reduced accordingly.

Serving Suggestions: This pie cries out for plain fresh berries or summer fruit sauces or compotes. Strawberry crush (page 49), sweet and sour cherry compote (page 155), or bourbon poached peaches (page 149) would be a good accompaniment. If it's off-season you can serve it with a raspberry sauce made with frozen berries.

Maple Bourbon Sweet Potato Pie

SERVES 8

When it comes to fall vegetable–based pies some individuals fancy pumpkin, while others (like me) are die-hard sweet potato fans. Both are autumnal, both marry well with the flavors of maple, spirits, and spice; but using sweet potatoes results in a denser, creamier texture. Originally created for an article in *Fine Cooking* magazine, this dessert is always one of my Thanksgiving pie offerings. I can't tell you how many people have said, as they down the last crumb, "and I thought I didn't like sweet potato pie."

INGREDIENTS

    1 9-inch basic pie crust (page 26), baked blind

    2 large or 3 medium-sized sweet potatoes

    4 tablespoons (2 ounces) butter, melted

    1 teaspoon vanilla

    3 eggs

    1 egg yolk

    ¾ cup cream

    ¼ cup + 2 tablespoons maple syrup

    ¼ cup + 1 tablespoon brown sugar

    ¼ cup bourbon

    ¼ teaspoon kosher salt

    ¼ teaspoon nutmeg (preferably freshly grated)

    ¼ teaspoon cinnamon

    ⅛ teaspoon ground cloves

    a few grinds black pepper

PREPARATION

1 Preheat oven to 425°. Pierce the sweet potatoes at each end with a fork and place them on a foil-lined baking sheet. Roast until the potatoes are soft, about 1 hour, turning them over halfway through the baking time. Cool, peel, and put the flesh through a food mill or mash smoothly with a potato masher. You should have 2 cups of purée.

2 Turn oven to 350°.

3 Combine the purée with all the remaining ingredients for the filling. Whisk until well combined and smooth. Pour the filling into the partially baked pie shell.

4 Bake at 350° for about 45 to 50 minutes, till the filling is just barely set. When the rim of the pie plate is nudged, the very center of the filling should barely move.

5 Cool the pie to room temperature. It can be made several hours or up to 1 day in advance.

Baker's Note: This is like a sweet potato custard, and you will want to take care not to overbake the filling. Check it frequently as it nears the end of its baking time and remember that it will set up a bit as it cools.

Serving Suggestions: Serve this pie with some lightly whipped cream or, for a slightly twisted take on a tried-and-true Thanksgiving combo, garnish with some marshmallow fluff (page 68).

Mocha Molasses Shoofly Pie

SERVES 8 TO 10

I first encountered shoofly pie as a child, at a Pennsylvania Dutch restaurant called The Plain and Fancy, and I have been enamored of it ever since. It's one of those thrifty down-home recipes that can be made straight out of your pantry. My variation on this classic pie adds a back note of coffee flavoring to the traditional molasses filling.

INGREDIENTS

1 9-inch basic pie crust (page 26), baked blind

1 cup flour

½ cup brown sugar

6 tablespoons (3 ounces) lightly chilled butter

1 cup hot brewed coffee

1 teaspoon baking soda

½ cup corn syrup

½ cup molasses

½ teaspoon vanilla

½ teaspoon kosher salt

powdered sugar for serving

PREPARATION

1 Preheat oven to 350°.

2 For the filling, combine the flour, brown sugar, and butter in a bowl. Rub with your fingertips or cut in with a pastry blender until you've formed uniform crumbs. Reserve.

3 Pour the hot coffee into a mixing bowl and add the baking soda. Whisk in the corn syrup, molasses, vanilla, and salt. Reserve.

4 Sprinkle the reserved crumb mixture evenly over the surface of the partially baked shell. Pour the reserved molasses filling over the crumbs. Be careful not to pour over the sides of the crust.

5 Bake at 350° for 35 to 40 minutes, until the filling appears puffed and set. Cool before serving. This is best made 8 to 10 hours in advance, and can be made 1 day ahead of time, but should be held at room temperature. Sprinkle generously with powdered sugar before serving.

Baker's Note: It is extremely important to make sure that your partially baked crust is well sealed. Brush the hot crust with egg white and repair all cracks before filling. If, as you're pouring the very thin filling into the shell, you panic and wonder what in the world thickens and sets the filling since the recipe doesn't call for eggs—fear not! The crumbs cause the filling to separate out into a cake-like top and a smoother, creamier bottom layer.

Serving Suggestions: This pie is intense—whipped cream or ice cream helps moderate the deep molasses flavor. If I want to provide a bit of plate interest, I'll add a drizzle of coffee syrup (page 52).

Key Lime Coconut Pie with Rum Cream

SERVES 8

A simple crumb crust combined with a filling that is quickly whisked together makes this dessert practically foolproof. I've added nontraditional accents of coconut and rum to create a unique version of this Florida favorite. If you have access to fresh key limes, by all means use them. I have substituted both bottled key lime juice and the more readily available Persian limes with delicious results.

INGREDIENTS FOR THE CRUST
   1⅓ cup graham cracker crumbs
   ⅓ cup sweetened shredded coconut (preferably the frozen kind, defrosted)
   2 tablespoons sugar
   6 tablespoons (3 ounces) butter, melted

INGREDIENTS FOR THE FILLING

    3 egg yolks

    ¼ teaspoon cream of tartar

    2 14-ounce cans of sweetened condensed milk

    1 cup key lime juice

INGREDIENTS FOR THE RUM CREAM TOPPING

    1½ cups heavy cream

    ¼ cup sugar

    ½ teaspoon vanilla

    2½ tablespoons dark rum

    3 tablespoons sweetened shredded coconut, toasted till light golden brown

PREPARATION FOR THE CRUST

1 Preheat oven to 350°. Lightly butter a 9-inch pie plate.

2 Combine the graham cracker crumbs, coconut, sugar, and melted butter in a mixing bowl and stir to combine. Press the mixture into the bottom and up the sides of the reserved pie plate, tamping down the crumbs to form an even crust. Bake at 350° for 8 to 10 minutes till lightly golden. Reserve and prepare filling.

PREPARATION FOR THE FILLING

1 In a mixing bowl, whisk together the egg yolks and cream of tartar. Whisk in the sweetened condensed milk. Gradually whisk in the lime juice till well combined. Pour the mixture into the prepared shell.

2 Bake at 350° for approximately 15 minutes, until the filling is just set. Remove from the oven, cool completely, and refrigerate for several hours or overnight.

PREPARATION FOR THE TOPPING

1 Whip the cream till lightly thickened and gradually whisk in the sugar. Beat to soft peaks and whisk in the vanilla and dark rum. Whip to medium stiff peaks.

2 Spread about two-thirds of the whipped cream over the pie filling. Place the remaining cream in a pastry bag fitted with a large open star tip and pipe a shell border or a series of whipped cream rosettes around the perimeter of the pie. Sprinkle the whipped cream with the toasted coconut. Refrigerate until ready to serve.

Baker's Note: If you don't want to bother with decorating the pie with a pastry bag, just serve slices of pie topped with a dollop of whipped cream and sprinkled with toasted coconut.

Serving Suggestions: Unless we're talking ice cream or whipped cream, I don't think pies need to be dressed up with extraneous garnishes. But if you really feel the occasion calls for more than a simple slice on a plate, for this pie you could add a drizzle of lime caramel (page 46) or some strawberry crush (page 49).

Chocolate Raspberry Fudge Pie

SERVES 8 TO 10

The uncommonly hot baking temperature given for this pie is not a misprint. While I was in the process of developing this recipe, I recalled a method of baking brownies that Maida Heatter uses. The result is a delicious truffle-like fudge pie with an unusually creamy texture. For devout chocoholics, I've included an optional chocolate glaze.

INGREDIENTS FOR THE PIE

1 9-inch basic pie crust (page 26), baked blind

4 ounces unsweetened chocolate

10 tablespoons (5 ounces) butter

2 eggs

2 egg yolks

1¾ cups sugar

¼ teaspoon kosher salt

1 teaspoon vanilla

½ cup flour

¼ cup raspberry purée (see raspberry red wine sauce, page 48, or use any seedless purée)

INGREDIENTS FOR THE OPTIONAL GLAZE

½ cup cream

4 ounces semisweet chocolate, finely chopped

1 teaspoon corn syrup

PREPARATION FOR THE PIE

1 Preheat oven to 425°.

2 Combine the unsweetened chocolate and butter in a double boiler and heat until melted. Reserve.

3 Combine the eggs, egg yolks, and sugar in a medium-sized mixing bowl and whisk until thick and light. Add the salt and vanilla and mix to combine. Whisk in the reserved chocolate. Add the flour and mix to blend. Add the raspberry purée and whisk just till well blended. Pour this mixture into the partially baked pie shell.

4 Bake at 425° for approximately 25 minutes. The filling will puff, be set, and start to pick up color and look somewhat crusty on top when it is done. Remove from the oven and cool completely before serving. Serve this pie at room temperature. It can be made 1 day ahead of time.

PREPARATION FOR THE OPTIONAL GLAZE

While the pie is baking, heat the cream to just under a boil. Stir in the chocolate and cook over low heat, constantly stirring, till the chocolate is completely melted. Remove from heat and add the corn syrup. Allow to cool slightly. Starting from the center of the pie and moving toward the edges, slowly pour the glaze over the cooled pie, being careful to just cover the surface. Use a small offset spatula to help spread the glaze if necessary. The object is to preserve as smooth a surface as possible. Allow the glaze to set for several hours at room temperature or quick chill it for 1 hour in the refrigerator if you prefer.

Baker's Note: If I plan to serve this pie à la mode, I don't glaze it. If, however, I opt for a whipped cream garnish, I usually do add that extra blast of chocolate.

Serving Suggestions: Raspberry red wine sauce (page 48), a scatter of fresh raspberries, and a bit of whipped cream turn this simple pie into a knockout dessert. For those who believe that pie requires ice cream, try a small scoop of not-just-plain-vanilla (page 261).

Lemon Pecan Tart

SERVES 8 TO 10

I love rich, gooey pecan pies, but I find them to be a bit too sweet for more than a bite or two. In his mouthwatering cookbook, *New Southern Kitchen*, Damon Lee Fowler includes a recipe for a lemon chess pie and pecan pie hybrid—the inspiration for this tart. A punch of zingy lemon against the buttery toasted nut filling is an unforgettable combination, and, yes, you can definitely eat a whole slice.

INGREDIENTS

1 10½-inch basic tart dough pastry shell (page 27), baked blind

4 tablespoons (2 ounces) butter

1 cup corn syrup

¾ cup brown sugar

2 eggs

3 egg yolks

grated zest of 2 lemons

1 teaspoon vanilla

¼ cup lemon juice

¼ teaspoon kosher salt

2½ cups pecan pieces, lightly toasted

¾ cup pecan halves

PREPARATION

1 Preheat oven to 350°.

2 In a small skillet, cook the butter over medium heat until lightly browned. Remove from heat and place in a medium-sized bowl.

3 Whisk the corn syrup and brown sugar into the melted butter. Whisk in the eggs and egg yolks and mix till well combined. Whisk in the grated lemon zest, vanilla, lemon juice, and salt.

4 Spread the toasted pecan pieces in the prepared tart shell. Arrange the pecan halves in a neat ring around the outer perimeter of the tart.

5 Gently pour about three-quarters of the filling over the nuts, being careful to cover them evenly. Transfer the tart to the bottom rack of the oven and add the remaining filling. Be careful not to overfill—you may wind up with a spoonful or so that won't fit, but you do not want the filling to run over your tart shell.

6   Bake at 350° for about 45 minutes. The tart will be slightly puffed, set, and lightly golden brown when ready. Remove and cool completely before serving. It can be made a day in advance.

Baker's Note: Lemon juice can vary quite a bit in strength and acidity levels. If you feel that your filling needs a bit more lemony flavoring, try adding a bit of Boyajian pure lemon oil (see the sources listing at the end of the book). This product adds intense citrus flavor without drastically altering the liquid content.

This tart is a close cousin to the browned butter date nut tart (page 101). Once certain techniques are learned and a basic recipe is mastered, the variations you can create are virtually unlimited. You can always substitute a different type of nut and vary the flavorings. For example, this can be turned into a delicious macadamia lime tart. Don't be afraid to experiment!

Serving Suggestions: Yummy just with whipped cream, but a bit of Lynchburg lemonade sauce (page 43) really accentuates the lemon flavor and looks pretty on the plate.

Fig Newton Zinfandel Tart

SERVES 10

My mother always said that Fig Newtons were a "healthy cookie," which is probably why I didn't appreciate them as a child. What can I say? I was an Oreo and Mallowmar gal. As an adult however, I am a big fan, and I pay homage to that American classic with this oversized cookie masquerading as a tart.

INGREDIENTS

18 ounces dried Calimyra figs, stem end removed, cut into pieces
½ cup orange juice
1½ cups Zinfandel wine
1 cup water
1 cup brown sugar
1 teaspoon vanilla
1 recipe Newton tart dough (page 32)
1 egg yolk combined with 1 teaspoon water

PREPARATION FOR THE FILLING

Combine the figs, orange juice, Zinfandel, water, sugar, and vanilla in a medium-sized nonreactive saucepan. Bring to a simmer. Cook over low heat, stirring occasionally, till the figs are completely soft and the remaining liquid is thick and syrupy. Toward the end of the cooking, mash the figs with a wooden spoon to further break them up. The final consistency should be jam-like. Remove from heat and cool. The filling can be made up to 2 days in advance.

PREPARATION FOR THE TART

1 Preheat oven to 375°.

2 Roll out the slightly larger piece of chilled Newton dough and fit into a 10½-inch removable-bottom tart pan, leaving about ½ inch of dough as overhang. Place the filling in the shell and spread evenly with a palette knife or spatula.

3 Fold the ½ inch of excess dough overhang in to enclose the filling. Brush this pastry border with some of the beaten egg yolk. Roll out the top crust and place over the top of the tart pan. Using your fingers, press down lightly around the tart perimeter to make sure the two crusts are sealed together well. Remove all excess dough to form a clean edge.

4 Brush the top crust well with beaten egg yolk. Use the tines of a fork to create a crosshatch pattern by very lightly dragging the back of the fork across the tart surface, being careful not to penetrate the dough. Wipe off the fork between each dragging. Score in one direction, turn the tart 45° and then repeat to form diamond-shaped markings. With a knife, cut 4 slits to form steam vents in the middle of the tart.

5 Bake at 375° for 45 to 50 minutes, until the top crust is golden brown. Cool completely before serving. The tart can be made 1 day in advance.

Baker's Note: For a nonalcoholic tart, substitute grape juice for the Zinfandel. You can vary the flavoring of this tart by keeping the proportions the same but changing the type of dried fruit and poaching liquid. Try apricots poached in an orange Riesling syrup or prunes poached in port and red wine.

Serving Suggestions: I would serve this with either whipped cream or crème fraîche (page 67). If you want an additional plate garnish, winter fruits poached in red wine syrup (page 157) would be a delicious accent.

Banana & Peanut Frangipane Tarts

MAKES 8 TO 10 TARTS

A classic sandwich combo translated into a killer all-American dessert (a.k.a., the Elvis)!

INGREDIENTS

1 recipe flaky puff-style pastry (page 29) or
   1 ½ pounds frozen puff pastry sheets
1 recipe peanut frangipane (page 57) at room temperature
7 ripe but not mushy bananas
¼ cup + 1 tablespoon sugar
1 scant teaspoon cinnamon
2 tablespoons (1 ounce) cold butter, cut into very small cubes

PREPARATION

1   Roll the pastry out to about ⅛ inch thick and cut into rounds 5½ inches in diameter. If you are using frozen puff pastry sheets, they should be about the right thickness. Place the rounds on parchment paper–lined baking sheets. You should be able to cut out 8 tarts. The scraps can be pieced together, rerolled one time and cut into 2 more tarts. Leaving a ½-inch outer perimeter on each tart, prick the centers several times with the tines of a fork. Chill briefly if the pastry seems at all soft.

2   Preheat oven to 425°. Leaving a ½-inch outer perimeter border, cover each tart with about 2½ tablespoons of peanut frangipane. Use an offset spatula to spread it to an even thickness. Slice the bananas about ⅓ inch thick and arrange the slices over the frangipane in overlapping concentric circles.

3   Sprinkle the outer pastry rim and the bananas of each tart with about 1½ teaspoons of sugar and a scant ⅛ teaspoon of cinnamon. Randomly dot the surface of each tart with butter.

4   Bake at 425° for about 25 to 30 minutes, until the pastry is puffed and golden brown. Cool slightly before serving. These tarts can be made several hours ahead of time and reheated briefly just before serving. If you would prefer to make 1 large or 2 medium-sized tarts instead of individual ones, by all means do so. The size of the tart is dictated by how large you cut the pastry base.

Baker's Note: Use this recipe as a basic guideline and vary the frangipane flavor and complementary fruit to create a multitude of variations. Some examples include sliced apricots with pistachio frangipane, pineapple with macadamia frangipane, and blueberries with hazelnut frangipane, but don't limit yourself to these combinations—try some of your own!

Serving Suggestions: These tarts should be served with a sprinkle of powdered sugar and some whipped cream. And I think they benefit from an addition of chocolate pudding sauce (page 38) or Concord grape syrup (page 50) to the plate. Some children and perhaps even some adults might wish to substitute marshmallow fluff (page 68) for the whipped cream.

Browned Butter Date Nut Tart

SERVES 10

This tart is all about autumn and the harvest season. Consider it as an alternative to the usual pecan pie at Thanksgiving. Fresh, plump Medjool dates, if you can find them in the market, would be my first choice for this dessert, but even the packaged varieties will work just fine.

INGREDIENTS

1 10½-inch basic tart dough pastry shell (page 27), baked blind
4 tablespoons (2 ounces) butter
2 eggs
2 egg yolks
¼ cup sugar
¼ teaspoon kosher salt
grated zest of 1 orange
¾ cup corn syrup
1 tablespoon orange juice
3 tablespoons brandy
1 cup dates, pitted and cut into medium dice
2 teaspoons flour
1½ cups walnut pieces, lightly toasted and skinned

PREPARATION

1 Turn oven to 350°.

2 Place the butter in a small saucepan and cook over medium heat until it just starts to brown and smell nutty. Remove from heat and reserve.

3 In a mixing bowl, combine the eggs, egg yolks, sugar, salt, orange zest, corn syrup, orange juice, and brandy. Whisk together till well combined. Blend in the reserved butter. Toss the dates with the flour and add to the liquid ingredients, along with the walnut pieces.

4 Pour the filling into the partially baked shell, making sure to distribute the dates and nuts evenly. You may have to break up any large sticky date "clumps" with your fingers. Do not overfill the shell.

5 Bake at 350° for about 40 to 45 minutes. The tart filling will puff up, brown, and be fairly set. Cool completely before serving.

Baker's Note: When making open-faced tarts or pies with a thin fluid filling, I often pour the last fourth of the filling into a small pitcher or liquid measure. If you place the partially filled tart on the oven rack and then add the last of the filling to it, you will run less risk of overflow or spillage. To cut dates, I often dip the blade of a knife or the kitchen shears in flour to facilitate the process.

Serving Suggestions: This tart is best served lightly chilled to accent the chewy, candy-like texture of the dates. Some excellent accompaniments include a dollop of crème fraîche (page 67) and/or a mixed citrus salad.

Chocolate Chip Cookie Tarts

MAKES 8 TO 10 INDIVIDUAL 4-INCH TARTS

I have experimented with using chocolate chip cookie dough in many different formats. Turning a standard dough into sophisticated individual tarts changes an all-American snack into an easy dinner dessert that's a real crowd-pleaser. After all, who doesn't like chocolate chip cookies?

INGREDIENTS

1 recipe of my favorite dough for individual tarts (page 28), rolled into 8 to 10 individual tart shells and baked blind

8 tablespoons (4 ounces) butter, at room temperature

½ cup brown sugar

¼ cup sugar

2 eggs

1 teaspoon vanilla

1¼ cups flour

¼ teaspoon kosher salt

¼ teaspoon baking soda

1 cup semisweet chocolate chips

PREPARATION

1   On a lightly floured surface, roll out individual pastry rounds ⅛ inch thick and about 6 inches in diameter and fit into 4-inch shallow flan rings. Trim excess pastry. Gather the scraps, chill, and reroll. This should generate a total of 8 to 10 tart shells. Place the shells on a parchment paper–lined baking sheet. Prick the bottoms once or twice with the tines of a fork. Freeze for at least 15 minutes before baking. Rolled shells can be made up to 1 month ahead and kept frozen.

2   Preheat oven to 375°. Bake the shells until they are a uniform light golden brown. Check the shells several times during the baking process to see if they are puffing up. Lightly tamp down the dough with your fingers to remove any air pockets that may form. Cool the shells before filling. The shells can be baked up to 24 hours in advance and held at room temperature if you wish.

3   Turn oven to 350°.

4   Using a mixer with a paddle, cream the butter, brown sugar, and sugar. Add the eggs and mix to incorporate, scraping the bowl down. Add the vanilla. Add the flour, salt, and baking soda and mix to blend in. Add the chocolate chips and mix just to incorporate.

5   Divide the dough between the baked shells. Bake the tarts at 350° for about 18 to 20 minutes, until the filling is lightly golden. The tops should still feel slightly soft when lightly touched. Serve warm. This can be made up to 24 hours in advance and lightly reheated before serving.

Baker's Note: I usually use homemade chocolate chips (page 54) when making these, but you can use any good-quality semisweet chip. Ghirardelli double chocolate chips are particularly good.

Serving Suggestions: I like to serve these à la mode, with a scoop of not-just-plain-vanilla ice cream (page 261) or milk chocolate malt ice cream (page 274). An optional drizzle of cocoa fudge sauce (page 37) can dress up the plate.

Chocolate Chestnut Tarts

MAKES 8 TO 10 SERVINGS

These double-decker individual tarts are a cinch to put together if you make the pastry and candied chestnut purée ahead of time. They are a perfect ending to a special autumn dinner.

INGREDIENTS

1 recipe of my favorite dough for individual tarts (page 28),
   rolled into 8 to 10 individual tart shells and baked blind
½ recipe candied chestnut purée (page 58)
⅓ cup flour
2½ teaspoons cocoa
⅛ teaspoon kosher salt
5 tablespoons (2½ ounces) butter
2½ ounces semisweet chocolate
¼ cup brown sugar
⅓ cup + 1 tablespoon sugar
1 egg
1 egg yolk
1 teaspoon vanilla
1 tablespoon dark rum
a few grinds black pepper

PREPARATION

1 Preheat oven to 350°.
2 Using a small offset spatula, spread the chestnut purée into the bottoms of the partially baked tart shells, filling one-third full. Place on a parchment paper—lined baking sheet and reserve.
3 Sift the flour and cocoa into a bowl. Add the salt and reserve.

4   Melt the butter and chocolate in the top of a double boiler. Whisk the brown sugar, sugar, egg, egg yolk, vanilla, rum and pepper into the melted chocolate. Add the reserved dry ingredients and mix just to combine.

5   Divide the chocolate mixture between the partially filled shells, spreading the mixture with an offset spatula to level.

6   Bake at 350° for approximately 15 minutes, until the chocolate filling is just set to the touch. Serve lightly warm or at room temperature. These can be made up to a day in advance if you reheat them at 350° for 5 minutes before serving.

Baker's Note: You can use this same recipe to bake a single large-format 10- to 11-inch tart.

Serving Suggestions: This is fabulous served with hot buttered rum raisin sauce (page 41) and whipped cream or not-just-plain-vanilla ice cream made with dark rum (page 261). A small pool of cocoa fudge sauce (page 37) and a liberal sprinkling of powdered sugar is another option.

Shelling Chestnuts

The appearance of creamy-fleshed chestnuts in the market signals that fall is well on its way. Choose glossy-shelled, unblemished nuts that are firm and heavy for their size. Shelling chestnuts can be a bit tricky, but this distinctive ingredient is worth the effort. Many recipes call for cutting an "x" in the stem end of each nut with a sharp paring knife and scoring through the curved side of the shell from tip to tip. This is followed by roasting the nuts in a single layer in a 350° oven for about 20 minutes, until the nuts start to steam and separate from their shells. At this point you should be able to completely remove the shells by peeling them back with a knife. This works well when you want to retain the natural texture of the nuts.

For many desserts, the shelled nuts undergo further cooking and will be chopped or puréed. If this is the case, I prefer to boil the nuts to remove their shells. With a cleaver or sharp, heavy knife, cut the chestnuts in half through the stem end. Discard any nuts that show evidence of interior bluish mold. Boil the nuts for approximately 5 minutes, until both the hard outer shell and papery inner shell can be removed. It is easiest to do this while the nuts are still very warm. Keep the nuts in the hot water and peel them one by one. Reheat them if necessary. I find that the fresher the chestnuts are the easier it is to peel them.

Nuts in their shells can be held for up to a week in a cool, dark pantry. Once shelled they should be used within 2 days.

Chocolate Grand Marnier Truffle Tart

SERVES 10 TO 12

This elegant tart looks impressive, tastes great, is not at all difficult to prepare, and can be made ahead of time. Sounds like a perfect entertaining dessert to me!

INGREDIENTS FOR THE TART
  1 prebaked 10½-inch basic
    tart dough pastry shell
    (page 27)
  8½ ounces semisweet
    chocolate
  11 tablespoons (5½ ounces)
    butter
  ¼ cup + 2 tablespoons sugar
  2 tablespoons flour
  3 eggs
  grated zest of 1 large orange
  ⅛ teaspoon kosher salt
  ¼ cup Grand Marnier

INGREDIENTS FOR THE
GANACHE GLAZE
  ¾ cup cream
  6 ounces semisweet chocolate,
    chopped into small pieces

1 Preheat oven to 350°.
2 Melt the chocolate and butter in a double boiler and reserve.
3 Whisk the sugar and flour into the melted chocolate. Whisk in the eggs one at a time, mixing till completely combined. Whisk in the grated orange zest, salt, and Grand Marnier and mix till just combined.
4 Transfer the filling to the prebaked shell. Please note that because the baking time for the filled tart is so short, the shell needs to have been baked all the way through before it is filled. Bake at 350° until the tart is just barely set, approximately 15 minutes. Remove the tart from the oven and let it cool while you prepare the glaze.

PREPARATION FOR THE GANACHE GLAZE

1 Heat the cream in a small saucepan until it is just under a boil. Add the chopped chocolate and, on very low heat, stir constantly until the chocolate is almost completely melted. Remove from heat and stir occasionally, until the chocolate is melted and the ganache is smooth. Cool slightly.
2 Strain the ganache through a fine-mesh strainer into a pitcher. Slowly pour the glaze over the center of the tart, allowing it to flow out to the edges. Do not overfill the tart. Chill the tart in the refrigerator to set the glaze, but serve at room temperature.

Baker's Note: The brand of chocolate you use will really affect the flavor of this tart. You can omit the orange zest and Grand Marnier if you wish and substitute another complementary alcohol—Kahlua, bourbon, rum, and Framboise are all excellent alternatives.

Serving Suggestions: I like to present this tart whole, with whipped cream piped around the outer perimeter. Artfully placed candied orange zest (page 60) and some chocolate shavings on top of the whipped cream add a nice touch.

Cranberry Linzer Tart

Cranberries most often are relegated to a supporting role on the Thanksgiving table, where they are a delicious foil to the traditional turkey. But they can perform the same supportive function in desserts. Paired with a rich, sweet ice cream, this rather tart tart would be a festive finale to any holiday meal.

INGREDIENTS

1 recipe walnut pastry dough (page 33) divided into
   two-thirds and one-third portions
2 generous cups cranberries
1 cup raisins
1 cup + 2 tablespoons sugar
⅛ teaspoon kosher salt
¼ cup orange juice
¼ cup water
¼ cup maple syrup
1 teaspoon vanilla
1½ tablespoons cream
1½ tablespoons additional sugar for finishing

PREPARATION

1 Combine the cranberries, raisins, sugar, salt, orange juice, water, and maple syrup in a medium-sized saucepan. Cook over medium heat, stirring often, until the berries pop and give off their juices. Simmer over medium heat until the juices turn syrupy and the mixture thickens considerably (about 10 to 15 minutes). Remove from heat, stir in the vanilla and cool to room temperature. This can be made several hours ahead and cooled slowly or it can be quick-chilled over an ice bath. Reserve.

2 Preheat oven to 375°. Roll out the larger piece of walnut dough, reserving the scraps and fit it into a 10½-inch removable-bottom tart pan. Chill it and then bake it blind. As soon as the shell is done partially baking, remove it from the oven and fill it with the reserved cranberry mixture.

3 Roll out the smaller piece of dough to form an approximately 12 × 7-inch rectangle and cut it into as many ¾-inch strips as you can. Lay 5 strips at

intervals lengthwise across the filling. Turn the tart and lay the remaining strips across the top in the opposite direction. Press the ends of the strips to the edge of the bottom crust to adhere. Gather all dough scraps and reroll for additional strips.

4   Using your finger, brush the strips with the cream, trying not to drip any cream into the filling. Sprinkle the strips with the additional sugar.

5   Place the tart on a lined baking sheet and bake at 375° till the filling is bubbly and the pastry is golden brown, approximately 45 to 50 minutes.

6   Remove the tart from the oven, allow it to cool for about 5 minutes, and loosen the sides of the pan by pushing up on the bottom. This will prevent the pan from sticking to the sides of the tart if any juices from the filling have bubbled over. Repeat this procedure one more time before removing the bottom of the pan completely. Serve the tart at room temperature. This is best served the day it's made.

Baker's Note: This filling can also be paired with cream cheese pastry (page 30). Cranberries are high in pectin, and the filling will thicken considerably as it cools. The finished product should have a jam-like consistency.

Serving Suggestion: Due to the tart nature of cranberries, you really need to serve this with something sweet, and I think ice cream is the best option. Burnt orange caramel ice cream (page 262) is the perfect match!

Lime Meringue Tart

SERVES 10

Meringue is kind of like the adult equivalent of cotton candy. There's just something endearing about the sweet fluffy stuff. This dessert has a shallow base of tart, lime-flavored baked custard crowned with extravagant poufs of toasted meringue. It's an impressive finale that will definitely generate ooohs and ahhs.

INGREDIENTS FOR THE TART
    1 10½-inch basic tart dough pastry shell (page 27), baked blind
    4 eggs
    1¼ cups sugar
    1 cup lime juice

⅛ teaspoon kosher salt
¼ cup cream

INGREDIENTS FOR THE MERINGUE TOPPING
¾ cup egg whites (about 6 whites)
¼ teaspoon cream of tartar
1 ½ cups sugar
½ cup water

PREPARATION FOR THE TART

1 Just before the tart shell has finished partially baking, combine all of the ingredients in a mixing bowl and whisk just to blend well.

2 Remove the tart shell from the oven. Turn oven to 350°. Make sure to repair any cracks or holes in the crust with egg white or extra pastry dough. This is critical with this tart because of the thin consistency of the filling.

3 Immediately fill the tart half full with the lime filling, transferring the remaining filling to a small pitcher. Place the partially filled shell on a lower oven shelf and carefully add the remaining filling, being careful not to overflow the shell.

4 Bake at 350° for about 20 minutes, until the filling is just set. It will still appear a bit jiggly in the very center. Allow to cool completely. The tart can be completed to this point several hours ahead of time.

PREPARATION FOR THE MERINGUE TOPPING

1 Combine the egg whites and cream of tartar in the bowl of a mixer with a whip attachment.

2 Place the sugar and water in a small heavy-bottomed saucepan and cook over medium heat until the syrup registers about 235° on a candy thermometer. At this point, start whipping the whites on medium speed while the sugar syrup continues to cook. When the syrup reaches 245°, carefully remove the candy thermometer. The egg whites should have started to thicken and peak at this point. With the mixer still running, carefully pour the hot syrup between the side of the bowl and the whip. Continue beating for about 3 to 4 minutes, until thick, medium firm peaks form. The meringue should still be warm to the touch.

3 Mound the meringue onto the cooled tart, making sure to completely cover the surface and paying particular attention to the edges, where the filling meets the crust. The meringue should be somewhat dome-shaped; use a small offset spatula to spread it. Form spiky decorative peaks by pulling the meringue up with the back of a large spoon.

4 My preferred method of browning the meringue is with a blowtorch. Alternatively, the entire tart can be placed under a preheated broiler. Turn the tart to make sure the surface browns evenly.

Baker's Note: My friend Brigid Callinan is the meringue queen. She makes a similar topping using brown sugar, a variation that you may wish to try. Even though "cooked" Italian-style meringues like this one are a bit more stable than traditional American meringue toppings, I would not attempt this tart on a humid day. To preserve its texture, it's also critical that the topping be completed no more than 5 hours ahead of time. You can, however, bake the filled tart base 1 day ahead.

Serving Suggestions: Serve this tart with fresh seasonal berries or strawberry crush (page 49).

Rustic Raspberry Tart

SERVES 8 TO 10

Rustic tarts are like French galettes or Italian crostatas—the pastry edges are folded up to partially enclose the filling, and they are fairly free-form in nature. In other words, they are really easy to make.

INGREDIENTS

    1 recipe cinnamon graham pastry (page 31),
       enough for a 9½-inch tart
    ½ cup sugar, divided
    3 tablespoons graham cracker crumbs
    1½ pints (3 cups) fresh raspberries
    1½ tablespoons (¾ ounce) butter,
       chilled and cut into small pieces
    ½ tablespoon cream

PREPARATION

1 Preheat oven to 400°.
2 On a lightly floured surface, roll the pastry out into a round about 12 inches in diameter. It should be about ⅛ inch thick. Transfer the dough to a parchment paper–lined baking sheet.
3 Sprinkle the surface of the dough with about 3¼ tablespoons of sugar. Sprinkle the graham cracker crumbs evenly over the sugar and arrange the raspberries over the dough, leaving a generous 1½-inch border around the outer perimeter. Dot the berries with the butter and sprinkle with an additional 3¼ tablespoons of sugar.

4 Fold the edges of the dough up over the filling, pleating and lightly pressing down to secure the edges to form a rustic tart. The finished tart should be about 9½ inches in diameter.

5 Brush the edges of the tart pastry lightly with the cream and sprinkle with the remaining 1½ tablespoons of sugar.

6 Bake at 400° for about 35 minutes. The tart is done when the pastry edges turn golden brown and the juices from the berries just start to bubble. Cool slightly before serving or serve at room temperature.

Baker's Note: This tart works equally well with blueberries or blackberries or a combination of berries. When berries are not in season, consider using sliced bananas as an alternative filling.

Serving Suggestions: I like to serve this simply with a dollop of sweetened whipped cream, but ice cream is also a possibility, as is Blenheim ginger ale sabayon (page 189).

Pink Grapefruit Soufflé Tarts

MAKES 8 TO 10 TARTS

The initial inspiration for these tarts came from a recipe attributed to Paula Oland in a piece by the great food writer Jeffrey Steingarten. The original recipe was lemon-based but a case of fabulous Texas Ruby Reds turned my thoughts to a grapefruit focus. These tarts are so light they practically levitate. Do not be intimidated by soufflé—if you can whip an egg white, you can make a soufflé. And you can make these ethereal beauties days ahead of time, freeze them, and pop them in the oven minutes before you are ready for dessert.

INGREDIENTS

1 recipe of my favorite dough for individual tarts (page 28),
    rolled into 8 to 10 individual tarts and baked blind
1⅛ cups fresh-squeezed pink grapefruit juice
4 eggs, separated
¾ cup sugar, divided
3 tablespoons + 1 teaspoon flour
2 tablespoons Campari

⅛ teaspoon baking soda
1 teaspoon vanilla
¼ teaspoon kosher salt
powdered sugar for service

PREPARATION

1 Strain the grapefruit juice into a nonreactive saucepan and reduce it by half
over medium heat. Reserve.

2 In a medium-sized stainless steel bowl, whisk the egg yolks with ½ cup of sugar
and the flour. Gradually whisk in the Campari and the reserved grapefruit
juice. Place this mixture in the top of a double boiler and cook, while whisking,
over medium heat until it thickens to the consistency of lemon curd. Remove
from heat and whisk in the baking soda and vanilla. Cool and reserve.

3 In a medium-sized stainless steel bowl whip, the egg whites and salt till foamy.
Gradually add the remaining ¼ cup sugar and whip to medium peaks.

4 Lighten the grapefruit custard by folding in one-third of the beaten egg
whites. Then fold in the remaining egg whites.

5 Place the partially baked tart shells on a parchment paper—lined baking sheet

and generously fill them with the grapefruit soufflé, mounding the mixture slightly. Place in the freezer and freeze until firm. Transfer the frozen tarts to a lidded freezer container and freeze in a single layer for several hours or up to 4 days.

6 When you're ready to bake the tarts, preheat oven to 375°. Bake the frozen tarts for about 15 to 18 minutes, until they are puffed, well browned, and set to the touch.

7 Remove the tarts from the oven, sprinkle with powdered sugar, and serve immediately.

Baker's Note: Grapefruit juice can vary quite a bit in taste—if you think your soufflé might need a flavor boost, you can add a few drops of Boyajian grapefruit oil to the cooked egg yolk base. Boyajian makes a terrific line of intense pure citrus oil that contribute quite a bit of flavor with a minimum of added liquid. Check your specialty stores for availability or see the sources listing at the end of the book.

   You can vary the flavor of this tart by making the soufflé base with lemon or lime juice. Substitute a complementary liqueur for the Campari if you wish.

Serving Suggestions: Serve this with some brown sugar—sweetened whipped cream and/or a garnish of grapefruit segments, fresh raspberries, and raspberry sauce.

Cherry Vanilla Turnovers

MAKES 12 TURNOVERS

Like food and wine, Fred and Ginger, and many other famous "pairs," cherries and vanilla have a natural affinity. They just seem to go together. Appropriate morning, noon, and night, these turnovers can be enjoyed as leftovers for breakfast after serving as dessert the night before. If you're not feeding a crowd or don't want the pastries to do double duty, you can easily halve the recipe.

INGREDIENTS

1 recipe cream cheese pastry (page 30) portioned into 12 2-ounce rounds
2 egg yolks
1½ teaspoons water
seeds of 1 vanilla bean or 1 teaspoon vanilla extract
⅔ cup sugar
2½ cups pitted Bing cherries
½ cup dried sour cherries
1 tablespoon + 2½ teaspoons cornstarch
⅛ teaspoon kosher salt
2 tablespoons sugar for finishing

PREPARATION

1   Preheat oven to 400°. On a lightly floured surface, roll each round of pastry into a circle approximately 6½ inches in diameter. Using a large circular cutter or an inverted 6-inch plate as a guide, cut out 6-inch rounds. Reserve. Chill briefly while preparing the filling.

2   Combine the egg yolks and water to make an egg wash. Reserve.

3   If using a vanilla bean, scrape the seeds and combine them with ⅔ cup sugar first. Mix to disperse the seeds. Reserve the pod for another use—like making vanilla sugar! Combine the sugar, cherries, cornstarch, and salt. If using vanilla extract, add at this point. Mix to blend.

4 To form the turnovers, brush the outer perimeter of the reserved rolled dough rounds with reserved egg wash. Place ¼ cup of the cherry filling in the center of each turnover. Fold the top half of the turnover over the filling, pressing to seal all along the bottom edge. Fold the very edge of the sealed pastry over onto itself to form a double thick rim. Press lightly along the edge of the pastry with the tines of a fork to seal. Repeat to form 12 turnovers. Place them on a parchment—paper lined baking sheet. Lightly brush the turnovers with egg wash and sprinkle each with about ½ teaspoon of sugar. Cut 3 small steam vents in the top crust of each turnover.

5 Bake at 400° for about 30 minutes, until the pastry is golden brown and the fruit juices are thickened and bubbling. Cool for 30 minutes before serving or serve at room temperature. These can be reheated at 350° for a few minutes if you wish.

Baker's Note: I often set up a turnover "assembly line." Roll out the pastry ahead of time, separating the cut rounds with plastic film. Lay out 4 to 6 rounds at a time, fill and turn the pastries in groups, and put them on the baking sheet. This definitely saves time!

If you're serving these as a breakfast pastry, you may want to forgo the final sprinkling of sugar on the exterior crust and instead drizzle a vanilla glaze on the baked turnovers. Combine 1 cup of confectioners' sugar with 1½ teaspoons of vanilla extract and enough milk or cream (about 1⅓ tablespoons) to make a fluid but not runny glaze.

Want to make turnovers but it's not cherry season? Blueberries or a combination of diced pears and sun-dried cranberries can be substituted.

Serving Suggestions: A scoop of not-just-plain-vanilla ice cream (page 261) or ruby port ice cream (page 268) would be the most appropriate accompaniment.

Rhubarb Cream Cheese Dumplings

MAKES 1 DOZEN DUMPLINGS

The flaky pastry that forms the base for these delectable dumplings is a simplified version of puff pastry. If you keep a stash of premade dough in your freezer and allow it to defrost overnight in your refrigerator, the final preparation is quick and easy.

INGREDIENTS

    1 recipe flaky puff-style pastry (page 29)

    2½ cups rhubarb, sliced ¼ inch thick (about 12 ounces of trimmed rhubarb)

    ¾ cup sugar, divided

    1 tablespoon orange juice

    4 ounces cream cheese, at room temperature

    ½ teaspoon ground ginger

    ¼ teaspoon vanilla

    1 egg yolk, beaten

    ½ teaspoon water

    powdered sugar for finishing

PREPARATION FOR THE FILLING

1 Combine the rhubarb, ⅜ cup of the sugar, and the orange juice in a sauté pan. Cook over medium heat, gently stirring, until the rhubarb starts to release some juices and becomes tender but not mushy. With a slotted spoon, remove the rhubarb from the pan and reduce any remaining juices until thick and syrupy. Pour the thickened juices over the rhubarb and chill over an ice bath until cool.

2 Combine the cream cheese with 3 tablespoons of the sugar, the ginger, and the vanilla. Mix until smooth.

3 Add half of the egg yolk to the cream cheese mixture and mix to combine. Make an egg wash by combining the remaining egg yolk with the water and reserve.

PREPARATION FOR THE DUMPLINGS

1 Preheat oven to 375°.

2 Roll the pastry into a rectangle approximately 18 × 14 inches. Using a pizza wheel or a large, sharp knife, trim the edges so that you have an even 16 × 12-inch rectangle. Cut the pastry into 12 4-inch squares. With a pastry brush, lightly brush the edges of each pastry square with the reserved egg wash.

3 Place a rounded tablespoon of the cooled rhubarb filling in the center of each pastry square. Place about ½ tablespoon of the cream cheese mixture on top of the rhubarb.

4 To form each dumpling, bring the opposite corners of the pastry square to meet in the center. Gently press the four edges of the seams that are formed to seal the pastry. Place the dumpling on a parchment paper–lined baking sheet.

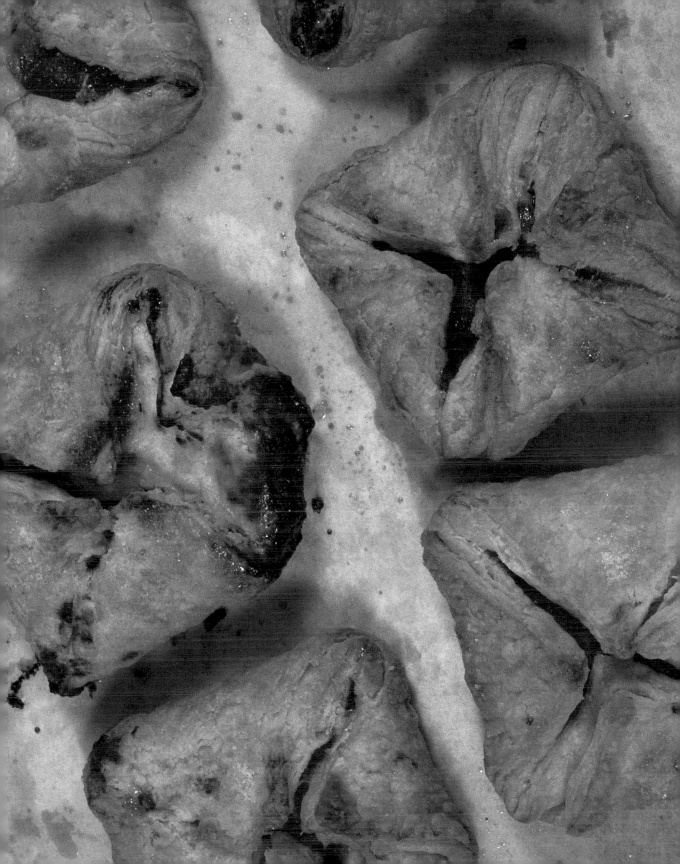

5 Sprinkle each dumpling with about ½ teaspoon of the remaining sugar.
6 Bake at 375° for 15 minutes and then turn the oven down to 350°. Bake for
   an additional 5 minutes, until the pastry is golden brown. Remove from the
   oven and allow to cool for 10 minutes. Sprinkle with powdered sugar and
   serve warm.

Baker's Note: When working with most pastries—and particularly puff pastry—
   I use a pounding motion to maneuver the dough into the basic size and shape
   I wish it to be. By vertically and horizontally pounding the dough (and, yes,
   exerting considerable heft and pressure at the same time), I find that I actually
   "work" the dough less and can accomplish the "rolling" process faster. Only
   toward the end of the process do I actually roll the dough in the traditional
   sense, to ensure even thickness.
       If rhubarb's not in season or you just don't care for it, you can use
   alternative fillings instead. Either peeled apples cut into large-dice and
   combined with some slivered dates or pitted cherries would be a good
   substitution. Lightly sugared summer berries can be used, but I would
   forgo cooking them and omit the orange juice.

Serving Suggestions: For brunch or tea, simply dust the warm dumplings with
   powdered sugar. For a plated dessert presentation, add a bit of strawberry
   crush (page 49) and a scoop of strawberry sorbet (page 279).

Fruit Somethings

Bourbon Peach Cobbler with Cornmeal Cream Biscuits

Deep-Dish Brown Sugar Plum Cobbler

Spiced Apple Cobbler with Cheddar Cheese Biscuit Topping

Blueberry Buckle with Coconut Streusel

Strawberry Rhubarb Caramel Crisp

Chocolate Strawberry Shortcakes with
   White Chocolate Cream

Pumpkin Shortcakes with Cranberry Orange Compote

Blueberry Cassis Shortcakes

Raspberry Nectarine Crumble

Blackberry Slump with Sweet Potato Dumplings

Sautéed Summer Berries

Strawberry Rhubarb Compote

Bourbon Poached Peaches

Cranberry Orange Compote

Oven Roasted Figs with Raspberries

Butterscotch Baked Bananas

Sweet & Sour Cherry Compote

Winter Fruits Poached in Red Wine Syrup

Fall Fruits Poached in Brandied Lemon Syrup

Peppered Bartlett Pears in Sherry Syrup

Golden Pineapple Soup

The first group of desserts in this chapter encompasses all of those fruit-based desserts with funny names: they include the familiar cobblers, crumbles, crunches, and crisps as well as the lesser-known buckles, grunts, slumps, and betties. What they all have in common is the employment of fruit that is layered, surrounded, or topped with some form of cake, crumb, or pastry. There are some regional differences in exact definitions, but in general *cobblers* are baked fruit topped with a pastry or biscuit crust. If it's a pastry crust, the dessert is sometimes called a *deep-dish pie*. Occasionally you will see cobblers with a bottom crust as well. *Crisps* fall into the category of fruit baked with a crumb topping (usually made from butter, flour, sugar, and, at times, nuts). If buttered, sweetened breadcrumbs are used, the dessert becomes a *betty*. *Crunches* and *crumbles* are closely related and usually contain oats. If you have a cake base that's topped with fruit and then covered with a layer of crumbs, you wind up with a *buckle*. *Grunts* and *slumps* are topped with steamed biscuits or dumplings and are cooked covered, on top of the range.

These are all genuinely American desserts—although they now turn up in the fanciest of restaurants, they are really humble, home-based sweets put together with a minimum of fuss. They are meant to be informal in preparation. In theory you can take almost any ripe, flavorful fruit, sugar it lightly, thicken it slightly, and give it a contrasting texture in the form of a biscuit topping, sweet buttered crumbs, or flaky pastry crust—you hardly need a recipe to make them, but I've included a few to be used as basic guidelines. I would encourage you to substitute fruits, interchange toppings, and vary spices and seasonings to suit your personal preference.

Ideally, these desserts should all be served within a few hours of baking—in fact, they're at their very best served warm, after only a fairly brief cooling period, from the oven. Some purists might like theirs plain and unadorned, while other folks say whipped cream is the proper garnish. I, however, *always* prefer my warm fruit somethings with a scoop of (preferably homemade) ice cream.

Here are a few key points to remember in making these wonderful fruit desserts:

- It's best to bake these comforting creations in sturdy, shallow ovenproof casseroles, gratins, or baking pans. Any recipe can be divided into individually baked portions if you wish. You'll probably need to increase the amount of pastry or crumb topping you make if you go for individual servings, though.

- Try to add only enough sugar to enhance the flavor of the fruit. Brown and white sugars can be used interchangeably, and sometimes substituting a bit of maple syrup or honey for a portion of the sugar can lend additional flavor.
- Try not to overthicken the fruit filling. These desserts should be juicy but not overly soupy in consistency. If you've combined the filling ingredients and the mixture seems dry, you can add a bit of fruit juice. On the other hand, if the mixture seems to be giving off excess liquid, you can add a bit more thickening. Some fruits, such as peaches and raspberries, are naturally much juicier than others (e.g., pears and apples) so if you're substituting fruits, you may need to adjust the amount of thickening called for. In all honesty, it's hard to screw these desserts up if you use good fruit—they are virtually guaranteed to be delicious.
- With the exception of the cake-based buckle, it is best to bake these desserts on a baking sheet lined with foil or parchment paper to avoid juicy overflows and messy cleanups.

The second part of this chapter includes simple recipes that highlight various fruits without a pastry component. If you think about it, straight-up, unadulterated fruit really was the original sweet stuff. The application of heat through poaching, sautéing, and roasting transforms fruit into marvelous compotes and gratins. What will make these desserts outstanding is seeking out the most flavorful fruit you can find. If you follow the mantra "think seasonally, buy locally" you should be very successful. Also worth exploring is the world of tropical fruits and items that in some markets might be considered specialty produce. While abundant in many locales, cherries, mangoes, figs, and rhubarb may be hard to find in some locations—it always pays to get to know your green grocer!

If you feel the need to embellish these luscious dishes, pair them with whipped cream, crème fraîche, ice cream, or sorbet. The contrast of a complementary cookie can also add complexity. Above all, use your imagination to create your own variations, and remember—there's always room for a fruit something.

Bourbon Peach Cobbler with Cornmeal Cream Biscuits

SERVES 8

In most parts of the country, life naturally seems to slow down during the summer season. It's the time for screen porch suppers, lazy beach weekends, and backyard barbecues. Social gatherings are relaxed and often spontaneous, centering around the simple pleasure of enjoying the company of family and friends. This low-fuss, but oh so delicious, dessert is one of my summertime favorites.

INGREDIENTS FOR THE FILLING

  10 medium ripe but firm peaches (about 2½ pounds or 6 cups sliced fruit)
  ¾ cup sugar
  ⅛ teaspoon kosher salt
  8 gratings fresh nutmeg
  3 tablespoons flour
  3 tablespoons bourbon

INGREDIENTS FOR THE BISCUITS

  1 cup flour
  ⅓ cup cornmeal (preferably stoneground yellow cornmeal)
  ¼ teaspoon kosher salt
  2 teaspoons baking powder
  2½ tablespoons sugar + 2 teaspoons for finishing
  2½ ounces butter (5 tablespoons), chilled and cut into pieces
  about ¾ cup cream + 1 tablespoon for finishing

PREPARATION

1 Preheat oven to 375°. Lightly butter a 2-quart shallow baking dish.
2 Blanch, peel, and pit the peaches and cut them into thick slices. Place them in a mixing bowl with the remainder of the filling ingredients. Toss to combine and place in the baking dish. Set aside while you make the biscuit topping.
3 Combine the flour, cornmeal, salt, baking powder, and 2½ tablespoons sugar in a mixing bowl. Cut in the butter until the mixture resembles coarse meal.

Stir in enough of the cream to form a moist but not sticky dough. Knead briefly on a lightly floured surface. Roll or pat the dough out to about ½ inch thick and, using a 2½-inch round biscuit cutter, cut out 9 biscuits. Reroll dough scraps if necessary. Place the biscuits on top of the prepared filling. Brush each with reserved cream and sprinkle with sugar.

4 Bake at 375° for about 45 minutes, till the fruit juices are bubbling and thickened and the biscuits are golden brown. If the biscuits appear to be browning too quickly, you can loosely cover the top of the cobbler with foil.

Baker's Note: Be sure to use ripe but firm, in-season peaches for optimum flavor. Remember, a good peach will smell like a good peach. You can substitute nectarines or plums for the peaches if you wish. This dish can also be made in 1-cup ramekins for individual portions.

Serving Suggestions: Serve warm with not-just-plain-vanilla ice cream (page 261) or bourbon molasses ice cream (page 264).

Deep-Dish Brown Sugar Plum Cobbler

SERVES 8

I can't understand why plums are not used more for baking in this country. Not only are they stunning in color, but because of their natural acidity, they add a rich, balanced complexity to desserts. I like to mix Black Friar and Red Casselman plums if those varieties show up in the market at the same time. Late-season Italian prune plums are also a good choice in this dessert.

INGREDIENTS

3 pounds ripe but firm plums, pitted and thickly sliced (about 7½ cups)

½ cup brown sugar

2 tablespoons cornstarch

grated zest and juice of 1 orange

¾ teaspoon cinnamon

¼ teaspoon kosher salt

1 recipe basic pie crust (page 26)

1 egg yolk combined with 1 teaspoon water

PREPARATION

1 Preheat oven to 375° and lightly butter an 8-cup baking dish.

2 Combine the plums, brown sugar, cornstarch, orange zest and juice, cinnamon, and salt in a mixing bowl and toss lightly. Place the mixture in the baking dish.

3 Roll the pastry out about ¼ inch thick and place over the filling, trimming the excess. Brush the pastry with the egg wash and cut 4 steam vents in the center of the pastry.

4 Bake at 375° till the pastry is golden brown and the juices are thickened and bubbling. Serve warm.

Baker's Note: I would encourage you to use this recipe as a basic guideline and substitute other stone fruits or a combination of stone fruits and berries if you wish. Some particularly delicious variations include apricots accented with a bit of fresh vanilla bean or a combination of peaches and blackberries.

Serving Suggestions: I always serve cobblers warm (but not hot, straight out of the oven) topped with ice cream. Not-just-plain-vanilla ice cream (page 261) is always appropriate, although ruby port ice cream (page 268) would also complement the flavor of plums. Lemon chiffon ice cream (page 271) is another alternative.

Spiced Apple Cobbler with Cheddar Cheese Biscuit Topping

SERVES 8

In some locales it's customary when serving wedges of warm apple pie to melt generous slabs of sharp cheddar cheese on top. To the uninitiated this might seem like a strange dessert pairing, but trust me—it's a terrific combo. The same flavor profile is given a different form in this easy-to-prepare deep-dish apple cobbler.

INGREDIENTS FOR THE FILLING

3¼ pounds apples (use a mix of types if possible)

¼ cup brown sugar

¼ cup maple syrup

1 ½ tablespoons cornstarch

½ teaspoon cinnamon

¼ teaspoon nutmeg

¼ teaspoon ground cloves

½ teaspoon kosher salt

¼ cup + 2 tablespoons apple cider

2 tablespoons (1 ounce) butter, cut into small pieces

INGREDIENTS FOR THE TOPPING

1 ½ cups flour

2 tablespoons sugar

2 teaspoons baking powder

½ teaspoon kosher salt

5 tablespoons (2 ½ ounces) butter, chilled and cut into pieces

¾ cup grated sharp white cheddar cheese (3 ounces)

¾ cup + 1 tablespoon cream

PREPARATION FOR THE FILLING

1   Preheat oven to 400°. Butter an 8 × 8 × 2-inch or 9 × 9 × 2-inch (or other 8- to 10-cup) ovenproof baking dish.

2   Peel and core the apples and slice them ½ inch thick; place in a mixing bowl. Add the brown sugar, maple syrup, cornstarch, cinnamon, nutmeg, cloves, salt and apple cider. Toss to mix well and place the apples in the prepared baking dish. Dot the top with the butter pieces. Reserve.

PREPARATION FOR THE TOPPING

1   Combine the flour, sugar, baking powder, and the salt in the bowl of a food processor with a steel blade. Pulse to combine. Add the chilled butter and cut in, pulsing until the mixture resembles coarse meal. Transfer the mixture to a mixing bowl.

2   Add the cheese to the flour mixture and mix to distribute evenly. Stir in the cream to form a soft but not too sticky dough. Lightly flour the dough while it's still in the bowl and knead a few times. Transfer the dough to a lightly floured surface.

3   Roll the dough out to about the dimensions of your baking dish. Place it on top of the apples. Cut several steam vents in the biscuit topping and place the dish in the oven.

4 Bake at 400° for about 20 minutes. Turn oven to 350° and bake an additional 30 to 35 minutes or until the apple juices are bubbling and thickened and the apples are soft. If the biscuit topping appears to be getting too brown, cover it lightly with foil. Allow to cool slightly before serving. This is best served shortly after being baked.

Baker's Note: Orange cheddar can be substituted for the white variety. I use the large holes on a box grater to grate the cheese. I usually mix Granny Smith apples with Cortlands, Empires, and/or Northern Spys for this recipe. You can substitute Bartlett pears for the apples and add some cranberries, dried fruit, or nuts to the filling if you wish. You can also bake this dessert in ovenproof 1-cup ramekins if you prefer individual portions.

Serving Suggestions: I would top this with a scoop of either ruby port ice cream (page 268) or a cinnamon-accented vanilla ice cream (page 261). A spoonful of crème fraîche (page 67) or frozen sourwood honey parfait (page 289) would be good alternatives.

Blueberry Buckle with Coconut Streusel

SERVES 10 TO 12

This is the kind of dessert that's ideal for informal family dinners, picnics, or a relaxed Sunday breakfast. While I'm not a huge fan of coconut, I do think its flavor is a different and delicious complement to fresh blueberries. I am a huge fan of crispy crumb toppings, so this buckle has an extra large proportion of crunchy streusel.

INGREDIENTS FOR THE STREUSEL
   ¾ cup flour
   ¾ cup brown sugar
   ½ teaspoon cinnamon
   ⅛ teaspoon kosher salt
   6 tablespoons (3 ounces) butter, chilled and cut into pieces
   ¾ cup sweetened flaked coconut (preferably the frozen kind, defrosted)

¾ cup + 2 tablespoons flour

¾ teaspoon baking powder

¼ teaspoon cinnamon

⅛ teaspoon kosher salt

3 tablespoons (1½ ounces) butter, at room temperature

⅜ cup sugar

½ teaspoon vanilla

1 egg

¼ cup milk

¼ cup sweetened flaked coconut (preferably the frozen kind, defrosted)

2 cups blueberries

PREPARATION FOR THE STREUSEL

1 Combine the flour, brown sugar, cinnamon, and salt in the bowl of a food processor fitted with a steel blade. Pulse to combine. Add the butter and cut in by pulsing until the mixture is crumbly. Be careful not to overprocess! This can also be done by hand—just rub the ingredients together to form coarse crumbs.

2 Place the streusel in a mixing bowl, add the coconut, and, using your hands, lightly rub the two together to combine. Reserve. The streusel can be made several days ahead if kept refrigerated. It can also be frozen for up to 2 months. Bring to room temperature before using.

PREPARATION FOR THE BUCKLE

1 Preheat oven to 350°. Butter a 9-inch springform pan.

2 Sift together the flour, baking powder, cinnamon, and salt. Reserve.

3 Using a mixer with a paddle, or by hand, cream the butter with the sugar till light. Add the vanilla and the egg. Mix to combine. Alternately add the sifted flour mixture with the milk and mix to blend. Add the coconut.

4 Evenly spread the batter in the prepared pan. Leaving a ¼-inch border around the outer perimeter, evenly distribute the blueberries over the batter. Sprinkle the blueberries with half of the prepared streusel. Bake at 350° for 15 minutes. Sprinkle the buckle with the remaining streusel and bake for approximately 35 minutes more, until the streusel is golden brown and the cake component tests done. Remove from oven and cool for at least 30 minutes. This can be served warm or at room temperature; and while it

can be made 24 hours in advance, ideally it should be served the same day it's prepared.

Baker's Note: For recipes calling for sweetened flaked coconut, I like using the frozen varieties. It tends to be a bit less sweet, is extra moist, and doesn't have additives or preservatives. It is, however, perishable and should be used within 2 to 3 days of defrosting.

Serving Suggestions: This is pretty yummy all on its own, but if you want to dress it up a bit, Lynchburg lemonade sauce (page 43) and a dollop of crème fraîche (page 67) will do the trick.

Strawberry Rhubarb Caramel Crisp

SERVES 6 TO 8

It is often said that opposites attract, and that is certainly the case with strawberries and rhubarb. I flat out love the sweet/tangy contrast that these natural dessert partners provide. Accented with caramel and topped with a simple streusel, this crisp can be put together in a matter of minutes with a minimal amount of fuss.

INGREDIENTS FOR THE TOPPING

8 tablespoons (4 ounces) butter, chilled and cut into pieces

1 cup flour

½ cup brown sugar

½ cup sugar

½ teaspoon cinnamon

⅛ teaspoon salt

INGREDIENTS FOR THE FILLING

2 pints strawberries

1½ tablespoons cornstarch

¼ teaspoon salt

grated zest of 1 orange

½ cup sugar

1 pound trimmed rhubarb, sliced ⅜ inch thick (3 heaping cups)

2 tablespoons orange juice, heated till warm

PREPARATION FOR THE TOPPING

Combine all the ingredients in the bowl of a food processor with a steel blade and pulse until the butter is evenly cut in and the mixture will come together if gently squeezed. The crisp topping should not be at all powdery, but it also should not form large clumps. Remove from the processor bowl. If not using right away, store covered in the refrigerator for up to 3 days. If chilled, allow to sit at room temperature for 15 minutes before using.

PREPARATION FOR THE FILLING

1 Preheat oven to 375°. Butter a 9-inch deep-dish pie plate or other 7-cup baking dish.

2 Hull the strawberries and cut in half, or in quarters if very large. Small berries can be left whole. Place the berries in a stainless bowl and add the cornstarch, salt, and grated orange zest. Reserve.

3 Sprinkle the sugar evenly into a large, wide, unlined sauté pan. Place over medium heat and cook, stirring gently only occasionally, till the sugar starts to caramelize. Tilt and swirl the pan to promote even browning. Once the sugar is dark amber in color, carefully add the orange juice. Add the rhubarb and cook lightly, stirring occasionally, just until the caramel is dissolved. It's OK if a few bits of caramel remain. The rhubarb should maintain its shape! Cool slightly and combine with the reserved strawberries. Toss gently and place the mixture in the prepared pie plate, mounding in the center.

4 Sprinkle the crisp topping evenly over the fruit. Place the pie plate on a foil-lined baking sheet. This crisp is very juicy and tends to bubble over.

5 Bake at 375° for approximately 35 minutes, until the fruit juices are bubbling and the crisp is golden. Cool 15 minutes before serving. This is best served shortly after baking.

Baker's Note: You can portion the filling into ¾- to 1-cup ovenproof ceramic ramekins for individual servings. This recipe can also be doubled very easily if you're feeding a larger group.

Serving Suggestions: I always serve fruit crisps with ice cream. Burnt orange caramel ice cream (page 262), not-just-plain-vanilla ice cream (page 261), or cream cheese ice cream made without the blackberry swirl (page 265) would be terrific. To simplify things you can also use a premium-quality store-bought ice cream.

Chocolate Strawberry Shortcakes with White Chocolate Cream

SERVES 8

Some purists might take offense at this gussied-up shortcake variation. While I do appreciate the virtues of a more traditional biscuit base, this softer cake, chocolaty but not too sweet, is a nice change.

INGREDIENTS FOR THE BERRIES

2½ pints strawberries

2 tablespoons sugar, or to taste

INGREDIENTS FOR THE SHORTCAKES

2 cups flour

½ cup cocoa

½ cup sugar + 1 tablespoon for finishing

2 teaspoons baking powder

½ teaspoon baking soda

½ teaspoon kosher salt

6 tablespoons (3 ounces) butter, chilled and cut into pieces

6 ounces semisweet homemade chocolate chips (page 54)
    or store-bought chips

1 egg

1 egg yolk

1 teaspoon vanilla

¾ cup milk + a bit extra for glazing

1 recipe white chocolate cream (page 67)

PREPARATION FOR THE BERRIES

Hull the berries and cut them into thick slices. Combine the berries and the sugar in a bowl and toss. Cover and refrigerate until ready to serve.

PREPARATION FOR THE SHORTCAKES

1 Preheat oven to 400°.

2 Place the flour, cocoa, ½ cup sugar, baking powder, baking soda, and salt in a food processor with a steel blade. Pulse to blend. Add the butter and pulse till

the butter is evenly cut in and the mixture resembles coarse meal. Transfer the mixture to a medium-sized mixing bowl. Stir in the chocolate chips.

3 Place the egg, egg yolk, vanilla, and ¾ cup milk in a small mixing bowl and whisk just to blend.

4 Combine the egg mixture with the flour mixture and mix just to combine, forming a moist but manageable dough. Do not overwork. Gather together and knead several times on a lightly floured surface.

5 On a lightly floured surface, with a floured pin, roll the dough out to about a ¾-inch thickness. Use a 3-inch round biscuit cutter to cut out shortcakes and transfer them to a parchment paper–lined baking sheet. You may gather the scraps of dough and reroll them one time.

6 Lightly brush the top of each shortcake with a bit of milk and sprinkle the tops with 1 tablespoon of sugar.

7 Bake at 400° for about 15 to 18 minutes, until the tops feel just set when lightly touched. Remove and cool slightly before serving. These can be made a few hours ahead and warmed slightly at 350° for service.

TO SERVE

When ready to serve, split the warm shortcakes in half horizontally with a serrated knife. Place the bottoms on serving plates. Divide about three-quarters of the berries and their juices among the shortcakes and top the berries with a generous dollop of white chocolate cream. Set the tops on each shortcake and top each with the remaining berries and another small spoonful of cream.

Baker's Note: You can make a dramatic giant shortcake if you wish and portion it by cutting it into wedges. The baking time will probably be closer to 25 to 30 minutes. If delicious strawberries are unavailable, consider substituting sweet and sour cherry compote (page 155), fresh raspberries, or even sliced bananas as an alternative filling.

Serving Suggestions: You could serve these with a bit of cocoa fudge sauce (page 37) on the plate. A dusting of confectioners' sugar and cocoa powder is a nice finishing touch.

Pumpkin Shortcakes with Cranberry Orange Compote

SERVES 8

While I like to use farmers' market fresh pumpkin for many savory dishes, I usually use canned purée in baked desserts for flavor and texture consistency. If you have any of these tender biscuits left over, try toasting them for breakfast and serve with cranberry conserve.

INGREDIENTS FOR THE SHORTCAKES

2¾ cups flour

¼ cup + 2 tablespoons brown sugar

1 tablespoon baking powder

1 teaspoon baking soda

½ teaspoon nutmeg

¼ teaspoon ginger

½ teaspoon kosher salt

8 tablespoons (4 ounces) butter, chilled and cut into pieces

½ cup pumpkin purée

1 teaspoon vanilla

¾ cup buttermilk

½ tablespoon cream

1 tablespoon sugar

¼ teaspoon cinnamon

INGREDIENTS FOR THE WHIPPED CREAM

1½ cups cream

1½ tablespoons sugar

INGREDIENT FOR SERVING

1 recipe cranberry orange compote (page 150)

PREPARATION FOR THE SHORTCAKES

1 Preheat oven to 425°.

2 Place the flour, brown sugar, baking powder, baking soda, nutmeg, ginger, and salt in a food processor with a steel blade. Pulse to combine. Add the cold

butter and pulse several times to evenly cut the butter in till the mixture resembles coarse meal. Add the pumpkin and pulse several times to distribute evenly. Transfer the mixture to a mixing bowl.

3 Combine the vanilla and the buttermilk and gently mix into the dry ingredients just until a soft dough forms. Gently knead the dough in the bowl several times, flouring it lightly. It should be soft but not sticky. Turn the dough out onto a lightly floured surface. Dust the top of the dough and a rolling pin lightly with flour and roll the dough out to a scant ¾ inch thick. Using a 2½- to 3-inch round cutter, cut out shortcakes and place them on a parchment paper–lined baking sheet. You can gather and reroll the scraps one time.

4 Brush the tops of the shortcakes with cream. Combine the sugar and the cinnamon and sprinkle a bit on top of each shortcake.

5 Bake at 425° for 5 minutes. Turn oven down to 400° and bake an additional 10 to 12 minutes, until both the tops and bottoms are golden brown. Allow to cool slightly before using or bake up to several hours in advance and reheat lightly before filling.

PREPARATION FOR THE WHIPPED CREAM
In a chilled bowl, with a chilled whip, beat the cream till lightly thickened. Add the sugar and beat the cream to medium soft peaks. Chill until ready to use. Rewhip to the proper consistency if necessary.

TO SERVE
Split the warm shortcakes with a serrated knife. Cover the shortcake bottom generously with cranberry orange compote, allowing some of the juices to lightly soak the biscuit. Spoon a generous dollop of whipped cream over the fruit and top with the shortcake tops.

Baker's Note: I like to garnish these shortcakes with candied pumpkin. Make a heavy sugar syrup by dissolving 1½ cups sugar in ¾ cup water with a cinnamon stick and slowly poach pumpkin that has been cut into medium dice until the pieces are soft and completely cooked through but not mushy. Quick chill over an ice bath. Store refrigerated in their syrup until ready to serve. Drain and scatter on dessert plates or add to the shortcake filling.

Serving Suggestions: If you'd like, you can substitute cognac-flavored vanilla ice cream (page 261) for the whipped cream. Sliced peppered Bartlett pears in sherry syrup (page 160), lightly sautéed spiced apples, or fall fruits poached in brandied lemon syrup (page 159) make good alternative filling options.

Blueberry Cassis Shortcakes

SERVES 6

Rounding out my trio of not-so-traditional shortcakes is a combination butter-milk (for flavor and tenderness) and cream (for richness) biscuit with a delicious cassis-accented blueberry compote. Blueberries are one of those fruits that really lend themselves to freezing, particularly if you plan to utilize them in a cooked ap-plication. Follow the farmstead mentality of putting up in-season crops for later use when the pickings are slim. Try preparing these in the chill of winter for an unexpected dose of summertime.

INGREDIENTS FOR THE BLUEBERRY COMPOTE

4 heaping cups blueberries, divided

3 tablespoons sugar

1 tablespoon lemon juice

2½ tablespoons crème de cassis

1 tablespoon cold water

1½ teaspoons cornstarch

INGREDIENTS FOR THE SHORTCAKES

2 cups flour

⅓ cup sugar + 1 tablespoon for finishing

2½ teaspoons baking powder

¼ teaspoon baking soda

½ teaspoon kosher salt

8 tablespoons (4 ounces) butter, chilled and cut into pieces

1 egg

¼ cup buttermilk

¼ cup cream + 2 tablespoons for glazing

Powdered sugar for serving

INGREDIENTS FOR THE WHIPPED CREAM

1½ cups cream

1½ tablespoons sugar

PREPARATION FOR THE BLUEBERRY COMPOTE

1 Combine 3 cups of blueberries with the sugar, lemon juice, and crème de cassis in a stainless saucepan. Cook over medium heat, stirring occasionally, until the berries pop and release their juices.

2 Combine the water with the cornstarch and stir into the simmering blueberry mixture. Simmer till thickened (about 1 minute) and remove from heat. Add the remaining 1 cup of blueberries. Taste the compote and adjust with sugar or lemon juice if necessary. Cool over an ice bath. This can be made up to 2 days in advance. Refrigerate until ready to use.

PREPARATION FOR THE SHORTCAKES

1 Preheat oven to 425°. Line a baking sheet with parchment paper.

2 Combine the flour, sugar, baking powder, baking soda, and salt in a food processor with a steel blade. Pulse to cut in the chilled butter until the mixture resembles coarse meal. Remove the mixture to a bowl. Combine the egg, buttermilk, and ¼ cup cream. Stir the buttermilk mixture into the dry ingredients to form a moist but somewhat stiff dough. You may need to add a bit of additional cream. On a lightly floured surface gently knead the dough several times.

3 Roll the dough out approximately ¾ inch thick and cut into 6 2½-inch rounds with a biscuit cutter. Gather the scraps, reroll and cut additional rounds. Place the shortcakes on the prepared baking sheet. Brush their tops with cream and sprinkle evenly with the remaining 1 tablespoon of sugar.

4 Bake at 425° for approximately 15 minutes, until lightly golden brown.

PREPARATION FOR THE WHIPPED CREAM

In a chilled bowl, with a chilled whip, beat the cream till lightly thickened. Add the sugar and beat the cream to medium soft peaks. Chill until ready to use. Rewhip to the proper consistency if necessary.

TO SERVE

Split the warm shortcakes with a serrated knife. Set the bottoms on individual serving plates. Divide the blueberry cassis compote among the shortcakes, allowing some to run off each shortcake onto the plate. Top the compote with a generous dollop of whipped cream. Cap with the top half of the shortcake. Sprinkle the plate and the top of the shortcake with powdered sugar and serve.

Baker's Note: I think these biscuits are best freshly baked, but you can make them several hours ahead and reheat them just before serving. Try using an all-purpose, Southern-style soft wheat flour (such as White Lily) if it's available in your market. For a different look, you can roll the dough into a rectangular shape and then cut it into 6 squares.

Serving Suggestions: This is a great all-purpose dessert shortcake that can be filled with almost any type of fresh berry or fruit compote. Think outside the box and use roasted plums, sautéed bananas, or poached apricots. You can also serve the shortcake with ice cream rather than whipped cream. Try lemon chiffon ice cream (page 271) for a delicious accompaniment to the blueberry cassis filling.

Raspberry Nectarine Crumble

SERVES 6

Juicy seasonal fruit is the starring attraction in this market-inspired dessert. Be flexible about your featured ingredients and buy whatever fruit seems to be at its peak. The suggested combination of nectarines and raspberries is delicious, but so are pairings of peaches and blueberries, apricots and cherries, or pears and rhubarb.

INGREDIENTS FOR THE TOPPING

1 cup flour
½ cup brown sugar
½ cup sugar
¼ teaspoon cinnamon
¼ teaspoon freshly grated nutmeg
¼ teaspoon kosher salt
½ cup old-fashioned oats
8 tablespoons (4 ounces) cold butter, cut into pieces

2 pounds (6–7 medium-sized) nectarines

1 pint raspberries

¼ cup sugar

2½ tablespoons cornstarch

1 teaspoon vanilla

2 teaspoons lemon juice

PREPARATION FOR THE TOPPING

Place the flour, brown sugar, sugar, cinnamon, nutmeg, salt, and oats in a food processor with a steel blade. Pulse several times to blend well. Add the butter and pulse until the mixture has the texture of rough meal and clumps together when squeezed lightly. Reserve chilled if not using immediately. The crumble topping can be made 3 days in advance. Bring to cool room temperature before using.

1 Preheat oven to 375°. Lightly butter a shallow 8-cup ovenproof baking dish.

2 Pit the nectarines and cut each of them into 8 slices. You should have about 4 cups of nectarines. In a mixing bowl, combine them with the rest of the filling ingredients. Toss gently and transfer the fruit to the baking dish.

3 Gently squeeze handfuls of the prepared crumble topping together and evenly sprinkle the topping over the fruit.

4 Bake at 375° for approximately 30 to 35 minutes, until the crumble topping is lightly browned, the fruit is tender, and the fruit juices are bubbling. Serve warm.

Baker's Note: This is one of the recipes that you can truly make your own. Vary the fruits (you should always have about 6 cups), add dried fruit to the filling, or substitute chopped nuts for the oatmeal and spice your crumble accordingly. This recipe can easily be doubled or tripled—if the topping is made ahead of time, you can stop at the market for fruit on your way home and have a freshly baked dessert for a crowd in under an hour. You can also make individual servings of crumble in 1-cup ceramic ramekins.

Serving Suggestions: Like all "warm fruit somethings," this crumble should, in my opinion, be served with ice cream. For something really special, try making cream cheese blackberry swirl ice cream (page 265), but substitute a raspberry swirl.

Blackberry Slump with Sweet Potato Dumplings

SERVES 8

I always imagine this dessert being cooked on an open hearth—I'm sure it was developed long before the kitchen range was commonplace. I've found mention of similar biscuit-topped, stewed fruit desserts in cookbooks from both New England and the South. While these regions are geographically disparate, their agrarian-based field-to-table cooking mentality is very similar. Try freezing some of the summer's bounty of blackberries and fix this hearty dessert in fall sweet potato season.

INGREDIENTS FOR THE STEWED BLACKBERRIES

4 cups blackberries

½ cup orange juice

1½ tablespoons water

½ cup + 2 tablespoons sugar

grated zest of half an orange

INGREDIENTS FOR THE DUMPLINGS

1½ cups flour

2 teaspoons baking powder

¼ cup sugar

½ teaspoon kosher salt

⅛ teaspoon cinnamon

⅛ teaspoon cloves

⅛ teaspoon freshly grated nutmeg

grated zest of half an orange

¼ cup + 2 tablespoons mashed cooked sweet potatoes

¾ cup milk

2 tablespoons (1 ounce) butter, melted

PREPARATION FOR THE STEWED BLACKBERRIES

Combine all of the ingredients in a shallow-sided, medium-sized saucepan or sauté pan (make sure you have a lid that will fit it). Bring the mixture to a simmer over medium heat and cook until the berries release their juices. Turn off heat and reserve while you prepare the dumplings.

PREPARATION FOR THE DUMPLINGS

1 Combine the flour, baking powder, sugar, salt, cinnamon, cloves, nutmeg, and orange zest in a medium-sized bowl.

2 Place the mashed sweet potatoes in a separate bowl and gradually mix in the milk until the mixture is smooth. Add the butter and then stir the sweet potato mixture into the dry ingredients until you have a dough that is well blended. The consistency should be that of a wet biscuit dough. Do not overmix.

3 Bring the stewed blackberries back to a simmer. Spoon 8 egg-shaped dumplings onto the surface of the simmering blackberries, leaving space between them. Immediately cover the pan and allow the dumplings to steam for approximately 12 minutes before checking them. When done, they will feel firm. Serve immediately. This dessert should be eaten while it is hot.

Baker's Note: Blueberries or a mixture of berries can be used instead of the blackberries.

Serving Suggestion: Serve in a shallow bowl, topped with not-just-plain-vanilla ice cream (page 261) or a generous splash of custard sauce (page 65).

Sautéed Summer Berries

SERVES 6

The application of a bit of heat to fresh berries seems to intensify their flavor. It's also a great way to doctor up less-than-stellar berries. You can add a touch more sweetness or acid, enrich them with additional butter, or add various herbs and spices as you see fit.

INGREDIENTS

2 tablespoons (1 ounce) butter

4½ cups mixed berries

2 tablespoons sugar

1 tablespoon Grand Marnier

1 teaspoon lime juice

a few grains kosher salt

PREPARATION

Melt the butter in a medium-sized nonreactive sauté pan over medium high heat. Add the remaining ingredients. Sauté, tossing a few times, until the berries have just started to release some of their juices and are warmed through.

Baker's Note: I'll often start sautéing berries such as blueberries or strawberries a moment or two before more fragile varieties such as raspberries. Please use this as a method rather than a strict recipe. You can sweeten with honey or brown sugar. Blueberries sautéed with a bit of maple syrup are also delicious. You can add a grating of citrus zest, a bit of vanilla, some chopped tarragon, or fresh ginger. You can season with nutmeg, a grind of black pepper, or a hint of fresh chili. This method also works for other fruits. Experiment with sliced bananas, nectarines, or figs.

Serving Suggestions: Warm sautéed berries are wonderful topped with a scoop of ice cream or sorbet. Check out the chapter on frozen desserts below to find a flavor pairing that appeals to you. These berries are also nice served alongside Cousin Steve's cheesecake (page 241) or Celebrity Dairy blintzes (page 334).

Strawberry Rhubarb Compote

MAKES 4 CUPS

Invariably, when I'm standing in line at my local market with an armful of rhubarb, someone will ask, "So what do you do with that stuff?" While excellent baked into simple pies, crisps, and crumbles, it can also be combined with strawberries in a juicy, flavorful fruit compote.

INGREDIENTS

1 cup orange juice
⅔ cup honey
1½ pounds rhubarb, sliced ⅓ inch thick (about 4 loosely packed cups)
1 teaspoon vanilla
½ teaspoon ground cardamom
3 cups hulled, thick-sliced strawberries
sugar, if needed

PREPARATION

1 Simmer the orange juice and honey in a medium-sized skillet over medium heat until the liquid is reduced by half. Add the rhubarb and cook, stirring until the rhubarb is just tender, about 3 minutes. Do not overcook or it will become mushy and disintegrate. Transfer to a mixing bowl and stir in the vanilla and cardamom. Cool (or quick chill over an ice bath if you're afraid that the rhubarb will overcook) and refrigerate if not using right away. Can be prepared up to 6 hours ahead.

2 Stir the strawberries into the chilled rhubarb just before serving. Season to taste, adding a bit of sugar or additional citrus if necessary.

Baker's Note: Some rhubarb (the field-grown varieties) can release a tremendous amount of liquid when cooked. If the rhubarb is tender and swimming in juices, you should drain the rhubarb and allow it to cool. Place the juices back on the heat and reduce them till thickened and slightly syrupy. Cool the juices and combine with the cooled rhubarb.

Serving Suggestions: I like to serve this in bowls, topped with a scoop of plain cream cheese ice cream (page 265), burnt orange caramel ice cream (page 262), or strawberry sorbet (page 279). It's also terrific served alongside buttermilk panna cotta (page 188) or not-afraid-of-flavor gingerbread (page 222).

Bourbon Poached Peaches

SERVES 8

The addition of a generous splash of good bourbon or sour mash whiskey gives these peaches an extra flavor dimension as well as a delightful Southern inflection.

INGREDIENTS

3 tablespoons sugar

1½ tablespoons lemon juice

½ teaspoon vanilla

¼ cup + 1 tablespoon bourbon

1 500 mg. vitamin C tablet

8 medium-sized, ripe freestone peaches

PREPARATION

1 Combine the sugar, lemon juice, vanilla, ¼ cup bourbon, and the vitamin C tablet in a nonreactive medium-sized sauté pan. Bring to a simmer over low heat, stirring to dissolve the sugar. Remove from heat and reserve.

2 Blanch and skin the peaches. Bring a saucepan of water to a boil. With a paring knife, cut a shallow x in the base end of each peach. Drop the peaches into the boiling water; after 30 to 45 seconds remove them to a bowl of ice water to stop the cooking. Using a paring knife, slip the skins off the peaches. Cut each peach into about 8 slices—you should have approximately 5 cups of sliced fruit.

3 Add the peaches to the bourbon syrup. Place over medium heat and cook, stirring gently, until the peach slices are just cooked through but are not falling-apart soft. Remove the peaches with a slotted spoon and place them in a bowl over an ice bath to stop them from cooking.

4 Depending on the juiciness of your peaches, you may have to reduce the juices. They should be thickened and syrupy. Add the remaining tablespoon of bourbon. Cool the syrup thoroughly and pour over chilled peaches. Refrigerate if not using immediately. This can be made up to 1 day ahead.

Baker's Note: Some people don't bother with peeling their peaches. I find East Coast peaches to have thicker skins than West Coast varieties, and I always peel mine.

You can substitute another type of alcohol, such as brandy or dark rum, for the bourbon if you wish. A teetotaler's version can also be made by using brewed tea in place of the bourbon.

A sauce with a smooth consistency can be made by puréeing the peaches, reduced juices, and bourbon. Strain through a fine-mesh strainer.

Serving Suggestions: This is a terrific topping to spoon over not-just-plain-vanilla ice cream (page 261). Add a few pecan shortbreads (page 302) and you have a complex, wonderful dessert. I also like to serve this with buttermilk panna cotta (page 188) and brown sugar sour cream cheesecake (page 243). Peaches pair well with the flavor of ginger, and this can also be served alongside not-afraid-of-flavor gingerbread (page 222).

The Wonders of Vitamin C

Utilizing Vitamin C tablets is a great way to prevent oxidation when cooking fruit. Certain fruits, such as pears, peaches, and apples, have a tendency to turn an unattractive brown even after they've been poached. This process can be slowed by the addition of a substantial amount of citrus juice, but I've found that I don't always want such a pronounced citrus flavor. By adding a 500 mg. vitamin C tablet to poaching liquid, cooked sorbet bases, or sauces, you can always preserve fruit's natural color.

Cranberry Orange Compote

MAKES ABOUT 4½ CUPS

This colorful compote is a wonderful adjunct to many cool-weather desserts—it's not bad right alongside your Thanksgiving bird either.

INGREDIENTS

8 navel oranges

2½ cups cranberries, picked over

¾ cup sugar

1½ tablespoons Grand Marnier

PREPARATION

1 Using either a serrated knife or a sharp paring knife, remove the skin and all of the white pith from the oranges. Working over a bowl to catch the juices, cut in between the membranes to release the orange segments. Reserve the segments and juice in separate bowls.

2 In a nonreactive saucepan, combine the cranberries, sugar, and ¼ cup of the reserved orange juice. Cook over low heat, stirring often, until the cranberries pop and soften (about 5 minutes). Remove from heat and stir in the Grand Marnier and reserved orange segments. Quick chill over an ice bath.

3 Taste and adjust the sugar if necessary. If the chilled compote seems too thick, you can add a bit more of the reserved orange juice. If it seems unusually soupy, you can strain off the excess juices, reduce them, and add them back to the compote. Once cool, the compote should be refrigerated until service.

Baker's Note: I occasionally add some sun-dried cranberries to this compote for a bit of textural contrast. Additions of some freshly grated ginger or some vanilla bean can bring yet another flavor.

Serving Suggestions: Use as a filling for pumpkin shortcakes (page 137) or serve alongside orange glazed cranberry sour cream poundcake (page 218) or cranberry crumb cake (page 229). You can also serve this compote topped with burnt orange caramel ice cream (page 262) or ruby port ice cream (page 268).

Oven Roasted Figs with Raspberries

SERVES 6

One of my favorite ways to prepare a variety of fruits is to roast them in a high-heat oven. Baking the fruit to the point where it's softened, warmed through, and lightly caramelized, this method is fast and easy and allows for an unlimited number of variations.

INGREDIENTS

12 medium-sized ripe but firm figs

juice of 1 orange

¼ cup honey

2½ tablespoons sugar

2 teaspoons fresh thyme

2 tablespoons (1 ounce) butter, cut into very small pieces

1½ cups fresh raspberries

PREPARATION

1   Preheat oven to 450°.

2   Butter a large shallow baking dish. Cut the figs in half and place them in the
    dish, cut side up, in a single layer. Squeeze the juice of 1 orange over the figs,
    drizzle them with the honey, and sprinkle them with the sugar and thyme.
    Dot the top of each fig with just a bit of butter.

3   Bake for about 8 minutes and then baste the figs with any accumulated
    pan juice. Place the pan back in the oven and bake for an additional 4 to
    5 minutes, until the figs just start to caramelize. Add the raspberries to the
    pan and bake for an additional 2 to 3 minutes, just to heat the raspberries
    through.

Baker's Note: I like to use Mission figs for this, but any variety can be substituted.
    Please use this as a conceptual recipe—the same methodology can be applied
    to many different types of fruits. Plums, apricots, pears, pineapples, grapes,
    etc., can all be oven roasted. You can also sweeten the fruit with brown sugar
    or maple syrup. Vary the citrus and add a touch of balsamic vinegar, a sweet
    dessert wine, or brandy depending on the flavor profile you wish to achieve.

Serving Suggestions: I like to serve the figs and raspberries with frozen sourwood
    honey parfait (page 289), crème fraîche (page 67), or a scoop of ice cream.
    A scatter of honeyed almonds (page 55) is a nice garnish. You can also pass
    a plate of cornmeal vanilla bean shortbreads (page 300) or almond butter
    cookies (page 308) when serving the fruits.

Butterscotch Baked Bananas

SERVES 8

Bananas are often the fruit that I turn to when we're "in between seasons" and other options are limited. This doesn't mean that they play second fiddle, though. Their versatility always has me coming up with new ways to use them. The 4 B's—bananas, butter, brown sugar, and bourbon—combine in this recipe with outstanding results.

INGREDIENTS

8 tablespoons (4 ounces) butter
½ cup brown sugar
1½ tablespoons bourbon
2 tablespoons water
½ teaspoon vanilla
a few grains kosher salt
⅛ teaspoon lemon juice
8 medium ripe, fragrant, fairly firm bananas

PREPARATION

1 Melt the butter in a small heavy-bottomed saucepan. Add the brown sugar and whisk continuously until smooth. It may take a minute or two for the mixture to emulsify—keep whisking!

2 Whisk in the bourbon, water, vanilla, salt, and lemon juice. Simmer, whisking often, for 3 minutes. Remove from heat and reserve. This can be made 3 days ahead up to this point if the brown sugar sauce is cooled and refrigerated. Rewarm and whisk well before using.

3 Preheat oven to 425°. Lightly butter a shallow baking dish large enough to hold the bananas in a single layer. Peel the bananas and slice them about ½ inch thick. Place them in the prepared baking dish and add the reserved brown sugar mixture. Toss lightly to coat the bananas.

4 Bake at 425° for about 5 minutes, until the juices are bubbling and the bananas are just warmed through but not mushy. Serve immediately.

Baker's Note: If you don't want to make this large a batch, simply allow 1 banana and 2 tablespoons of brown sugar per portion. You can vary the liquor used in this recipe or leave it out entirely. An alternative cooking method is to bring the brown sugar sauce to a simmer in a sauté pan, add the bananas, and heat them on top of the range. The end results are identical.

Serving Suggestions: These bananas (and the resulting "pan juices") are wonderful topped with ice cream of layered sundae-style. Try them in combo with peanut butter ice cream (page 266) or bourbon molasses ice cream (page 264). These can also be served as a filling for chocolate shortcakes (page 135) or as a garnish for black walnut angel food cake (page 226), in which case whipped cream would be the appropriate accompaniment.

Sweet & Sour Cherry Compote

MAKES ABOUT 2 CUPS

I dearly remember the sour cherry tree my grandmother had in her Brooklyn backyard. When we could beat the birds to those precious fruits, she often put up a cherry compote that was later turned into blintzes and strudel filling. Consider yourself lucky if you live in an area with native sour cherries—most of us have to make do with the dried or canned varieties.

INGREDIENTS

2½ cups pitted Bing cherries
¾ cup dried sour cherries (Montmorency or Morello are both good)
3 tablespoons sugar
¼ cup cherry cider or juice (check your local natural foods store for this, but cranberry juice or a fruity red wine can be substituted)
¼ cup orange juice, divided
⅛ teaspoon kosher salt
a few grinds black pepper
1 tablespoon balsamic vinegar
1 teaspoon cornstarch

PREPARATION

1 In a medium-sized nonreactive saucepot combine the Bing cherries, dried cherries, sugar, cherry cider, 3 tablespoons of the orange juice, salt, pepper,

and balsamic vinegar. Bring to a simmer over medium low heat and cook, stirring occasionally, until the Bing cherries have softened and given off some of their juices. It should take about 10 to 12 minutes.

2 Combine the cornstarch with the remaining 1 tablespoon of orange juice and stir this into the cherries. Simmer 1 minute, allowing the juices to thicken slightly. Remove from heat and adjust the seasonings to your taste. You may need a bit more sugar or orange juice.

3 Cool over an ice bath. If, once cool, the mixture seems a bit too thick, you might want to add a touch more cherry cider or orange juice. This can be made up to 2 days in advance.

Baker's Note: Adding a hint of savory seasoning like balsamic vinegar and black pepper to fruits is a wonderful way to round out flavors and add complexity. These flavors also work well with peaches, apricots, and strawberries.

Cherry season is often preciously short. To take full advantage of it, I will buy pounds of fruit when the season is at its peak, pit the cherries, and freeze them for future use. You may also find bags of individually quick-frozen cherries (sans syrup) in your grocer's freezer case.

Serving Suggestions: Serve with buttermilk vanilla bean custard pie (page 85) or use as a filling for chocolate shortcakes (page 135). This compote also works well with orange coconut sorbet (page 284) or ruby port ice cream (page 268).

Winter Fruits Poached in Red Wine Syrup

SERVES 6 AS A PRIMARY DESSERT OR 12 AS A DESSERT GARNISH

I love poached fruits for their versatility. They can be used as the main attraction or serve in a supporting role. A cut glass bowl heaped with jewel-like fruits makes a beautiful addition to a holiday brunch or dessert buffet.

INGREDIENTS
    2 cups red wine
    ½ cup ruby port
    1 cup water

¼ cup orange juice

½ cup sugar

2 tablespoons honey

6 ripe Bartlett pears

12 pitted prunes

12 dried apricots

2 tablespoons golden raisins

2 tablespoons dark raisins

½ cup seedless red grapes

PREPARATION

1 In a medium-sized saucepan, combine the red wine, port, water, orange juice, sugar, and honey. Bring to a boil and then turn down to a slow simmer. Meanwhile, prepare an ice bath.

2 Peel the pears and remove their cores with a small melon baller. Cut each pear into 6 to 8 slices and add to the poaching liquid. Poach the pears, turning them occasionally, until just cooked through. If necessary, poach the pears in 2 batches. Remove the pears from the syrup with a slotted spoon and quick cool over the ice bath.

3 Add the prunes, apricots, and both kinds of raisins to the poaching liquid and simmer till plumped and softened (about 10 minutes). Remove from heat and allow the dried fruits to cool in the syrup. Combine the syrup, dried fruits, and pears. Add the grapes and toss gently to combine. Serve at room temperature. This can be made 48 hours in advance and stored covered in the refrigerator. Bring to room temperature before serving.

Baker's Note: Feel free to vary the variety of fruits used. Dried cherries, dried figs, roasted chestnuts, fresh orange segments, and Granny Smith apples all lend themselves to being poached in red wine syrup.

Serving Suggestions: These fruits are wonderful paired with creamy Maytag blue cheesecakes (page 254). The fruits can also be used as a simple dessert accompanied by a dollop of crème fraîche (page 67) and a crisp cookie. Alternatively, they can be topped with a scoop of burnt orange caramel ice cream (page 262) or served with frozen sourwood honey parfait (page 289).

Fall Fruits Poached in Brandied Lemon Syrup

SERVES 8

I've included several poached fruit variations in the book because I think that they really add an interesting dimension to desserts and can be reflective of what's best and freshest in the market in any given season. Be imaginative and personalize your mix by adding nontraditional fruits or even vegetables. For this autumnal mélange, I've used diced pumpkin, but dates, quince, or fennel could also be used in combination with the usual pears and dried fruits.

INGREDIENTS

    1 cup sugar
    ½ cup lemon juice
    ½ cup brandy
    1 cup water
    ½ cup apple cider
    1 cinnamon stick
    4 ripe but firm Bartlett pears
    ¾ cup medium-diced fresh pumpkin
    ⅓ cup sun-dried cherries
    ⅓ cup dried apple slices
    ½ cup raisins

PREPARATION

1 Combine the sugar, lemon juice, brandy, water, apple cider, and cinnamon stick in a saucepan and bring to a simmer.

2 Peel and core the pears and cut them into ½-inch thick slices. Poach the pears in the syrup until they are just tender. Remove the pears with a slotted spoon and chill them over an ice bath.

3 Add the diced pumpkin to the syrup and poach until the pumpkin is tender. It should be soft but still retain its shape. With a slotted spoon, remove the pumpkin to the ice bath.

4   Add the cherries, apple slices, and raisins to the syrup and allow the mixture to simmer 2 to 3 minutes. Remove from heat and let the mixture cool to room temperature.

5   Remove the cinnamon stick from the syrup and add the cooled dried fruits and syrup to the pears and pumpkin. Mix lightly to combine. Chill lightly before using. This can be made up to 2 days ahead of time.

Baker's Note: To cut pumpkin make sure you have a sharp, heavy knife and a sturdy cutting board set on top of a damp towel to prevent slipping. I like to use small "pie pumpkins." Cut the pumpkin in half and lay it on the cutting board with the flat, cut side down. Remove the outer skin—I find a serrated knife is great for doing this. Using a spoon, scoop out the pumpkin seeds and interior "guts." Cut into thick slices and then cut the slices into medium-sized cubes.

If you find that your syrup is reducing too much during the poaching process, add a bit of extra water to dilute it slightly.

Serving Suggestions: This is a great garnish for pumpkin cognac cheesecake brûlée (page 247) and can be used to fill pumpkin shortcakes (page 137). You can also serve this simply topped with a bit of crème fraîche (page 67) that's been lightly sweetened and whipped with a pinch of cinnamon. Hazelnut sandies (page 314) would make an excellent "side cookie."

Peppered Bartlett Pears in Sherry Syrup

SERVES 6 TO 8

I recommend using Lustau's East India Sherry, if you can find it, in the poaching syrup. It is a delicious, nutty-tasting sherry that is terrific both in desserts and as an aperitif.

INGREDIENTS

2 cups sugar

1½ cups water

2 cups sherry

½ cup Amaretto

1 cup orange juice

2 bay leaves (fresh or dried)

1 500 mg. vitamin C tablet

2 cinnamon sticks

8 whole black peppercorns

6–8 ripe but firm Bartlett pears

freshly ground black pepper for service

PREPARATION

1 Combine the sugar, water, sherry, Amaretto, orange juice, bay leaves, vitamin C tablet, cinnamon sticks, and peppercorns in a nonreactive saucepan large enough to hold the pears in a single layer. If you have a piece of cheesecloth you can tie the spices into a sachet to make their removal easier, but doing so is not essential.

2 Place the saucepan over medium heat and cook, stirring once or twice, till the sugar has dissolved. Turn the heat to low. While the liquid is heating, peel the pears (leaving the stems on if you're going to serve them whole) and core them from the bottom end, using a melon baller or small spoon. As you peel and core them, place the pears in the warm poaching syrup. Once you have prepared all the pears, bring the syrup back to a slow simmer. Poach the pears, occasionally turning them gently and basting them so they cook evenly. The cooking time can vary quite a bit, but it usually takes about 12 to 15 minutes for the pears to get done.

3 To check for doneness, insert a cake tester or toothpick into the pears. They should offer no resistance but should still hold their shape and maintain some texture.

4 Remove the cooked pears to a bowl and chill over an ice bath. Separately cool the poaching liquid and then pour it over the pears. Refrigerate for up to 2 days before serving. These are best served lightly chilled. Grind a bit of fresh black pepper over the pears just before serving.

Baker's Note: If I'm going to slice the pears or serve them halved, I find it easier to cut them in half with a paring knife before coring and poaching. I then cut a shallow v-shaped channel down the center to remove the stem blooming end and the hard stringy core.

Serving Suggestions: Try serving these sliced and fanned out, topped with some shaved Manchego cheese and honeyed almonds (page 55). Or serve a whole pear drizzled with some poaching liquid that has been reduced down to a syrup along with almond butter cookies (page 308) and some sherry-flavored whipped cream.

Golden Pineapple Soup

SERVES 6

For me, 82° and sunny constitutes the perfect climate—in another life, perhaps I will reside in Hawaii. In the meantime, during warm-weather months I frequently make this intense, pure, tropical essence. When paired with a scoop of sorbet, it's one of the most refreshing ways I can think of to conclude a meal.

INGREDIENTS

  1 large, fragrant, ripe pineapple
  2 tablespoons orange juice
  2 tablespoons lime juice
  1½ cups sugar
  1½ cups water
  1 vanilla bean
  2 teaspoons peeled and chopped fresh ginger
  ⅛ teaspoon kosher salt
  2 tablespoons dark rum or Kirsch (optional)

PREPARATION

1 Preheat oven to 375°.
2 Cut both ends off the pineapple and place it, along with the orange and lime juices, in a roasting pan. Cover the pan with foil and roast for approximately 1½ hours, until the pineapple core is soft and easily pierced with a knife. Allow to cool.
3 While the pineapple is cooling, place the sugar in a large heavy-bottomed saucepan. In a separate pan, heat the water to just under a boil. Allow the sugar to caramelize over medium high heat until it reaches deep amber and

then immediately stop the caramelization by carefully adding the hot water. Continue cooking to dissolve any caramel bits. Reserve.

4 Remove the exterior skin from the cooled pineapple and cut the flesh into chunks. Discard the inner core. Place the pineapple in a food processor with a steel blade and pulse until finely chopped. Alternatively, you can do this by hand. Add the chopped pineapple and any accumulated juices to the caramel syrup. Scrape the seeds from the vanilla bean and add them and the scraped pod to the caramel. Add the chopped ginger and salt. Allow this mixture to simmer over low heat, stirring occasionally, for 30 minutes. Remove from heat and, if you like, add the rum or Kirsch.

5 Strain the entire pineapple mixture through a large fine-mesh strainer, allowing the juices to drip through naturally and applying no heavy pressure to the pineapple mixture. A china cap—style strainer is the best tool for this. It's OK to give the mixture a stir now and then. Depending on the size of your strainer, this process can take quite a long time. When the mixture is finished straining, you should be left with a thin, clear consommé-like pineapple essence. Discard the remaining solids.

6 Cool the pineapple soup down over an ice bath and taste for seasoning. You might need to add a bit of additional citrus. Serve chilled. This can be made 3 days ahead of time and can be frozen.

Baker's Note: Try to choose a ripe, fragrant, fresh pineapple. The fruit should give just a bit when pressed and should be free of soft spots. There should be no evidence of mold on the stem end. The best indicator of a good pineapple is its aroma—it should smell sweet and fruity and not at all fermented.

Serving Suggestions: A scoop of orange coconut sorbet (page 284) or strawberry sorbet (page 279) would be delicious floated in a shallow bowl of this soup— surround with a simple tropical fruit garnish. You could also top grilled, rum-basted slices of pineapple with a scoop of not-just-plain-vanilla ice cream (page 261) and surround that with the soup. If you wanted a complex plate, pineapple fritters (page 350) would make a terrific side garnish.

Custards & Puddings
Low & Slow Is the Way to Go

Banana Pudding Cream Puffs

Bourbon Crème Caramel with Brûléed Bananas

Coffee Anise Crème Caramel

Baked Butterscotch Pudding

Persimmon Pudding

Coconut Rum Raisin Bread Pudding

Sally Lunn

Deep Dark Chocolate Pudding

Key Lime Soufflé Pudding

Buttermilk Panna Cotta

Blenheim Ginger Ale Sabayon

Summer Cherry Berry Pudding

Ginger Crème Brûlée

There are few things in this world more comforting than a creamy smooth custard. Simple mixtures of dairy products, sugar, and eggs, custards are prime examples of thrifty, homey desserts. Ironically, the more enriched versions are thought of as being luxurious and indulgent — crème brûlée is not considered grandma food.

A custard's richness and texture are largely dependent on the type of liquid called for and the resulting ratio of that liquid to eggs. Using higher butterfat dairy products (cream or half-and-half as opposed to milk) and a higher percentage of egg yolks to that liquid will give you the silkiest, most luscious custards. It is entirely possible to make a custard of milk set with whole eggs (or even whole eggs plus egg whites), but it will not have the trademark feel of a truly great custard when you spoon it into your mouth.

While the ingredients and general makeup of custards are key, the primary secret to perfect custards lies in the baking process. It's really as simple as the custard itself — custards must be baked for extended periods of time in moist, low-heat baking conditions (a.k.a., low and slow). This gentle heating will allow the eggs to set gradually, producing a characteristic uniformly smooth texture. Whatever you do, watch a baking custard carefully and do not overcook it! The finished product should be barely gelled and still a bit jiggly toward the center. As with all baked goods, a fair amount of carry-over cooking time during the cooling down process should be factored in.

Puddings are close cousins to custards, and while the two are similar in texture, the cooking process for them can be a bit different. Most puddings are starch thickened and heated on top of the range, and many are egg enriched as well. Although they are cooked over direct heat, I think that the same "low and slow" principle applies — you are better off cooking a stirred pudding a longer period of time over moderate heat to achieve optimum consistency. This will also prevent scorching or curdling. A stirred custard that is cooked on top of the range that is strictly egg thickened is a custard sauce or "anglaise." A frozen anglaise that has been churned becomes ice cream. Custards can also form the base of soufflés and bread puddings. What is critical to all of these desserts in all of their varying permutations is that the end result be as smooth as possible. Follow these basics and you will wind up with a perfect custard every time.

- Have your ingredients at room temperature.
- Be sure to gradually temper an egg base with hot liquid to prevent the eggs from cooking too quickly on initial contact.
- Whisk the custard base thoroughly but gently. You want to make sure all the ingredients are well combined, but you want to avoid adding excess air to the mix.
- Strain custards through a fine mesh strainer to remove any bits of coagulated egg or shell. Skim off any resulting surface foam as well.
- Custards should be tightly covered with aluminum foil before baking. This will allow them to steam slightly and prevent a surface skin from forming. One exception to this is with bread puddings, on which a toasty, lightly caramelized top is often desirable.
- Always bake custards in a water bath, starting with hot water. This will allow the eggs to set gradually and evenly.
- Bake custards on a lower oven rack. I find a temperature of 325° to be ideal. I generally bake bread puddings at 350° since structurally they are not as fragile as a plain custard.
- Once the outer edges of a custard begin to set, check it frequently. When done, the center of a custard should be jiggly, with no traces of unbaked liquid. Bread puddings are a bit more stable and will puff and feel firm to the touch.
- Cool custards (preferably on a rack) to room temperature before chilling completely in the refrigerator—refrigerate several hours before serving.
- Cover cooled custards with plastic wrap to prevent surface condensation and the penetration of any refrigerator odors.

Banana Pudding Cream Puffs

SERVES 8

Banana pudding is a homey dessert dear to the hearts of virtually all Southerners. This updated version crosses the traditional assembly of bananas, pudding, and Nilla Wafers with a cream puff.

INGREDIENTS FOR THE CREAM PUFF SHELLS

6 tablespoons (3 ounces) butter

¾ cup water

¼ teaspoon kosher salt

1½ teaspoons sugar

¾ cup flour, sifted

3 eggs

INGREDIENTS FOR THE PUDDING

1 cup milk

1 cup half-and-half

4 egg yolks

⅔ cup sugar

¼ teaspoon kosher salt

¼ cup cornstarch

2 tablespoons (1 ounce) butter

1¼ teaspoons vanilla

2 tablespoons bourbon

INGREDIENTS FOR ASSEMBLY

6 medium ripe bananas

powdered sugar

1 recipe caramel sauce (page 36) or cocoa fudge sauce (page 37)

1 recipe pecan praline (optional) (page 56)

PREPARATION FOR THE CREAM PUFF SHELLS

1 Preheat oven to 400°.

2 Combine the butter, water, salt, and sugar in a heavy-bottomed saucepan. Over medium heat, bring the mixture to a rolling boil. Add the flour all at once and quickly stir it with a wooden spoon to incorporate all of the flour. The dough will come together to form a ball and will be smooth and stiff. Continue to stir over heat for 1 minute. Remove from heat and transfer to the bowl of an electric mixer fitted with a paddle attachment.

3 On medium speed, allow the dough to mix for about 30 seconds. Add the eggs one at a time, waiting until each is fully incorporated into the dough before adding the next.

4   Fit a pastry bag with a large open tip and fill with the dough. If you don't have a bag and tip, the puffs can also be spooned into mounds.

5   On a baking sheet lined with parchment paper, pipe 8 equal mounds, approximately 2¼ inches wide and 1½ inches high, leaving several inches of space between the puffs. If the puffs form pointed peaks, lightly wet your finger and gently flatten the points.

6   Bake at 400° for 15 minutes, until the puffs are golden brown. Turn oven to 325° and bake an additional 10 minutes. Remove the puffs from the oven and prick each one with the tip of a sharp knife. Place them back in the oven and allow them to dry out for an additional 5 minutes. Remove them from the oven and let them cool. You can make the puffs several hours in advance and recrisp them for 3 minutes in a 375° oven shortly before filling.

PREPARATION FOR THE PUDDING

1   Combine the milk and half-and-half in a medium-sized heavy-bottomed stainless steel saucepan. Bring to just below a simmer.

2   Combine the egg yolks, sugar, salt, and cornstarch in a stainless steel bowl and whisk to combine. While whisking, add about one-third of the hot milk mixture to the yolks to temper. Transfer the yolk mixture back into the saucepan and cook over medium heat, stirring constantly, until the mixture thickens and just starts to bubble.

3   Remove from heat and gently stir in the butter, vanilla, and bourbon. Strain the mixture into a storage container, chill over an ice bath till cool, cover the surface with plastic wrap, and refrigerate until needed. The pudding can be made up to 2 days in advance. Stir the pudding lightly before using to restore its smooth texture.

TO ASSEMBLE

1   Recrisp the puffs if they were made in advance. Cool slightly. With a serrated knife, slice the top third of the puff off to form a cap. Remove any spongy, doughy interior that still remains.

2   Slice the bananas and layer them, alternating with the pudding, until the puffs are generously filled. The pudding should be slightly mounded over the top of the puff. Place a cap on top of each puff. Sprinkle the cream puff caps generously with powdered sugar.

3   Serve with a generous puddle of either cocoa fudge sauce or caramel sauce.

4   If desired, sprinkle the plate with some chopped pecan praline.

Baker's Note: Convection ovens are ideal for baking cream puff shells. If that option is available to you, be sure to adhere the corners of the parchment paper to the baking sheet with a few dabs of the cream puff paste. You will also want to reduce the suggested baking temperature by 25°.

Cornstarch-thickened creams should not be vigorously beaten once they have reached their thickened state. If stirred too much they have a tendency to thin out.

Serving Suggestions: I have given the option of using either cocoa fudge sauce or caramel sauce with this dessert. Of course, it wouldn't be objectionable if you wished to use both! Miniature versions of these puffs can also be made for dessert buffets.

For a classic rendering of banana pudding, without the puffs, you can layer the pudding with freshly sliced bananas and brown edge wafers (page 305) in a medium-sized bowl or individual coupes. Top with lightly sweetened whipped cream. A more involved parfait presentation can also incorporate drizzles of one of the suggested sauces and layers of chopped pecan praline.

Bourbon Crème Caramel with Brûléed Bananas

SERVES 6

Bakers often have their personal flavor favorites, and one of mine is a pairing of bourbon and bananas. It's always a challenge to utilize a set of ingredients in un-accustomed ways. Like the preceding recipe, this dessert is an updated take on beloved banana pudding. The flavor profiles on the two desserts are similar, but the presentations are completely different.

INGREDIENTS FOR THE CARAMEL
   ¾ cup sugar
   4 tablespoons water, divided
   2 tablespoons bourbon

INGREDIENTS FOR THE CUSTARD
  1 cup + 3 tablespoons half-and-half
  2 tablespoons cream
  2 eggs
  2 egg yolks
  ¼ cup + ⅛ cup sugar
  ¼ teaspoon kosher salt
  ½ teaspoon vanilla extract
  3 tablespoons bourbon

INGREDIENTS FOR SERVING
  3 small ripe but firm bananas
  sugar for caramelizing bananas
  6 mint sprigs for garnishing

PREPARATION FOR THE CARAMEL
1 Combine the sugar and 3 tablespoons water in a small saucepan and bring to
   a boil over high heat. Cook without stirring until the mixture begins to color.
   Meanwhile, combine 1 tablespoon water and the bourbon in a separate
   saucepan and heat just to warm through.
2 As the caramel begins to pick up color, swirl gently and cook until it turns
   medium amber. Remove from heat and immediately and carefully add
   the warm water-bourbon mixture. Swirl to combine and divide between
   6 4-ounce ovenproof ramekins or aluminum utility cups. Reserve.

PREPARATION FOR THE CUSTARD
1 Preheat oven to 325°.
2 Combine the half-and-half with the cream in a small saucepan and heat to
   just under a boil.
3 Combine the eggs, egg yolks, sugar, salt, vanilla, and bourbon in a stainless
   bowl and whisk just to combine. Slowly pour some of the hot half-and-half
   mixture into the eggs, whisking to temper. Whisk in the remaining half-and-
   half mixture. Pass through a fine-mesh strainer and evenly divide between
   the reserved caramel-filled ramekins.
4 Place filled ramekins in a hot water bath. Cover with foil and transfer to the
   oven.

5 Bake for approximately 40 to 45 minutes, until the custards are just set. Remove the ramekins from the water bath and cool. Refrigerate several hours or up to 2 days.

TO SERVE

1 Run a paring knife around the crème caramels to loosen. Turn out onto individual dessert plates, allowing the bourbon syrup to surround the custards.

2 To make the banana garnish, slice the bananas ¼ inch thick at a slight angle and place them on a baking sheet. Sprinkle the bananas evenly with sugar and, using a propane torch, caramelize them until golden brown. Alternatively, you can caramelize them under a broiler. Place the caramelized bananas around the crème caramels. Garnish each with a mint sprig.

Baker's Note: If you don't own ovenproof ceramic ramekins and can't find individual aluminum utility cups, try using disposable muffin tins for this recipe. You can cut them apart with a sharp pair of scissors before you line them with caramel.

Serving Suggestion: If you'd like an extra plate garnish, consider sticking a brown edge wafer cookie (page 305) into each custard or passing a plate of them at the table. This completes the banana pudding experience.

Coffee Anise Crème Caramel

SERVES 8

Crème caramel is one of those desserts that is usually served perfectly straight up. And it's wonderful that way, but, as an upstart pastry chef, I can't resist fiddling around with flavors. A hint of anise and a back note of coffee gives this mellow classic a whole new dimension.

INGREDIENTS FOR THE CARAMEL
    1 ½ cups sugar
    ½ cup water
    additional ¼ cup + 2 tablespoon hot water

INGREDIENTS FOR THE CUSTARD

   3 cups half-and-half

   2 teaspoons whole anise seeds

   1½ tablespoons instant coffee

   4 eggs

   4 egg yolks

   ¾ cup sugar

   ¼ teaspoon kosher salt

   2 teaspoons vanilla

   1½ tablespoons Sambuca

PREPARATION FOR THE CARAMEL

1 Combine the sugar and water in a heavy-bottomed saucepan. Place on medium heat and cook, swirling the pan occasionally, till a medium amber caramel forms. In a second saucepan have at the ready the additional water, heated to barely simmering. Remove the caramel from the heat and use the additional water to stop the caramelization—add it slowly and carefully, swirl the caramel, and pour it into a large, 8- to 10-cup ceramic soufflé dish, tilting the dish to coat the sides as well as the bottom. Reserve.

PREPARATION FOR THE CUSTARD

1 Preheat oven to 325°.

2 Place the half-and-half and anise seeds in a saucepan and heat to just under a boil. Add the instant coffee and stir to dissolve. Remove from heat and reserve.

3 In a stainless bowl, combine the eggs and egg yolks. Whisk in the sugar and salt. Whisk in the vanilla and Sambuca.

4 Temper the egg mixture with a portion of the hot half-and-half. Gradually whisk in the remaining half-and-half.

5 Strain the custard through a fine-mesh strainer into a pitcher. Pour the strained custard into the reserved caramel lined soufflé dish. Skim any foam that may have formed on the surface and place the soufflé dish in a shallow roasting pan. Cover the soufflé dish with aluminum foil and place the roasting pan on the lower oven rack. Add to the pan enough hot water to reach halfway up the soufflé dish.

6 Bake at 325° for approximately 1¼ hours but start checking for doneness at 60 minutes. The actual baking time can vary tremendously. The custard

is done when the sides are set and the center is slightly jiggly but not at all liquidy. Doneness is best judged by visual clues—not by baking time!

7   Remove the custard from the water bath. Remove the foil and cool to room temperature. Refrigerate for 6 hours or up to 2 days before serving.

8   Unmold the custard up to 2 hours before serving. To remove the crème caramel from its pan, carefully loosen the sides of the custard with a paring knife. Cover the soufflé dish with a shallow-rimmed dessert platter. Holding both the soufflé dish and the platter, swiftly turn them over. The custard should slip out of the soufflé dish along with a generous quantity of caramel syrup. Refrigerate if not serving immediately.

Baker's Note: When testing custards, I have baked the same recipe over and over and come up with widely differing baking times. The exact temperature of the ingredients, exact sizing of the eggs, exact placement in the oven, and exact temperature of the water bath will all affect timing. My rule of thumb is to start checking for doneness early. Once you see the exterior portion of the custard setting, check frequently—you are usually within 15 minutes of proper doneness at this point.

Individual custards can also be made in 1-cup ceramic ramekins. The baking time should be reduced accordingly—the approximate time is probably closer to 50 minutes.

This recipe calls for a generous amount of caramel syrup. I've found that a thickly coated soufflé dish makes removal of the custard easier—and, besides, I love caramel. Excess syrup can be strained and spooned over ice cream.

Serving Suggestion: Try serving a wedge of this on the same plate as peppered Bartlett pears in sherry syrup (page 160).

Baked Butterscotch Pudding

SERVES 6

Simply put, this is a mighty fine pudding. A silky, creamy custard lavishly flavored with brown sugar, caramelized sugar, and a wee bit of Scotch whiskey—it's a wonderful, easy-to-make entertaining dessert.

INGREDIENTS

2 cups cream
1 cup milk
¾ cup sugar
8 egg yolks
¼ cup brown sugar
1 teaspoon vanilla
¾ teaspoon salt
2½ tablespoons Scotch whiskey

PREPARATION

1 Preheat oven to 325°.

2 Combine the cream and milk in a saucepan and heat until just under a boil. While the cream is heating, place the sugar in a medium-sized saucepan and cook over medium heat till the sugar turns a medium amber. Tilt and swirl the pan rather than stirring the sugar until all the sugar dissolves.

3 Once the sugar has properly caramelized, remove from heat and stop the caramelization with the hot cream mixture—add the cream slowly and be careful because it will bubble up and give off a great deal of steam. Place the pan back on the burner and dissolve any bits of caramel.

4 In a medium-sized stainless bowl, whisk together the egg yolks, brown sugar, vanilla, salt, and scotch. Temper the eggs with a portion of the hot caramel cream. Whisk in the remaining cream.

5 Strain the custard through a fine-mesh strainer into a pitcher and divide between 6 6- to 8-ounce ramekins or custard cups. Place the filled ramekins in a shallow roasting pan and place the pan on a lower oven shelf. Form a hot water bath by adding to the pan enough hot water to reach halfway up the sides of the ramekins. Cover the pan with a sheet of aluminum foil.

6 Bake at 325° for about 50 to 55 minutes. Start checking the custards early—they are done when the edges are set and the center is jiggly but not liquidy. Remove the ramekins from the water bath, let the custards cool, cover them with plastic, and refrigerate at least 4 hours or up to 2 days before serving.

Baker's Note: This recipe doubles and even triples beautifully if you're feeding a large group. You can substitute bourbon for the scotch if you wish. It's possible to omit the alcohol component as well, but I think the liquor helps temper the innate richness of the pudding.

Serving Suggestions: You can top the servings of this pudding with a dollop of whipped cream and a drizzle of caramel sauce (page 36). I've also finished them by covering the surface with overlapping concentric circles of banana slices, sprinkling the bananas with sugar, and then caramelizing the fruit with a blow torch or under the broiler.

Persimmon Pudding

SERVES 10

Persimmons are a peculiar fruit—when ripe, their intense, lush honey flavor is spectacular. If eaten when anything less than dead ripe, they can provide you with a mouth-puckering, tannic taste experience that you'd be hard pressed to forget. Every fall I try to introduce a few converts to this American heritage dessert because you simply don't see it served much these days. Deeply flavored and at the same time quite delicate in texture, it's well worth getting to know. I hope you'll try it and become a fan.

INGREDIENTS

1¼ cups flour

¾ teaspoon baking soda

¾ teaspoon baking powder

½ teaspoon ginger

½ teaspoon cinnamon

⅛ teaspoon nutmeg

⅛ teaspoon cloves

½ teaspoon kosher salt

7 tablespoons (3½ ounces) butter, at room temperature

¾ cup + 1½ tablespoons sugar

3 eggs

1½ cups half-and-half

1½ cups strained persimmon purée

2 tablespoons apricot jam

PREPARATION

1 Preheat oven to 350°. Butter a 10-inch round cake pan (or a 9 × 9-inch square pan). Line the bottom of the pan with parchment paper and butter the paper.

2 Sift together the flour, baking soda, baking powder, ginger, cinnamon, nutmeg, and cloves. Add the salt and reserve.

3 Using a mixer fitted with a paddle, cream the butter with the sugar. Add the eggs one at a time, scraping the bowl several times. Alternately add the sifted dry ingredients with the half-and-half. Add the persimmon purée and the apricot jam. Mix to blend.

4 Pour the mixture into the prepared pan and place the pan in a water bath. Bake at 350° for approximately 70 minutes, till the pudding is firm and golden brown. When tested with a toothpick, the pudding should be moist but not wet. Remove from the oven and cool for 30 minutes. Turn out onto a parchment paper–lined baking sheet and reinvert onto a service platter. Serve while warm. This can be made 1 day ahead and reheated.

Baker's Note: Persimmon season is often irregular and fleeting, but persimmon purée freezes very well. I have substituted apricot purée in this recipe, and it is equally delicious.

Serving Suggestions: Serve with vanilla bean custard sauce (page 65) or frozen sourwood honey parfait (page 289). You can also keep it simple with a dollop of toasted pecan cream (page 63) or plain whipped cream.

Persimmons

In many parts of the country, the appearance of native persimmons is a sure sign that cool weather is on its way. Indigenous to a good part of the East Coast as well as the Midwest and Texas, these small jewel-like fruits rarely make it to farmers' markets, and I have yet to see them marketed commercially. In order to be eaten, they must ripen to the point where they are meltingly soft and are literally falling off the tree. At that point, they taste like an intense combination of a date and an apricot, with honey overtones. Unripe, persimmons are amazingly tannic and altogether unpleasant to taste. Native persimmons tend to be fairly seedy, and I find that it's easiest to run them through a food mill to produce a smooth purée. The resulting purée can then be frozen.

Japanese-originated Hachiya persimmons are now grown in California and are fairly common these days. Although quite different from the tiny American native persimmons, you can usually substitute them in most recipes. Hachiyas are large, slightly elongated, brightly colored fruits, which, like native persimmons, must be ripened to the point where they are soft. Do not confuse them with Fuyus, another Japanese variety that is round, squat, and crisply textured and is best eaten raw, sliced into salads.

When I plan on puréeing them, I usually freeze both native persimmons and Hachiyas overnight, defrost them, and then purée them. Because they are so soft when ripe, no cooking is needed. In the South, it's said that persimmons won't fully ripen until after the first hard frost. And perhaps there really is something to the frost theory—freezing them does seem to break down their cell structure and intensify their flavor.

Try adding persimmon purée to apple or pear sauces, mix chopped pulp into muffins, and by all means, try making persimmon pudding!

Coconut Rum Raisin Bread Pudding

SERVES 12 (MAKES 1 LARGE OR 2 SMALL PUDDINGS)

The first bread pudding I can recall eating was one served at a marvelous restaurant in New York City called the Coach House. Sadly, this landmark dining spot is now closed, but I've always viewed their classic rendition of this dessert as a standard-bearer. You wouldn't think that old bread and eggs could be turned into much, but a well-made bread pudding is a fitting end to even the most sophisticated meal.

INGREDIENTS
2 loaves Sally Lunn bread (recipe follows)
1 cup raisins
approximately ¾ cup dark rum, divided

1½ cups sweetened shredded frozen coconut, defrosted

5 cups half-and-half

grated zest of 1 orange

1 15-ounce can sweetened coconut cream (Coco López)

7 eggs

9 egg yolks

¾ cup sugar, divided

1 teaspoon vanilla

1 cup orange juice

PREPARATION

1 Preheat oven to 350°.

2 Put the raisins and ½ cup rum in a small saucepan and bring to a boil. Remove from the heat and allow the raisins to plump for 30 minutes.

3 Trim the crusts off the Sally Lunn bread. Cut the bread into ½ inch thick slices. Cut each slice in half lengthwise to form 3 × 1-inch "sticks." Lay the bread out on cookie sheets and toast lightly in the oven for 8 minutes, turning the bread slices over midway through the baking time. Alternatively, you could cut the bread into sticks 1 day before making the pudding and allow them to dry out at room temperature, uncovered, overnight.

4 Butter an 11 × 9½ × 2½-inch baking dish (14-cup capacity). You can also bake this pudding in 2 7-cup casseroles if you wish. Arrange a third of the bread in the baking dish, leaving some space between the slices but avoiding any large gaps. Sprinkle half the coconut over the bread.

5 Drain the raisins, reserving the rum, and sprinkle half of them over the coconut. Place another layer of bread (again using one-third of the sticks) in the baking dish, arranging the sticks in the opposite direction of the first layer. Sprinkle with the remaining coconut and raisins and cover with the last layer of bread.

6 Combine the half-and-half with the grated orange zest and bring to just under a boil.

7 Combine the coconut cream, eggs, egg yolks, ½ cup sugar, vanilla, and orange juice in a mixing bowl and whisk well to blend. Gradually whisk in the hot half-and-half. Measure the reserved rum from the drained raisins and add to it enough additional rum (it will likely require about ¼ cup) to measure ½ cup. Add the rum to the custard.

8 Strain the custard through a fine-mesh strainer and pour the custard over the layered bread. Sprinkle the top of the pudding with the remaining ¼ cup sugar. Allow the pudding to soak for 15 minutes, pushing down on the top layer of bread once or twice to remoisten it.

9 Place the pudding in a water bath and bake at 350° till the pudding is puffed and golden brown and feels springy to the touch (about 90 minutes). Test the center of the pudding with a cake tester or skewer. The custard should be set, with no traces of liquid.

10 Remove from the oven and cool slightly before serving. The pudding can be made up to 2 days ahead of time. If made ahead, bring it to room temperature and then reheat for 15 minutes in a 350° oven.

Baker's Note: Brioche or challah can be substituted for the Sally Lunn bread. If you want to streamline the process of assembling the pudding, you can cut the bread into cubes, allow it to dry slightly, and then mix it together with the coconut, raisins, and custard. I prefer the structure and ingredient distribution that the layering process provides, but it is not essential. If the bread is cut into cubes, the pudding can also be baked in individual ramekins.

Serving Suggestions: Serve with tangerine anglaise (page 65) and garnish with candied orange zest (page 60).

Sally Lunn

MAKES 2 8½ × 9 × 2½-INCH (6-CUP) LOAVES

Sally Lunn is a rich batter bread with properties similar to brioche. Its culinary history has been the subject of much debate, but we know that American recipes for it have been in existence since colonial times. I prefer egg-enriched breads for making bread pudding, and this one is extremely easy to put together—no kneading required! (Although you do need to think a day in advance to allow for an overnight chilling period.)

INGREDIENTS

1 cup milk
1 package dry yeast (1 scant tablespoon)
¼ cup sugar

3¾ cups flour

1½ teaspoons kosher salt

4 eggs

8 tablespoons (4 ounces) butter, melted

PREPARATION

1 Heat the milk until it is just warm to the touch. Dissolve the yeast and the sugar in the milk and allow the yeast to proof for 10 minutes.

2 Place the flour in the bowl of a mixer with a paddle attachment. Add the yeast mixture and mix just to blend. Add the salt, eggs, and melted butter and mix till a thick, smooth batter is formed. Make sure to scrape the bowl once or twice.

3 Scrape the batter into a large buttered bowl, cover with plastic wrap, and allow to rise in a warm spot until doubled in volume.

4 Rap the bowl on a countertop to deflate the dough, re-cover the bowl tightly with plastic wrap, and place it in the refrigerator overnight.

5 Remove the chilled dough from the refrigerator. Butter 2 6-cup loaf pans. Turn the dough out onto a lightly floured surface. Divide the chilled dough in half and form into loaves. Cover the loaves with a tea towel and allow them to rise till doubled.

6 Preheat oven to 350°. Bake the risen loaves till they are golden brown on top. Turn a loaf out of the pan—it should be browned on the bottom as well and sound hollow if tapped. Baking time is generally about 45 minutes. Cool the bread on a rack.

Baker's Note: This truly is a batter bread—do not be tempted to add additional flour. If the dough is properly chilled and you work quickly, you shouldn't have any problems forming it into loaves.

Serving Suggestions: Apart from being wonderful in the preceding bread pudding recipe, Sally Lunn makes excellent French toast, which in turn makes an excellent dessert if topped with fruit (fresh, sautéed, or poached) and cream (whipped or in the form of ice cream or custard sauce).

Deep Dark Chocolate Pudding

MAKES ABOUT 3½ CUPS; SERVES 4

In my opinion, chocolate pudding can hold its own against any fancy-schmancy mousse. As comforting as comfort food gets, this ultrarich version of the childhood favorite can be quite elegant when placed in crystal glasses and served with a slender, long-handled spoon.

INGREDIENTS

2¼ cups milk, divided
½ cup sugar
¼ teaspoon kosher salt
5 tablespoons cocoa
2 tablespoons cornstarch
3 egg yolks
7 ounces semisweet chocolate, finely chopped
2 teaspoons butter
1 teaspoon vanilla

PREPARATION

1   Heat 2 cups of the milk in a heavy-bottomed stainless saucepan to just under a boil.

2   Combine the sugar, salt, cocoa, and cornstarch in a stainless bowl. Whisk in the remaining ¼ cup milk until smooth. Slowly whisk in the hot milk and transfer the mixture back into the saucepan. Cook, stirring, over medium heat until the mixture thickens and just starts to bubble.

3   Place the egg yolks in a small stainless bowl. Whisk in about ½ cup of the hot cocoa mixture to temper the yolks and transfer the mixture back into the saucepan. Cook, whisking over low heat, for 1 minute more. Remove from heat and gently stir in the finely chopped chocolate, butter, and vanilla. When the chocolate and butter are melted, mix one more time, and strain the mixture into a pitcher. Pour into individual glasses and cover the surface of each pudding with a piece of plastic wrap. Cool slightly and then refrigerate for several hours before serving. This can be made 2 days in advance.

Baker's Note: Two generous tablespoons of cognac, bourbon, Grand Marnier, or dark rum make a tasty addition to this pudding if your audience is age appropriate. It is extremely important to take that extra step of putting the pudding through a fine-mesh strainer before portioning it. This will guarantee a wonderful, oh so smooth texture. Please note that I am not a "skin" fan, but if you like the slightly chewy crust that forms on top of puddings when they're exposed to air, you can ignore the step of placing plastic wrap directly on the pudding surface.

Once the pudding has thickened, be careful not to overheat or vigorously stir it. Either will cause a cornstarch-thickened pudding to thin out and become runny in texture.

Serving Suggestions: A large dollop of softly whipped cream is a must. I have also served this pudding accompanied by warm mini-sized chocolate chip cookies (downsized from the giant celebration cookies, page 295).

Key Lime Soufflé Pudding

MAKES 6 PORTIONS

This dessert is a variation on the traditional American pudding cake or sponge custard. During the baking process the batter separates into two distinct strata—a creamy custard-like bottom layer and an airy cake-like top. It is zingy in flavor and in texture. In my mind it is a near-perfect dessert and an all-time personal favorite. It is extremely important to have all the ingredients at room temperature before starting to make this. The cream and milk can be brought to proper temperature by heating them separately until they are just barely warmed through.

INGREDIENTS

4 tablespoons (2 ounces) butter, at room temperature

¾ cup sugar

grated zest of 2 limes

3 egg yolks, at room temperature

⅓ cup flour

½ cup cream, at room temperature

1 cup milk, at room temperature

⅓ cup key lime juice

3 egg whites, at room temperature

¼ teaspoon kosher salt

PREPARATION

1 Preheat oven to 350°. Butter 6 1-cup ceramic ramekins.

2 In the bowl of a mixer with a paddle attachment, beat the butter, sugar, and lime zest till very creamy and well combined. Add the egg yolks and mix to blend, scraping the bowl once or twice.

3 Alternately add the flour and cream, stopping to scrape the bowl.

4 Gradually add the milk, scraping the bowl once or twice. Add the lime juice and mix to combine. Remove the mixture to a large mixing bowl.

5 Place the egg whites in a clean stainless bowl and combine with ¼ teaspoon salt. Whip the whites to medium peaks. Do not overbeat.

6 Lighten the egg yolk base with ⅓ of the beaten whites. Quickly fold in the remaining whites, being careful not to overfold.

7 Using a ladle, divide the mixture between the ramekins, being careful to get a representative scoop of batter in each ladleful. The top of the batter tends to be foamy, the bottom thinner in consistency. Plunge the ladle down to the bottom of the batter and bring it straight up to get the proper mix. You may have some batter left over. The batter at the very bottom of the bowl is sometimes quite thin, lacking in egg white "foam." If this is the case, do not use the last bit—the layers to the pudding will not separate properly if you do.

8 Place the ramekins in a water bath and bake at 350° for approximately 40 minutes or until the puddings are golden brown. Remove the ramekins from the water bath. With the tip of a sharp paring knife, loosen the edges of the puddings. Allow to cool completely. The puddings can be stored at room temperature for several hours or covered and refrigerated for up to 24 hours.

9 To serve, reheat the puddings at 350° for 2 to 3 minutes. Run a paring knife around the sides of the puddings. Turn each upside down into the palm of your hand or onto a wide flat spatula and then turn right side up onto individual serving plates.

Baker's Note: Fresh key limes are becoming easier to find these days—check your local specialty produce purveyor. For this recipe you can use bottled key lime juice or juice squeezed from regular limes if you wish. You can also vary the flavor profile of this dessert by substituting lemon juice or seedless passion fruit purée for the key lime juice.

Serving Suggestions: Sprinkle the pudding with powdered sugar and serve with whipped cream and a garnish of fresh, seasonal berries. If fresh berries are unavailable, a simple lightly sweetened seedless raspberry sauce made from frozen berries or cinnamon spiced blueberry sauce (page 45) made with individually quick frozen berries can be used.

Buttermilk Panna Cotta

SERVES 6

Panna cotta has become a dessert classic for a number of reasons. It's exceptionally creamy in texture, but because it doesn't employ eggs, it's much lighter than your average custard. Its simplicity allows it to pair well with any number of garnishes, and it's very quick and easy to make. This barely set version, which incorporates the refreshing tang of buttermilk, is my personal favorite.

INGREDIENTS

  2 cups heavy cream, divided
  1 tablespoon gelatin
  ¾ cup sugar
  ½ vanilla bean
  2 cups buttermilk

PREPARATION

1 Place ½ cup cream in a small bowl. Sprinkle the gelatin over the cream, set aside, and allow the gelatin to soften for 5 minutes.

2 Place the sugar in a medium-sized saucepan. Split the vanilla bean and scrape the seeds into the sugar. Gradually whisk in the remaining 1½ cups of cream. Add the vanilla bean pod and cook over medium heat, whisking occasionally, until the cream is just under a simmer and the sugar is dissolved. Add the reserved gelatin and stir until it is dissolved. Remove from heat and stir in the buttermilk.

3　Strain the mixture through a fine-mesh strainer into a pitcher. Divide the mixture among 6 8-ounce dessert cups or ramekins, cover with plastic wrap, and refrigerate for several hours (or up to 2 days) until set.

4　To serve, loosen the panna cotta by dipping the ramekins in very hot water. Turn out onto individual dessert plates, garnish, and serve.

Baker's Note: These panna cottas are set with the barest minimum of gelatin. If I know that the weather is going to be quite warm and that the dessert will sit out unrefrigerated for more than a few minutes, I sometimes add a bit more gelatin (an additional half teaspoon).

　　When I once had to make 300 of these for an event and didn't have enough ramekins, I molded them in 9-ounce clear plastic cups (the kind available at your supermarket). If you use cups, once the panna cotta is set, remove by turning the cups upside down onto individual plates. Stick the blade tip of a small, sharp paring knife through the bottom of each plastic cup to break the "air seal." The panna cotta should just drop out onto the plate, though it's possible that it will need a bit of nudging.

　　You can also forgo the unmolding process entirely and serve the panna cotta in pretty dessert glasses.

　　You can substitute sour cream for the buttermilk in this recipe if you wish.

Serving Suggestions: Fresh berries, cinnamon spiced blueberry sauce (page 45), bourbon poached peaches (page 149), or sweet and sour cherry compote (page 155) would be great with this. Perhaps a crisp cookie for some crunch? Try cornmeal vanilla bean shortbreads (page 300) or pecan shortbreads (page 302).

Blenheim Ginger Ale Sabayon

SERVES 6

Dessert sabayons, or zabagliones, are ethereal, foamy sauces that are based on whipped egg yolks, sugar, and a liquid. Using a spicy ginger ale in the base allows this European standard to take on an American slant. Blenheim is a small, old-fashioned soft drink producer in South Carolina that makes a potent, extra flavorful beverage. Other ginger ales can be used, but try to find one that has a punchy flavor profile. Reed's is a good alternative.

INGREDIENTS

6 egg yolks

½ cup sugar

⅛ teaspoon kosher salt

½ cup + 1 tablespoon ginger ale

your choice of seasonal fruit

1 cup lightly sweetened whipped cream (optional—see the Baker's Note)

PREPARATION

1 Combine the egg yolks, sugar, salt, and ginger ale in a large stainless steel bowl. Whisk with a balloon whip to combine.

2 Place the bowl over a slowly simmering pot of water. The water should not touch the bottom of the bowl. Whip the sabayon mixture vigorously and continuously, making sure to scrape the bottom and sides of the bowl. After several minutes, the sabayon will become thick and triple in volume. Continue to whip until the sabayon feels very warm to the touch but be careful not to overcook it and scramble the eggs. Remove from the heat and serve immediately.

3 This is best served in balloon glasses, spooned over seasonal fruit. Strawberries would be my preferred pairing but other berries, sliced peaches, plums or tropical fruits would also be delicious.

Baker's Note: A chilled mousse-like version of this sabayon can be made by allowing the whipped base to cool completely (it will deflate) and then folding 1 cup of lightly sweetened whipped cream into it. Once the cream has been folded in, the chilled sabayon can be held in the refrigerator for several hours before using. You lose the temperature contrast and a bit of the flavor intensity of the hot version, but this does facilitate advance preparation.

Serving Suggestions: Warm sabayon can be served over plain fresh fruit or strawberry rhubarb compote (page 148). The cool variation can also be used to enrich a sorbet dessert. Try serving it with a scoop of purple plum rum sorbet (page 282) or layering it with sliced strawberries and strawberry sorbet (page 279).

Summer Cherry Berry Pudding

SERVES 6

The British influence on American sweets is quite strong, particularly in the realm of traditional dessert "puddings." As unlikely as it may seem, the basis for this dessert is fresh seasonal summer fruit and a loaf of commercial white bread. While it must be made a day in advance, the preparation process is very simple—and the results are very delicious.

INGREDIENTS

- 1 loaf sliced white bread (preferably Pepperidge Farm Original White), crusts trimmed
- 2 cups pitted Bing cherries
- 1 cup blueberries
- 7 tablespoons sugar
- ½ tablespoon lemon juice
- 1 tablespoon orange juice
- 1 tablespoon Grand Marnier
- ¼ teaspoon kosher salt
- 1 cup blackberries
- 1 cup raspberries

PREPARATION

1 Snugly line 6 1-cup ceramic ramekins with plastic film, allowing several inches of overhang to facilitate turning the pudding out for service.

2 Using a plain biscuit or cookie cutter with the same diameter as the bottom of the ramekins, cut out 12 circles of white bread. Cut as close to the edge as possible in case you need to use trimmings to line the sides of the ramekins. Cut each of the remaining slices of bread into 3 strips. Place one round in the bottom of each ramekin. Line the sides of each ramekin with the bread strips. They should fit together closely with no gaps. Reserve.

3 In a medium-sized nonreactive saucepan, combine the cherries, blueberries, sugar, lemon juice, orange juice, Grand Marnier, and salt. Bring to a simmer over medium heat, stirring occasionally. Turn heat to low and cook until the cherries are softened and the blueberries pop and give off their juices.

4 Add the blackberries and raspberries and cook over low heat for a few minutes

until the fruit is heated through—you do not want the berries to disintegrate. Remove from heat and drain the fruit, reserving the juices.

5 Divide the berries among the reserved ramekins, pushing down to pack the fruit tightly. Pour several tablespoons of the juices into each ramekin to saturate the bread. Dip the remaining bread rounds in the juices and place on top of the berries, pressing down firmly. The bread should feel moist and the "puddings" should be juicy. Reserve all remaining fruit juices. Cover the ramekins by folding up the overhanging plastic wrap and place in the refrigerator for 24 hours.

6 To serve, lift the plastic liner out of the ramekin—the pudding should dislodge easily—and invert the pudding onto a plate. If the fruit juices have not stained the bread all the way through, take a pastry brush and dab the puddings with some of the reserved juices.

7 Serve cold, with whipped cream.

Baker's Note: You can also make 1 large pudding in a 6-cup bowl or soufflé dish if you wish. The procedure is exactly the same, although lining the mold with bread becomes more of an exercise in patchwork.

Any type or proportion of berries can be used in this dessert. I have also made this with a combination of strawberries and poached rhubarb.

You may be tempted to try something other than white bread for lining your molds—I was. I have tried brioche, poundcake, and genoise, but I've gone back to the basic white loaf—its lower fat content and neutral flavor allow the berries to shine.

Serving Suggestions: As recommended, a dollop of whipped cream is lovely. If you have the time to make it, you might consider serving a Grand Marnier–flavored custard sauce (page 65) along with or in lieu of the whipped cream.

Ginger Crème Brûlée

SERVES 4 (IN 4-OUNCE RAMEKINS), BUT SEE THE BAKER'S NOTE

A well-made classic vanilla crème brûlée is hard to improve upon, but goodness knows pastry chefs have kept themselves busy for a long time coming up with some pretty strange flavor variations. Although untraditional, the infusion of fresh ginger adds a fabulous, refreshing flavor in contrast to the richness of the cream.

INGREDIENTS

3 tablespoons peeled, medium chopped fresh ginger
1 cup cream
½ cup half-and-half
3 egg yolks
¼ cup + 2½ tablespoons sugar
⅛ teaspoon ground ginger
⅛ teaspoon kosher salt
¾ teaspoon vanilla
additional sugar for brûléeing

PREPARATION

1 Place the chopped ginger in a small nonreactive saucepan, cover with water, and bring to a simmer. Remove from heat and drain, using a fine-mesh strainer, discarding the water.

2 Place the ginger back in the saucepan and add the cream and half-and-half. Bring the mixture to just under a simmer. Remove from heat, cover the pan with a lid, and allow the ginger to steep for 30 minutes.

3 Preheat oven to 325°.

4 Strain the ginger-cream mixture through a fine-mesh strainer, pressing on the ginger to extract all "juices." Discard the ginger and place the strained cream back into the saucepan. Heat until it's hot to the touch.

5 Combine the egg yolks, sugar, ground ginger, salt, and vanilla in a mixing bowl and whisk lightly to blend. Gradually whisk in a portion of the cream to temper the yolk. Add the remaining cream. Strain the mixture through a fine-mesh strainer into a pitcher.

6 Divide custard among 4 (preferably shallow) 4-ounce ceramic ovenproof ramekins, filling them ⅞ full. Skim off any foam that may have been generated.

7   Place the ramekins in a hot water bath and cover the top of the water bath with aluminum foil. Bake at 325° for approximately 45 to 50 minutes but start checking for doneness early. The custards are done when they are set around the sides and still a bit jiggly in the center. The baking time will be greatly affected by the exact size and shape of your ramekins.

8   Remove the custards from the water bath. Cool, cover with plastic wrap, and refrigerate till completely chilled (several hours or up to 2 days).

9   There are two ways to brûlée the custards—using a blowtorch or using an overhead broiler. In either case you will need to sprinkle a layer of sugar evenly over the custards, completely covering the surface. I have not specified an exact amount of sugar because it can vary depending on the dimensions of the ramekins. I like using a blowtorch to caramelize sugar because the heat is very direct, very hot, and can be easily adjusted. A broiler will also work, but you will probably have to move the custards around a bit to get an even caramelization. Brûlée until the sugar is evenly caramelized to a deep amber color.

Baker's Note: Ginger is very high in acid and can potentially make dairy products curdle—I found this out the hard way when making ginger ice cream one time. If you blanch the ginger before adding it to the cream base, the possibility of this happening seems to be eliminated.

This is a very rich dessert, and for most people a modest 4-ounce portion is just right. You can, however, make the custards in any size ramekin ranging from a mini 2-ounce to a big-boy 8-ounce. I like a shallow, wider ramekin because it provides a greater surface area for the crunchy caramelized sugar topping, but any shape (including standard soufflé-style cups) will work.

Serving Suggestions: These are perfect when garnished with a cluster of fresh raspberries and a mint sprig. They really don't need any further adornment, but if you must, accompany them with a couple of my Milanos (page 305) on the side.

Let Them Eat Cake!

Devil's Food Cake with Whipped Ganache

Blackout Cake

Chocolate Wafer Cookies

Dark Chocolate Peppermint Pattie Cake

Chocolate Chestnut Cream Roll

Milk Chocolate Chip Poundcake

Orange Glazed Cranberry Sour Cream Poundcake

Double Lemon Custard Cake

Not-Afraid-of-Flavor Gingerbread

Banana Upside Down Cakes

Black Walnut Angel Food Cake with Sorghum Syrup

Cranberry Crumb Cake

Big Island Fruitcake

Cinnamon Apple Date Babycakes

Chocolate-Dipped Banana Buttermilk Cupcakes

Plain or fancy, special-occasion or everyday, cakes are desserts that evoke powerful memories. My husband's family still talks about a particular "brownstone front cake" that hasn't been eaten for over 20 years—I'm still trying to unlock the secrets behind that one. The image that leaps to many people's minds when you say the word "cake" is a picture-perfect three-layer model with a buttery crumb, swathed in a generous quantity of sweet icing. There is something quintessentially American about these tall beauties, but I must confess that I have a personal preference for plainer poundcakes or fudgey chocolate cakes that have a minimum of extraneous dressing. Maybe I'm just not a frosting kind of gal—I prefer for the cake itself to be the focal point of the dessert.

Cakes of all types have amazing powers—they are like people magnets. Set one out at the office or bring one to a picnic or potluck, and you will have a buzzing crowd around you in no time. I often find myself baking cakes for social gatherings, and that usually necessitates a large number of servings. I tend to bake larger-scale cakes so there is more to share. Homemade cake, even leftover homemade cake, is always appreciated. A generously proportioned Bundt cake should, theoretically, feed an extended family (or a couple of teenage boys), but even with a small group, by the time everyone "evens out the cake by cutting off just another thin slice," the cake magically seems to disappear.

Baking is highly variable and dependent on technique when it comes to pastries. With cakes though, it's more of an exact science. Great cakes are based on specific formulaic recipes that have just the right ingredients in just the right proportions. If one measures properly and has ingredient consistency, a cake should come out according to recipe time and time again. When someone tells me that a proven cake recipe didn't work, I always start sleuthing. Often it turns out that the person substituted regular flour for cake flour, only had 5 eggs in the house when the recipe called for 6 ("one egg shouldn't make that much of a difference"), or thought a little maple syrup instead of the sugar would taste good. Every typical cake ingredient plays a specific role, and for a full scientific (but readable) explanation of cake chemistry, I recommend that you consult Shirley Corriher's book *Cookwise*. The book also contains a recipe for what is, hands down, the world's best coconut layer cake.

Next in importance to the ingredients you use is how you put the cakes together.

The actual process of creaming the fat and sugar components or the art of whipping and folding directly affects the ultimate texture of the cake. Undercreaming and overfolding are two of the more common mistakes made in cake-baking.

The type and size of pans you use are also critical to successful cakes. Individual recipes specify pan sizes, and ideally what's called for is what should be used. If, however, you wish to bake a recipe that calls for a 10-inch springform pan and you have only a 9-inch pan, you don't need to run out and purchase new bakeware. But you do need to refrain from using the full amount of batter the recipe produces. For most recipes, cake pans should be filled one-half to two-thirds full. If too much batter is used, the pan will overflow (which is one reason why a recipe might tell you to form a collared parchment extension as you would in making a soufflé). If too little batter is placed in the pan, you will not attain proper volume and the texture will be affected. Consult a volume chart if you wish to make a small pan-size deviation, use common sense, and adjust the baking time accordingly.

Cakes are susceptible to oven variations. I never, repeat *never*, assume that a recipe's stated baking time is totally accurate. In the recipes that follow, I have tried to provide visual clues to when a cake is done, and usually it will be done at a time reasonably close to that suggested in the recipe. If a recipe tells you to bake for 45 minutes, but the cake doesn't look, feel, or smell done, let it continue to bake unless you are given specific indications to expect it to seem underdone. A moist, chocolate soufflé-type cake, for example, ought, in fact, to appear slightly underdone when it is in fact done.

Here are a few more specific suggestions that will help you create your own lasting cake memories.

- Have all of the ingredients (especially butter and eggs) at room temperature. If necessary, chilled eggs can be brought to proper temperature by allowing them to sit, covered with hot tap water, for a few minutes.
- Make sure to measure ingredients accurately in proper wet and dry measures. Professional bakers usually weigh ingredients, and I always do weigh butter, shortening, and chocolate, using an ounce scale. For the small amounts of dry ingredients used in home baking, I find the "fill and level" method of cup measuring easiest. Remember, if the ingredient pours (dairy products, molasses, liquor, etc.), measure it in a marked see-through, liquid pitcher-type measure. Place the measure on a flat surface before filling. Dry, solid ingredients should always be measured with standardized dry cup measures.

- Preparing a proper *mise en place* is very important in cake-making. If everything is measured and at hand, you are less likely to leave an ingredient out.
- Taste the batter before placing it in a baking pan—if you've made a glaring error of omission or mismeasurement, it may become apparent to you at this point and may still be correctable. Virtually every young baker I've trained has doubled a recipe without doubling the sugar or forgotten the lemon juice in the lemon cake at least once.
- Whenever feasible, line pans with parchment paper.
- Bake cakes in the lower third or middle of your oven, reversing or turning pans midway through the baking process if your oven has significant hot spots.
- Many cake recipes will tell you to remove the cake from the oven when it "tests done." Unless otherwise specified, this usually means that the cake is springy and set to the touch and is just starting to pull away from the sides of the pan. If a skewer or toothpick is inserted into the center of the cake, no traces of unbaked batter should adhere to it.
- Some cakes are delicious served warm (not hot!), but I often find that their flavors and textures are better if cakes are allowed to cool completely and are then briefly reheated before serving.

A Note on Creaming, Whipping, and Folding

The successful outcome of a dessert can depend on whether the process of creaming, whipping, or folding is done properly. All are fairly basic steps that are called for in many recipes. Every baker's technique may vary somewhat, but here are my general guidelines for accomplishing these tasks successfully.

CREAMING. Creaming involves the blending of fat and sugar. This serves to incorporate air and form a smooth, emulsified mixture, which is critical to realizing proper texture when putting together many cake batters and cookie doughs. To do this, it is important that the butter (or other fat) be at cool room temperature. If it is too soft, the blend will be greasy and the end product heavy. If the butter is too cool, the mixture will not aerate properly and the butter will not be evenly distributed. The creaming process can be accomplished by hand with a sturdy wooden spoon, in a standing mixer with a paddle attachment, or with a portable mixer outfitted with beaters. The exact time needed to achieve proper consistency will vary with each method. Ingredients are properly creamed when they lighten in color and become fluffy in texture.

WHIPPING. The process of whipping is generally used to incorporate air into a mixture. This is most often done with heavy cream or egg whites but can also be called for with egg yolk–rich mixtures such as sabayons. For tips on whipping cream, please see page 63. For whipping egg whites, make sure to use an extremely clean whip and a large, clean bowl. A copper bowl is great for whipping whites but not essential. Some recipes have you add lemon juice or cream of tartar to egg whites, as the incorporation of a bit of acid will help them whip to greatest volume. Egg whites are most easily separated from yolks when cold, but they should be whipped at room temperature. To hasten their coming to proper temperature, you can lightly warm the egg whites by placing them in a bowl and gently whisking them over a pot of simmering water for a minute or two. Most of the time, egg whites need to be beaten to soft or medium peaks. They will just hold their shape but still be moist-looking. Overbeaten egg whites look grainy and dry—they are difficult to incorporate into batters and will not provide maximum rise when baked. If I'm whipping egg whites by machine, I like to take them to the point where they are almost, but not quite, ready and then finish the last few strokes by hand. You are far less likely to overbeat them this way. Occasionally (usually when sugar is added) a recipe will instruct you to beat to firm peaks. At this point the whites should be glossy, smooth, and firm.

FOLDING. The technique of folding is often used in recipes where beaten egg whites or cream is incorporated into another mixture. Occasionally melted butter, chocolate, or dry ingredients (such as flour) are also folded into a base mixture. The point of folding—as opposed to stirring or mixing—is to try and retain as much air as possible. This procedure needs to be done gently but thoroughly and quickly. Use a large bowl with a rounded bottom and a medium-sized to large, long-handled rubber spatula. In almost all recipes that require folding, the lighter mixture is incorporated into the heavier base. It is usually best to partially fold about one-third of the lighter mixture in first to "lighten" the base before folding in the remaining portion of whites or cream. To fold, place the lighter mixture on top of the heavy one and, using the spatula with the rounded side toward the bottom of the bowl, cut down through the center, bringing the blade up against the side of the bowl and out over the top. As you complete this motion, turn your wrist so the mixture at the bottom of the bowl is brought up along with the spatula, allowing it to gently fall over on itself. With each "fold," give the bowl a quarter turn. The finished mixture should be fairly well blended (a few streaks are fine) and retain an airy quality.

Devil's Food Cake with Whipped Ganache

SERVES 12 TO 16

Many years ago, my husband and I spent a summer working on Cape Cod, where I fell in love with a chocolate cake we ate in a Provincetown restaurant. Ben sweet-talked the restaurant's pastry chef into telling him what went into the cake, and he recreated it for my next birthday. The original was filled with whipped cream, but I've opted for a layer of rich whipped ganache. This super moist, devilishly delicious cake is a great dessert to serve to die-hard chocoholics.

INGREDIENTS

1½ cups + 2½ tablespoons flour

¾ cup cocoa

2 teaspoons baking soda

1 teaspoon baking powder

½ teaspoon kosher salt

2 eggs

2 cups sugar

½ cup vegetable oil

1 cup buttermilk

1 cup brewed coffee, at room temperature

1 teaspoon vanilla

1 recipe chocolate ganache (page 53)

1 recipe cocoa fudge sauce (page 37), optional for serving

PREPARATION

1 Preheat oven to 350°. Butter a 10 × 2-inch round cake pan (see the Baker's Note for alternative pan option) and line the bottom with parchment paper. Line the sides of the pan with a parchment "collar" that extends 1½ inches above the sides of the pan. Butter the parchment paper and dust the pan with cocoa, tapping out the excess.

2 Sift together the flour, cocoa, baking soda, and baking powder; add the salt. Reserve.

3   In a mixer, using a whip attachment, beat the eggs with the sugar until the mixture is thick and light (about 4 to 5 minutes). Reduce the speed and beat in the vegetable oil. Alternately, add the reserved dry ingredients with the buttermilk, pausing to scrape the bowl several times. Add the coffee and the vanilla and mix to blend. Be forewarned that this is a very thin batter. Transfer the mixture to the prepared baking pan.

4   Bake at 350° for approximately 55 to 60 minutes or until the top of the cake is springy to the touch and a toothpick inserted into the center tests clean. Cool the cake in the pan for 20 minutes.

5   Remove the parchment collar and turn the cake out onto a cardboard cake circle.

6   Prepare the whipped ganache by placing the cooled ganache in a mixer bowl—its consistency should be solid but creamy and malleable—and whip until the ganache just starts to thicken and lighten in color slightly. It should be of spreadable consistency.

7   Slice the cooled cake into two layers and spread the bottom layer with whipped ganache. Top with the remaining layer, pressing down lightly. Unless the weather is very warm, keep this cake at room temperature before serving. It can be made up to 2 days ahead of time. If refrigerated, bring it to room temperature to serve. I like to cut wedges of this cake and pour a light glaze of cocoa fudge sauce over the top of each portion, allowing a bit to drip down the sides, just before serving. If you would like to leave the cake plain, sprinkle some powdered sugar over the top just to give it a more finished look.

Baker's Note: You can also bake this cake in 2 8-inch cake pans. If you choose this option, there is no need to collar the pans; just line the bottoms with parchment. Cut each 8-inch layer in half and use 3 of the layers, spreading the ganache between two of them to form a three-layer cake. Snack on the remaining layer.

Serving Suggestion: Serve with a scoop of icy-cold milk sherbet (page 287).

Blackout Cake

The blackout cake was the creation of Ebinger's, a famous New York–based neighborhood bakery chain. An indecently rich, dark, tower of chocolate, this cake has become something of a Holy Grail for many bakers. Devoted blackout aficionados believe that this is the cake to end all chocolate cakes. Cult-like fans went through blackout withdrawal when the bakeries closed down and The Cake disappeared. Many have tried to recreate this cake, and I feel that with this version I've come close. Making it is a multistep process (remember, this was a bakery specialty), but the process can easily be broken down into components. Astute recipe readers may notice that the cake component is my basic devil's food, as presented in the preceding recipe. If you want to make an easier (but very delicious) chocolate cake, check out that recipe for devil's food cake with whipped ganache. If you or someone you love has nostalgic blackout memories, I hope you'll try this version at least once.

INGREDIENTS FOR THE CHOCOLATE PUDDING FILLING

1½ cups milk, divided

⅓ cup sugar, divided

¼ teaspoon kosher salt

2 tablespoons cocoa

1 tablespoon + 1 teaspoon cornstarch

1 egg

1 egg yolk

4 ounces semisweet chocolate, finely chopped

1½ tablespoons (¾ ounce) butter, at room temperature

INGREDIENTS FOR THE CAKE

1½ cups + 1½ tablespoons flour

¾ cup cocoa

2 teaspoons baking soda

1 teaspoon baking powder

½ teaspoon kosher salt

2 cups sugar

2 eggs

½ cup vegetable oil

1 cup buttermilk

1 cup brewed coffee, at room temperature

1 teaspoon vanilla

INGREDIENTS FOR THE ICING

8 ounces semisweet chocolate

2½ tablespoons (1¼ ounces) butter

¼ cup hot brewed coffee

2 teaspoons corn syrup

½ teaspoon vanilla

INGREDIENT FOR ASSEMBLY

2½ cups chocolate wafer cookie crumbs (see Baker's Note)

PREPARATION FOR THE CHOCOLATE PUDDING FILLING

1 Combine 1 cup milk with 2 tablespoons sugar in a small saucepan and bring to just under a boil.

2 In a mixing bowl, combine the remaining sugar with the salt, cocoa, and cornstarch. Whisk in the remaining ½ cup unheated milk. Gradually whisk in the hot milk and place the entire mixture back into the saucepan. Cook, over medium heat, stirring, until the mixture thickens and just starts to bubble. Whisk in the egg and egg yolk.

3 Cook for 30 seconds. Remove from heat and whisk in the chopped chocolate and butter. When both are melted, strain the pudding through a fine-mesh strainer, cool, cover with plastic wrap, and reserve in the refrigerator.

PREPARATION FOR THE CAKE

1 Preheat oven to 350°. Lightly butter 2 8-inch round cake pans, line with parchment paper, butter the paper, and flour the pans, shaking out the excess flour.

2 Sift together the flour, cocoa, baking soda, and baking powder; add the salt. Reserve.

3 In a mixer, using a whip attachment, beat the eggs and sugar until thick and lemon-colored. Beat in the vegetable oil. Alternately add the dry ingredients with the buttermilk, scraping the bowl once or twice. Add the coffee and vanilla to form a thin batter. Divide the batter among the prepared cake pans.

4   Bake at 350° for approximately 40 to 45 minutes, until the cake tests clean when a toothpick is inserted. Cool in the pans for 15 minutes. Invert onto cooling racks, peel off the parchment paper, and cool completely.

5   When cool, split each cake into two layers with a serrated slicing knife. Spread what will be the bottom layer of the cake with half of the reserved chocolate pudding. Place a second layer on top and spread with the remaining pudding. Top with a third cake layer and prepare the icing. Reserve the fourth layer for a post-assembly treat.

PREPARATION FOR THE ICING AND ASSEMBLY

1   In the top of a double boiler, melt the chocolate with the butter. Remove from heat and whisk in the brewed coffee, corn syrup, and vanilla.

2   Place the icing over an ice bath and chill, whisking often, till the mixture is of thin but spreadable consistency. Working quickly, ice the sides and top of the cake. Press the chocolate cookie crumbs onto sides and top of cake.

3   Serve at room temperature. If holding for more than 2 hours, store in the refrigerator for up to 24 hours but bring back to room temperature before serving.

Baker's Note: When I first started working on this recipe, I used the extra cake layer to form the blackout's characteristic crumb coating. While this is perhaps the easiest method, I was never entirely happy with it—the cake is so moist that, even with some drying-out time, the resulting crumbs were not quite as fine as I wanted them to be. I'm sure that the bakeries used a mixture of leftover chocolate cake and cookie crumbs, and this led me to using ground-up chocolate wafer cookies. You can make your own (see the following bonus recipe) or you can use store-bought Nabisco chocolate wafers. Yes, it's another step to prepare a separate crumb coating, but as a reward you get to snack on the extra cake layer!

This cake can also be made in a single, collared 10 × 2-inch cake pan. If you do this, split the baked cake in half and fill with all of the pudding. The rest of the recipe remains the same.

Serving Suggestions: Blackout cake is meant to be served simply, on its own. If you want to dress individual plates, perhaps add a drizzle of cocoa fudge sauce (page 37) and a sprinkle of cocoa.

Chocolate Wafer Cookies

MAKES 3 DOZEN COOKIES, 5 CUPS OF CRUMBS

INGREDIENTS

1¼ cups flour

½ cup cocoa

¼ teaspoon salt

½ teaspoon baking soda

½ teaspoon baking powder

1¼ cups sugar

8 tablespoons (4 ounces) butter, chilled

1 egg

1 egg yolk

½ teaspoon vanilla

PREPARATION

1 Preheat oven to 350°.

2 Combine the flour, cocoa, salt, baking soda, baking powder, and sugar in a food processor with a steel blade. Pulse to combine.

3 Add the butter and pulse to cut in.

4 Add the egg, egg yolk, and vanilla and mix by pulsing just until the dough comes together to form a mass.

5 Form rounded walnut-sized balls of dough and place them on a parchment paper—lined baking sheet. Flatten the balls with the bottom of a metal measuring cup dipped in sugar between each flattening. Bake at 350° for about 12 minutes, reversing the sheets midway, until the cookies feel set to the touch. They will puff up and then fall and flatten back out. Cool completely.

6 Place the cooled cookies in a processor and, using the pulse button, process to medium-sized crumbs.

Baker's Note: These cookies make a great chocolate crumb crust for pies, cheesecakes, and ice cream cakes—as well as a wonderful coating for the blackout cake above.

Dark Chocolate Peppermint Pattie Cake

SERVES 12

If you're one of those individuals who always opts for the chocolate-covered Thin Mints when your local Girl Scout representative comes calling, this dessert is for you. The refreshing peppermint counterpoint takes the edge off the intense fudge-like cake.

INGREDIENTS FOR THE CAKE

    14 ounces semisweet chocolate
    16 tablespoons (8 ounces) butter
    ¼ cup + 2 tablespoons cream
    6 eggs, separated
    1 cup sugar
    1 cup flour
    ½ teaspoon kosher salt
    2 teaspoons vanilla
    1 cup (6 ounces) small-diced Peppermint Pattie candies

INGREDIENTS FOR THE GANACHE TOPPING

    1 cup cream
    8 ounces semisweet chocolate, finely chopped

PREPARATION FOR THE CAKE

1 Preheat oven to 350°. Butter a 9½- to 10-inch springform pan, line the bottom with parchment paper, butter the paper, and flour the pan, tapping out the excess flour.
2 Melt the chocolate with the butter and cream in the top of a double boiler. Reserve.
3 In the bowl of a mixer with a whip, beat the egg yolks with the sugar until very thick and light (about 5 minutes).
4 Add the melted chocolate mixture to the egg yolks and mix till just blended. Add the flour, salt, and vanilla and mix till combined, scraping the bowl once or twice. Transfer the batter to a large mixing bowl and stir in the Peppermint Pattie pieces. The mixture will be quite thick.

5 In a clean mixing bowl, with a clean whip, beat the egg whites to medium soft peaks. Lighten the batter by stirring in about one-third of the egg whites. Fold in the remaining whites and place the batter in the prepared pan.

6 Bake at 350° for approximately 45 to 50 minutes. The top of the cake will feel set, and very fine hairline cracks will just start to form around the edges. Remove and cool in the pan on a rack.

PREPARATION FOR THE GANACHE TOPPING AND ASSEMBLY

1 Heat the cream in a heavy-bottomed saucepan to just under a boil. Add the chopped chocolate and, over very low heat, constantly stirring, cook the mixture until it is completely smooth. Strain through a fine sieve into a bowl and cool, stirring occasionally, until thickened and spreadable. This can take several hours. You can make the topping up to 3 days ahead, refrigerate it, and allow it to come to room temperature for several hours before using. You can also hasten the cooling process by placing the melted ganache over an ice bath and gently stirring it till thickened; however, the resulting texture may not be quite as smooth and creamy.

2 Place the cooled cake upside down on a cardboard cake circle or a service plate. Remove the sides and bottom of the springform pan. Remove the parchment liner. Using an offset spatula, decoratively spread the ganache over what is now the top of the cake, drawing the ganache all the way out to the edges of the cake. Using the offset spatula, level the edges to give the cake a finished look. Serve at room temperature.

Baker's Note: To facilitate cutting the Peppermint Patties, I often freeze them first. Use a hot, dry long-bladed knife to cut perfectly clean slices of the cake.

Serving Suggestion: Serve with whipped cream, cocoa fudge sauce (page 37), and a drizzle of mint syrup (page 51).

Chocolate Chestnut Cream Roll

SERVES 12

By popular demand, this cake has been making a regular appearance at the Barker family Christmas Eve dinner table. It's based on the late Dione Lucas's classic

Roulage Leontine, but I have taken the liberty of giving the delicate chocolate cake a sumptuous chestnut-flavored filling.

INGREDIENTS FOR THE CAKE ROLL

cocoa for dusting parchment paper
8 ounces semisweet chocolate, chopped into pieces
8 eggs, separated
1 cup sugar
⅓ cup orange juice
½ teaspoon kosher salt

INGREDIENTS FOR THE CHESTNUT CREAM

3 cups heavy cream
¼ cup sugar
1 teaspoon vanilla
1¼ cups candied chestnut purée (page 58) or 1 (8.75-ounce) can
  sweetened chestnut *spread* (do not use unsweetened chestnut purée
  or overly sweet chestnut "crème")

PREPARATION FOR THE CAKE ROLL

1 Preheat oven to 350°. Butter a 15 × 12 × 1-inch half sheet pan or jelly roll pan. Line the pan with parchment paper, allowing the paper to extend over the short edges of the pan. Butter the parchment paper and coat the pan and the paper with cocoa, knocking out the excess. Also liberally sprinkle a sheet of parchment paper or a cotton tea towel that is larger than the cake with cocoa and reserve.

2 Place the chocolate in the top of a double boiler and heat till melted. Reserve.

3 Combine the egg yolks with the sugar in the bowl of a mixer with a whip, beating until very thick and light (about 5 minutes). Whisk the orange juice into the melted chocolate and add this to the egg yolk mixture. Mix to blend. Transfer this mixture to a large mixing bowl.

4 In a clean bowl, with a clean whip, beat the egg whites and salt to medium peaks. Fold a third of the whites into the chocolate mixture to lighten. Fold in the remaining whites and gently place the batter in the prepared pan. Lightly spread with an offset spatula.

5 Bake at 350° for about 18 minutes, reversing the pan midway through the baking time. The cake will set to the touch and will just start to pull away from

the sides of the pan a bit when done. Remove from oven and loosen the cake from the sides of the pan with a paring knife. Cool for 1 minute. Fold the excess parchment paper back against the pan and quickly turn the pan upside down onto the reserved cocoa-dusted parchment paper or tea towel. Lift up the pan and gently remove the parchment paper. Allow the cake to cool completely.

PREPARATION FOR THE CHESTNUT CREAM

Whip the cream with the sugar to medium stiff peaks. Combine the vanilla and the candied chestnut purée and whisk till smooth. Whisk the chestnut purée into the cream, being careful not to overwhip it. Chill until you're ready to fill the cake.

ASSEMBLY

1 Keeping a long side of the cake in front of you and leaving a 1-inch border along the long side furthest from you, with an offset spatula evenly spread three-quarters of the chestnut cream onto the cake. Grasp the parchment paper or tea towel and use it as an aid to quickly roll the cake up lengthwise— it should roll over on itself 1½ times. Be fearless! The trick is not to stop in mid-roll.

2 Transfer the rolled cake to a serving platter by gradually easing it off the parchment paper or tea towel.

9 Place the remaining chestnut cream in a pastry bag fitted with a large open star tip and decorate the top by piping rosettes down the center. Refrigerate until ready to serve. This can be made up to 10 hours ahead of time.

Baker's Note: You can turn this roll into an impressive Bûche de Noël. Slice a third of the cake off one end at a steep bias and snug it up to the cake on the opposite side to form a "log." Heat some chocolate ganache (page 53) until it is just barely fluid and drizzle it over the top of the cake and along the seam where the cake segments meet. Chill the cake briefly to set the ganache and sprinkle it lightly with cocoa. Garnish with meringue mushrooms (page 319). When making Bûche de Noël, bypass the step of piping chestnut cream on top of the roll—as a result you will need only 2 cups of cream and a scant ½ cup of purée for the filling.

Serving Suggestions: Slices of this cake can be served with a drizzle of cocoa fudge sauce (page 37) or hot buttered rum raisin sauce (page 41).

Milk Chocolate Chip Poundcake

SERVES 16 TO 20

This is a variation of the brown sugar pear poundcake recipe that appeared in the dessert chapter of my and Ben's earlier book, *Not Afraid of Flavor*. That cake was a variation of Maida Heatter's Kentucky Poundcake. (For those of you unfamiliar with Maida Heatter's amazing dessert cookbooks, you owe it to yourself to read every word the woman has written—yes, her recipes are that good!) As for this recipe, our line cooks at Magnolia Grill have given this cake the "Best Smelling Dessert in America" award. The aroma of the warm glaze being brushed onto the poundcake is indeed tantalizing.

INGREDIENTS FOR THE POUNDCAKE

    fine, dried, unseasoned breadcrumbs for coating the pan

    3½ cups flour

    1½ teaspoons baking powder

    ½ teaspoon kosher salt

    24 tablespoons (12 ounces) butter, at room temperature

    1⅜ cup light brown sugar

    1⅜ cup sugar

    5 eggs

    2 teaspoons vanilla

    ¼ cup + 1 tablespoon dark crème de cacao

    ¾ cup milk

    2¼ cups homemade milk chocolate chips (page 54)

INGREDIENTS FOR THE GLAZE

    ⅓ cup sugar

    ⅓ cup dark crème de cacao

PREPARATION FOR THE POUNDCAKE

1 Preheat oven to 350°. Butter a 10-inch, 12-cup Bundt pan and dust the pan with breadcrumbs, shaking out any excess crumbs.

2 Sift together the flour and baking powder. Add the salt. Reserve.

3 In the bowl of a mixer fitted with a paddle, cream the butter till light and fluffy. Gradually add both the brown and granulated sugar and beat for several minutes, occasionally scraping the bowl.

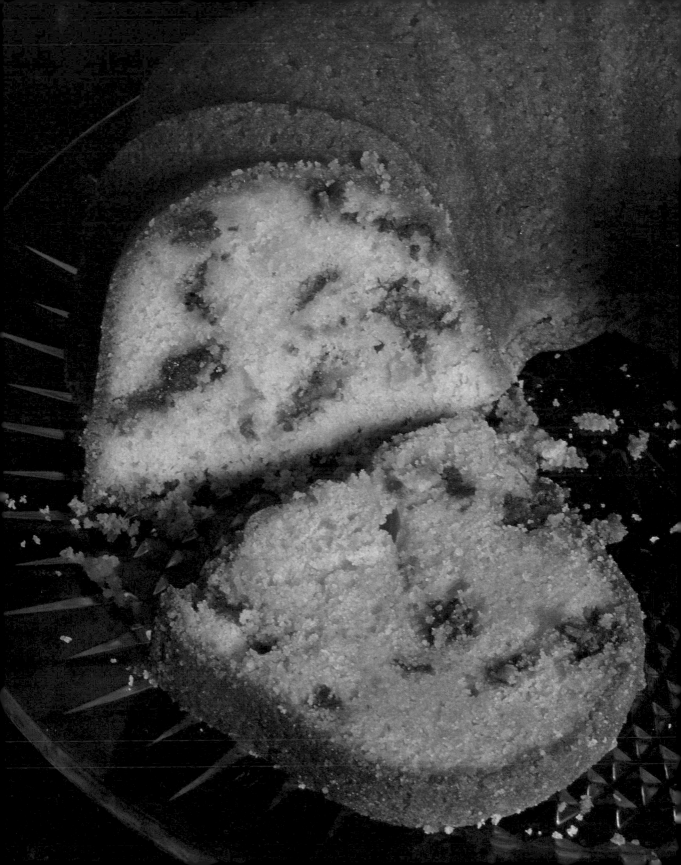

4   Add the eggs one at a time, briefly beating and scraping the bowl after each addition. Add the vanilla and crème de cacao and mix to combine.

5   Alternately add the reserved dry ingredients with the milk and mix just to combine. Stir in the milk chocolate chips. Transfer the batter to the prepared pan.

6   Bake at 350° for approximately 1 hour and 20 minutes. When done, the cake will be golden brown and will test done if checked by inserting a toothpick. Remove from oven and allow the cake to cool for about 15 minutes while you prepare the glaze.

PREPARATION FOR THE GLAZE AND ASSEMBLY

1   Combine the sugar and crème de cacao in a small saucepan and cook over low heat till the sugar is just dissolved.

2   Turn the cake out onto a cooling rack and immediately brush the warm cake with the warm glaze. Allow to cool completely before serving. This cake is best if made 24 hours in advance.

Baker's Note: One of the many great tips I've learned from reading Maida Heatter is to coat pans used for baking poundcakes with breadcrumbs. This almost imperceptible coating gives the cake an extra crunchy crust, which contrasts beautifully with the soft, buttery interior, particularly if you serve the cake lightly toasted.

Serving Suggestions: This cake can be served simply on its own or with a multitude of garnishes. I like to toast pieces lightly and then plate them individually with butterscotch baked bananas (page 154), a scoop of milk chocolate malt ice cream (page 274), and a drizzle of cocoa fudge sauce (page 37). Another possible combination would be the cake, not-just-plain-vanilla ice cream (page 261), and creamy peanut butter and honey sauce (page 39).

Orange Glazed Cranberry Sour Cream Poundcake

SERVES 16 TO 20

Jewel-like cranberries provide bursts of both flavor and color in this big, beautiful poundcake. Baked in a festive Bundt pan, this dessert is perfect for a holiday brunch or open house buffet.

INGREDIENTS FOR THE POUNDCAKE

fine, dried, unseasoned breadcrumbs for coating the pan

3 cups flour

½ teaspoon baking soda

½ teaspoon kosher salt

16 tablespoons (8 ounces) butter, at room temperature

grated zest of 2 oranges

2 cups sugar, divided

6 eggs, separated

1½ teaspoons vanilla

1 cup sour cream

2¼ cups cranberries

INGREDIENTS FOR THE GLAZE

2 tablespoons sugar

3 tablespoons orange juice

INGREDIENTS FOR THE ICING

⅞ cup confectioners' sugar

1½ tablespoons orange juice

PREPARATION

1 Preheat oven to 350°. Butter a 12-cup, 10-inch Bundt pan and coat the interior with the breadcrumbs. Turn the pan over and tap to remove excess crumbs.

2 Sift the flour and baking soda together. Add the salt and reserve.

3 In the bowl of a mixer with a paddle attachment, cream the butter with the grated orange zest. Gradually add 1¾ cups sugar and beat until light and

fluffy. Add the egg yolks (reserving the whites) in 3 additions, stopping to scrape down the bowl several times. Add the vanilla.

4 Alternately add the flour mixture and the sour cream, stopping to scrape down the bowl several times. Transfer this mixture to a large mixing bowl and stir in the cranberries. Reserve.

5 In a clean mixing bowl, whip the egg whites till frothy. Gradually add the remaining ¼ cup sugar and beat the whites to medium peaks. Lighten the reserved cake batter by folding in one-third of the egg whites. Fold in the remaining whites. Transfer the batter to the prepared pan.

6 Bake at 350° for approximately 65 minutes, until the cake is golden brown, just starts to pull away from the pan, and tests done. Place the pan on a cooling rack and cool for about 15 minutes.

7 While the cake is cooling, prepare the orange glaze by combining the sugar and orange juice in a small saucepan or sauté pan. Cook over medium heat until the sugar is dissolved. Turn the partially cooled cake out onto a cooling rack and place over a baking sheet. Brush the warm glaze on the warm cake. Allow the cake to cool completely.

8 To make the orange icing, place the confectioners' sugar in a small mixing bowl and whisk in the orange juice. The icing should be thick but of fluid consistency. Spoon it over the cooled cake, allowing it to drip irregularly down the sides. Allow the icing to set before serving. The icing is best applied 1 to 2 hours before serving the cake, but the cake can be baked up to 1 day in advance.

Baker's Note: To adapt this cake recipe to another season, try substituting blueberries or raspberries for the cranberries.

Serving Suggestion: If you want to turn this cake into an individually plated dessert, try arranging slices with some cranberry orange compote (page 150) and topping them with some whipped cream.

Double Lemon Custard Cake

This is technically a lemon curd cake, but I have never liked the sound of that British term for the sumptuous spread. "Curd" is too close to "curdled," which is not a good thing in the world of desserts. This cake has an out-of-this-world, super moist, custardy texture, so I feel completely justified in taking liberties with the "menu speak."

INGREDIENTS

    1 cup cake flour
    1 teaspoon baking powder
    ¼ teaspoon kosher salt
    8 tablespoons (4 ounces) butter, at room temperature
    grated zest of 1 lemon
    1 cup sugar
    ½ teaspoon vanilla
    1 tablespoon lemon juice
    2 eggs
    1 cup lemon curd/custard (page 59)

PREPARATION

1. Preheat oven to 350°. Butter an 8 × 8-inch pan, line the bottom with parchment paper, and butter the paper. Dust lightly with flour, tapping out the excess.

2. Sift the flour and baking powder together. Add the salt and reserve.

3. Using a mixer with a paddle, cream the butter with the lemon zest and sugar until light and fluffy. Add the vanilla and lemon juice and mix to blend. Gradually add the reserved flour mixture and mix to blend, scraping down the bowl. Add the eggs and mix till smooth and incorporated.

4. Transfer the batter to the prepared pan and spread with an offset spatula. Leaving a ¼-inch border around all four sides, dollop the lemon curd evenly over the surface of the cake. Using an offset spatula or butter knife, lightly swirl the curd into the cake. Do not overmix!

5 Bake at 350° for 40 to 45 minutes, until the cake is set and lightly browned. Cool completely before removing from the pan. To remove, invert onto a parchment paper–lined baking sheet and reinvert so that the cake is right side up. This cake is best served the day it's made.

Baker's Note: You can vary this recipe by substituting tangerine or lime juice and zest for the lemon in both the cake and the curd.

Serving Suggestions: This is wonderful for brunch or tea with just a sprinkling of powdered sugar. To turn it into a full-fledged dessert, plate it cut into individual portions, topped with cascading lightly sugared berries and a dollop of whipped cream.

Not-Afraid-of-Flavor Gingerbread

SERVES 10 TO 12

The motto of Magnolia Grill is "Not Afraid of Flavor," and desserts, like the rest of the food we serve there, are true to that pronouncement. This moist, spicy cake is a symphony of well-orchestrated flavors. Gingerbread is often thought of as an autumnal or winter dessert; however, it also pairs well with summer fruits such as peaches, plums, and blueberries.

INGREDIENTS
  2½ cups flour
  ½ teaspoon cinnamon
  ½ teaspoon cloves
  ½ teaspoon freshly ground black pepper
  ½ teaspoon ground ginger
  ¼ teaspoon dry mustard
  ½ teaspoon kosher salt
  8 tablespoons (4 ounces) butter
  1 cup sugar
  2 tablespoons peeled, very finely chopped fresh ginger
  2 tablespoons finely chopped crystallized ginger
  2 eggs
  ½ cup canola or other vegetable oil

1 cup molasses
½ cup brewed coffee
2 teaspoons baking soda
½ cup orange juice

PREPARATION

1 Preheat oven to 350°. Butter a 9 × 9 × 2-inch pan or a 10 × 2-inch round cake pan and line the bottom with parchment paper. Butter the parchment paper.

2 Sift the flour together with the cinnamon, cloves, black pepper, ginger, and dry mustard. Add the salt. Reserve.

3 In the bowl of a mixer with a whip attachment, cream the butter with the sugar and the fresh and crystallized ginger. Add the eggs and mix to blend.

4 Add the vegetable oil and the molasses and mix to blend.

5 Gradually add the reserved sifted dry ingredients and mix just to blend, scraping the bowl once or twice.

6 In a small saucepan, bring the coffee to just under a boil. Add the baking soda and stir to dissolve. Gradually add this mixture to the mixing bowl. Scrape the sides of the bowl and add the orange juice. Mix to combine.

7 Pour the batter into the prepared pan and bake at 350° for approximately 60 to 65 minutes. The gingerbread will test done when checked with a skewer, and it will feel set and springy to the touch. It will just start to pull away from the sides of the pan. Cool completely before serving. Once it is cool, turn the gingerbread out onto a parchment paper–lined cake circle, remove the parchment paper, and reinvert onto a serving platter.

Baker's Note: Try to use young, fresh ginger in this recipe. It will be less fibrous, "juicier," and have better flavor.

Serving Suggestions: You can serve this perfectly plain (dusted with a bit of powdered sugar) or with a fruit sauce and whipped cream. Bourbon poached peaches (page 149) or peppered Bartlett pears in sherry syrup (page 160) would work well with this cake, as would a very simple Granny Smith applesauce (page 47). You could also serve this cake with a dollop of lemon curd/custard (page 59).

Banana Upside Down Cakes

SERVES 8

Upside down cakes are wonderful examples of top-notch home-style baking. Here, brown sugar, bananas, and a light buttermilk cake come together in a simple dessert that is undeniably delicious.

INGREDIENTS

20 tablespoons (10 ounces) butter, at room temperature, divided
¾ cup brown sugar
4 large ripe (speckled but not mushy) bananas
1½ cups cake flour
1 teaspoon baking powder
¼ teaspoon baking soda
½ teaspoon cinnamon
¼ teaspoon kosher salt
1 cup sugar
2 eggs
2 teaspoons vanilla
½ cup + 2 tablespoons buttermilk

PREPARATION

1 Preheat oven to 350°. Butter 8 1-cup ramekins.
2 In a medium-sized saucepan, over medium heat, combine 12 tablespoons (6 ounces) of the butter with the brown sugar, whisking until smooth and well combined. Immediately pour into the bottoms of the ramekins, dividing evenly. Peel the bananas and slice them a scant ¼ inch thick; arrange the slices in an overlapping layer that covers the bottom of each ramekin. Reserve.
3 In a bowl, sift together the cake flour, baking powder, baking soda, and cinnamon. Add the salt. Reserve.
4 Using a mixer with a paddle attachment, cream the remaining 8 tablespoons (4 ounces) of butter with the sugar. Add the eggs and the vanilla and mix to combine, scraping down the bowl once or twice. Alternately add the reserved sifted dry ingredients with the buttermilk and mix till smooth and combined. Divide the batter among the ramekins and arrange the ramekins on a rimmed baking sheet.

5   Bake at 350° for about 35 to 40 minutes, rotating the sheet after 20 minutes, until the cakes are firm to the touch and the juices are bubbling. Remove and let cool for a while on a rack but serve while still warm. To serve, run a paring knife around the inside edge of each ramekin to loosen the cake and invert onto a plate. Gently lift off the ramekin and reposition any stray banana slices. These cakes can be made 1 day ahead of time and reheated in a 350° oven to warm through.

Baker's Note: I prefer the look of small individual cakes, but you can use a 9 × 2-inch round pan (or any round or square pan that has an 8-cup capacity) and make a larger cake. The baking time will need to be adjusted (it will probably take about 45 to 50 minutes).

Use this cake as a basic recipe and vary it by substituting different fruits. I have used blueberries, plums, fresh pineapple, and cranberries with great success.

Serving Suggestions: I love upside down cakes served with a complementary ice cream. With this banana version, try a scoop of peanut butter ice cream (page 266), milk chocolate malt ice cream (page 274), or—my favorite—bourbon molasses ice cream (page 264).

Black Walnut Angel Food Cake with Sorghum Syrup

SERVES 12

I wanted to include a recipe for angel food cake in this collection because it's one of the best ways I know of to utilize the surplus egg whites that bakers always seem to wind up with. Light in texture, these fluffy, low-fat confections often seem, to me, a bit light in the flavor department as well. The addition of small quantities of black walnuts and sorghum syrup gives the very traditional angel food an exciting new personality.

INGREDIENTS
1 cup lightly toasted, finely chopped black walnuts
½ teaspoon cinnamon

1 cup + 2 tablespoons cake flour

1½ cups sugar, divided

¼ teaspoon kosher salt

1¾ cups egg whites (12–14 whites), at room temperature

1½ teaspoons cream of tartar

3 tablespoons sorghum syrup

1 teaspoon vanilla

PREPARATION

1 Preheat oven to 350°.

2 In a small bowl, combine the walnuts with cinnamon and reserve.

3 Triple sift the cake flour with ½ cup of the sugar. Add the salt and reserve.

4 Using a mixer with a whip attachment, beat the egg whites till foamy. Add the cream of tartar and beat until soft peaks just start to form. Gradually add the remaining 1 cup of sugar, ¼ cup at a time, and beat till medium peaks form. Transfer the beaten whites to a large mixing bowl.

5 In 3 additions, sprinkle the reserved flour mixture over the whites and delicately but thoroughly fold to combine. Fold in the sorghum syrup and vanilla.

6 Place a third of the batter in a 10-inch tube pan with a removable bottom (but not a nonstick pan!). Sprinkle with half of the reserved walnut mixture. Top with another third of the batter, spreading lightly with a small offset spatula if necessary. Sprinkle with the remaining walnuts and top with the remaining batter.

7 Bake at 350° for 35 to 40 minutes, until the cake is golden brown and springy to the touch. Remove from oven and immediately invert. If your pan has little "feet" on the bottom, you can simply turn the pan upside down to cool. If not, hang the inverted pan over a narrow-necked wine bottle or a large funnel to cool. Allow to cool completely (2 to 3 hours).

8 To remove the cake from the pan, run a long thin-bladed knife around the outer perimeter of the pan to loosen the sides. Push up on the removable bottom to remove the cake. Loosen the cake from the center tube by again inserting a thin-bladed knife and tracing around the tube. Loosen the bottom of the cake as well. Turn the cake out onto a parchment paper–lined baking sheet. Cover with a service platter and reinvert so that the cake is right side up. To serve, slice with a serrated knife. This cake should be served the day it's made.

Baker's Note: Black walnuts are a dark, very hard shelled variety of nut with a distinctive taste that is stronger and richer than that of the more common English walnut. They will often show up in farmers' markets during the fall harvest season and are becoming more widely available. I have recently found commercially grown Diamond brand black walnuts in my local supermarket. Hickory nuts, hazelnuts, or regular walnuts can be substituted. Maple syrup or molasses can be substituted for the sorghum syrup.

Serving Suggestions: Try pairing this cake with bourbon poached peaches (page 149) or sliced peppered Bartlett pears in sherry syrup (page 160) and whipped cream. It's also good lightly toasted and served with Granny Smith applesauce (page 47) and not-just-plain vanilla ice cream (page 261). An extra drizzle of sorghum syrup is always welcome.

Cranberry Crumb Cake

SERVES 9 TO 12

At one time, most American neighborhoods had small storefront bakeries that turned out the sweet stuff childhood memories are made of. One commonly found offering was squares of buttery crumb-strewn coffee cake covered with a drift of powdered sugar. My re-creation adds a counterpoint of tart cranberries.

INGREDIENTS FOR THE CRUMB TOPPING
   1¾ cups + 2 tablespoons flour
   ¾ cup brown sugar
   1½ teaspoons cinnamon
   ¼ teaspoon kosher salt
   10 tablespoons (5 ounces) butter, melted

INGREDIENTS FOR THE CAKE
   1½ cups flour
   ½ cup sugar
   2¼ teaspoons baking powder
   ¼ teaspoon cinnamon
   ¼ teaspoon kosher salt
   1 egg

½ cup + 2 tablespoons milk

2 tablespoons vegetable oil

1½ teaspoons vanilla

1½ cups cranberries

2 tablespoons confectioners' sugar

PREPARATION

1 Preheat oven to 350°. Butter a 9 × 9 pan, line the bottom with parchment paper, and butter the paper. Lightly flour the pan, tapping out the excess flour.

2 Prepare the crumb topping by stirring together the flour, brown sugar, cinnamon, salt, and melted butter. At first it might look as if the crumb mixture is too wet, but don't worry—it will become more "crumbly" once it sits for a few minutes. Reserve.

3 Sift the flour, sugar, baking powder, and cinnamon into a medium-sized bowl. Add the salt and reserve.

4 Combine the egg, milk, vegetable oil, and vanilla and mix till blended. Stir this mixture into the reserved dry ingredients and mix till just smooth and blended. Spread the batter evenly in the prepared pan with a small offset spatula. The batter will just cover the bottom of the pan. Place the cranberries in a single even layer over the batter, leaving a ¼-inch border around the outer perimeter of the pan. Scatter the crumb topping evenly over the cake, breaking up any large chunks. Press the crumbs down lightly.

5 Bake at 350° for about 50 minutes or until the cake tests done. To remove this cake from its pan, allow it to cool completely, loosen the sides with a paring knife, then cover with a parchment paper–lined baking sheet, and turn the pan over; when the cake comes free, remove the parchment paper liner. Cover the cake with a service platter and reinvert. Sift the confectioners' sugar over the top of the cake. This can be made 1 day in advance. Store at room temperature.

Baker's Note: You can also bake this recipe in a 10-inch springform pan. Blueberries or raspberries can be substituted for the cranberries.

Serving Suggestions: This cake is wonderful for breakfast, brunch, lunch, or a snack just as it is, but it can be dressed up a bit and served as a homey dinner dessert too. I would suggest serving it lightly rewarmed with a scoop of cream cheese ice cream made with a cranberry swirl (page 265) or Granny Smith applesauce (page 47) and whipped cream.

Big Island Fruitcake

MAKES 1 9 × 5 × 3-INCH LOAF OR 5 MINI LOAVES;
AS A ROUND CAKE, IT CAN BE MADE IN A 9-INCH SAVARIN
RING MOLD OR AN 8½-INCH SPRINGFORM PAN

The object of many jokes, fruitcakes seem to have developed a rather negative reputation. I too confess to turning up my nose at these often maligned cakes—particularly the ones with commercially dyed candied fruits. My husband insisted that an updated recipe based on top-notch ingredients could be delicious and challenged me to make one. A jumbo bag of macadamia nuts that I received after doing a cooking event in Hawaii was the inspiration behind this nontraditional tropical version. This recipe can be baked in any pan that has a 7½- to 8-cup capacity and doubles well for holiday gift-giving. Plan ahead because this cake is best made at least 2 weeks in advance.

INGREDIENTS

¾ cup (4 ounces) dried pineapple

¾ cup (4 ounces) dried mango

⅜ cup (2 ounces) dried papaya

⅜ cup (2 ounces) candied orange peel
   (page 61, or use a good commercial product)

¾ cup (4 ounces) dried cherries

½ cup frozen sweetened shredded coconut, defrosted

¾ cup (4 ounces) macadamia nuts

½ cup (3 ounces) Brazil nuts

¼ cup (1½ ounces) whole almonds

1½ cups flour, divided

½ teaspoon baking powder

1 teaspoon ginger

½ teaspoon kosher salt

12 tablespoons (6 ounces) butter, at room temperature

1 cup brown sugar

3 eggs

1 teaspoon vanilla

3 tablespoons golden rum (I use Appleton's)

additional ¼ cup + 2 tablespoons golden rum
    to soak the finished cake, divided

cheesecloth

PREPARATION

1 Preheat oven to 325°. Butter the pan, line the bottom with parchment paper, butter the paper, and flour the pan, knocking out the excess flour.

2 Cut the pineapple, mango, papaya, and orange peel into ¼-inch dice. Combine in a bowl with the cherries, coconut, macadamia nuts, Brazil nuts, almonds, and ¼ cup of flour. Mix to blend and reserve.

3 Sift the remaining 1¼ cups flour with the baking powder and ginger. Add the salt. Reserve.

4 In the bowl of a mixer fitted with a paddle, cream the butter with the sugar. Add the eggs one at a time, scraping the bowl after each addition. Alternately add the reserved sifted flour mixture with the vanilla and 3 tablespoons of golden rum. Mix until just blended. Stir in the reserved fruits and nuts. Place the batter in the prepared pan. Bake at 325° till the cake is golden brown and springy to the touch. This should take about 90 minutes. (If baked as mini loaves, the cakes should test done after 60 to 70 minutes.) Allow the cake to cool in its pan for 15 minutes before turning out onto a wire rack.

5 Brush the cake with 2 tablespoons of golden rum. When completely cool, wrap the cake in cheesecloth and brush the cheesecloth with ¼ cup of rum. Wrap in aluminum foil and store refrigerated or in a cool place for at least 2 weeks. This recipe can be made up to a month in advance, in which case rebrush the cake with an additional ¼ cup of rum at least once. For optimum texture and flavor, however, a weekly moistening is suggested.

Baker's Note: Try to find plump, unsulfured, excellent-quality dried fruit to make this cake. You can vary the fruits and nuts to change the profile of the cake, but the ratio of fruits and nuts to batter should stay the same.

Serving Suggestions: Serve this cake at room temperature, cutting it into thin slices to be presented along with a holiday cookie assortment. It's also quite tasty lightly toasted and topped with a scoop of not-just-plain-vanilla ice cream (page 261).

Cinnamon Apple Date Babycakes

MAKES 8

These small individual cakes look rather lonely on their own and are meant to be garnished for a plated presentation. By topping them with a scoop of ice cream and drizzling a bit of sauce around them, it's easy to turn plain into pretty special.

INGREDIENTS

1½ cups flour

¾ teaspoon baking soda

1 teaspoon cinnamon

¼ teaspoon kosher salt

½ cup chopped dates

¼ cup apple cider

12 tablespoons (6 ounces) butter, at room temperature

1 cup sugar

2 eggs

1¾ cups peeled, medium-diced Granny Smith apples

¾ cup medium chopped, lightly toasted skinned walnuts

PREPARATION

1   Preheat oven to 350°. Butter 8 1-cup ramekins and line the bottoms with parchment paper. Butter the parchment paper.

2   Sift together the flour, baking soda, and cinnamon. Add the salt and reserve.

3   Combine the dates and the apple cider in a small saucepan and heat just till the cider comes to a boil. Remove from heat and allow the dates to plump. Reserve.

4   In the bowl of a mixer with a paddle attachment, cream the butter with the sugar. Add the eggs and mix till combined. Gradually add the reserved flour mixture and beat till combined, scraping the bowl once or twice. Add the reserved dates and cider and mix till combined. Add the apples and walnuts and mix just to blend. This will be a very thick, chunky batter.

5   Divide the batter among the prepared ramekins. An ice cream scoop is great for doing this. Place the ramekins on a baking sheet and bake at 350° for 35 to 40 minutes, until the cakes are well browned and springy to the touch.

6 Cool to warm before serving or cool completely and reheat before serving. These can be made up to 2 days ahead of time. To remove the cakes from the ramekins, run a paring knife around the outer perimeter of the cake, turn the ramekin over, and shake forcefully to pop the cake out into the palm of your hand. Remove the parchment paper liner from the bottom of the cake and place the cake upright on a service plate. If the cakes have been made ahead, reheat them in their ramekins for 5 minutes in a 350° oven before turning them out.

Baker's Note: I sometimes call these chunky cakes because they are so packed with fruit and nuts. You can change this recipe by substituting pears for the apples and varying the nuts and spicing. Raisins or dried figs can also be substituted for the dates. This cake can also be baked in an 8-inch springform or cheesecake pan, but the baking time will have to be increased.

Serving Suggestions: Although these work as sturdy lunchbox or picnic cakes, I do like to serve them warmed, topped with ice cream and surrounded by sauce. Try them with not-just-plain-vanilla ice cream (page 261) or bourbon molasses (or sorghum) ice cream (page 264) and cider-flavored fruit caramel (page 46), applesauce (page 47), gingered maple walnut sauce (page 42), or caramel sauce (page 36). You can, of course, opt for good-quality store-bought products as well.

Chocolate-Dipped Banana Buttermilk Cupcakes

MAKES 18 TO 24 CUPCAKES (DEPENDING ON THE SIZE OF YOUR TINS)

Although small in size, a cupcake can pack a whole lot of flavor into a portable single-serving treat. Ideal for picnics, bake sales, after-school snacks, and, yes, birthday parties—cupcakes make everyone smile.

INGREDIENTS FOR THE CUPCAKES
  2½ cups cake flour
  1 teaspoon baking soda
  1 teaspoon baking powder

½ teaspoon kosher salt

12 tablespoons (6 ounces) butter, at room temperature

1½ cups sugar

3 eggs

1½ teaspoons vanilla

⅔ cup mashed bananas (2 medium-sized bananas)

½ cup + 2 tablespoons buttermilk

INGREDIENTS FOR THE CHOCOLATE GLAZE

½ cup cream

6 ounces semisweet chocolate, chopped

1 tablespoon corn syrup

PREPARATION FOR THE CUPCAKES

1 Preheat oven to 350°. Place paper liners in the cups of muffin tins.

2 Sift the cake flour, baking soda, and baking powder together. Add the salt and reserve.

3 Using a mixer fitted with a paddle, cream the butter with the sugar. Add the eggs and mix to blend well, scraping the bowl once or twice.

4 Combine the vanilla, mashed banana, and buttermilk and mix to blend. Alternately with the reserved dry ingredients, add this mixture to the batter in 2 additions, starting and ending with the dry ingredients.

5 Mix the batter just until the ingredients are combined. Divide the batter among the lined muffin tins, filling each cup two-thirds full.

6 Bake at 350° for approximately 20 minutes, until the cupcakes are golden brown and just firm to the touch. Cool in the pan for 2 to 3 minutes and then carefully remove the cupcakes and allow them to cool completely on a rack.

PREPARATION FOR THE CHOCOLATE GLAZE

1 In a small saucepan, bring the cream to just under a boil. Add the chocolate and, over very low heat, stir until it is just melted. Remove from heat and stir in the corn syrup. Cool slightly.

2 Glaze each cupcake by completely dipping the top in the glaze. As you remove the cupcake, give it a twist to prevent the glaze from dripping down the sides. Place the glazed cupcakes upright on a baking sheet or plate and chill briefly in the refrigerator to set the glaze. Serve at room temperature.

Baker's Note: Using a spring-loaded ice cream scoop is the easiest and quickest way to portion the batter among the cups of the muffin tins.

Serving Suggestions: A festive platter of cupcakes is a great alternative to a large-format iced cake. The chocolate glaze, when set, makes a perfect background for piping out a Happy Birthday message. Use a commercial icing tube or make your own thick confectioners' sugar icing and pipe out 1 letter per cupcake, leaving a plain glazed cupcake between words. Candles, sprinkles, and sparklers are optional.

Everything You Always Wanted to Know about Cheesecake

While it's often said that America's favorite dessert is apple pie, in a recent nationwide poll cheesecake was a very close contender. Most cheesecake recipes are inherently simple and even the gussied-up, multiflavored versions are just variations on a basic theme. Why, then, do so many people have problems making cheesecake? One of the most frequently asked baking questions I get is, "How do you keep cheesecakes from cracking?" In my opinion, cheesecake is not really a cake—in reality it's a baked custard, and, as with other custards, low and slow is the way to go when it comes to baking cheesecakes.

There are two methods of baking cheesecakes that I've found to be highly effective in eliminating earthquake-like faults. They differ according to the type of pan you use. One way to bake cheesecakes is utilizing the water bath method and a "cheesecake pan." Cheesecake pans come in several diameters, and they are solid, seamless, and 3 inches deep. When using these pans, I always lightly butter the pan, line both the bottom and the sides with lightly buttered parchment paper, and bake the cake in a larger, shallow-sided pan that is filled with enough warm water to reach at least 1 inch up the sides of the cheesecake pan. The water bath allows the cake to bake evenly and slowly, ensuring a luxurious, creamy texture. This procedure can be used for both crustless and crumb-crusted cakes. So how, you may wonder, does one get the cake out of the pan? Once chilled, the cake is very easy to turn out. Simply heat the pan by holding it briefly over an open flame, dipping it in very hot water, or heating the sides with a blowtorch or hair dryer. Cover the pan with a sheet of parchment paper, place a platter or cardboard cake circle on top of the parchment paper, and flip the pan so that it's upside down. Lift up the pan, remove the parchment paper from the bottom of the cake, and re-invert the cheesecake onto a service platter.

Many cheesecake recipes call for using a springform pan. Often they instruct you to wrap the bottom of the pan with aluminum foil and bake the cake in a water bath. I find this problematic because no matter how well you wrap the pan, there's often some water seepage. This is particularly troublesome with cakes that have a crumb crust. When making cheesecakes in a springform pan, I use a graduated heat method of baking and forgo the water bath. This means starting the cake at a preheated 350° and turning the temperature of the oven down by 50° every 20 minutes. The cake usually finishes baking on the oven's "low" setting (or 225° if your oven doesn't have this calibration). Baking times tend to vary a bit more using this process, so it is important to check the cake frequently toward the end of the recommended baking time. To facilitate the absolutely clean removal of a cheesecake from its pan, I line the lightly buttered pan with buttered parchment paper, even when using a springform pan. If you are going to serve the cake directly from the pan bottom, you can omit this step. If you want to remove the cake from the bottom, use the parchment. Once the cheesecake is chilled, briefly pass the bottom of the pan over a gas or electric burner. This causes the chilled butter used to grease the pan to melt slightly. Remove the pan sides. Insert a long-bladed slicing knife or a long offset spatula between the crust and the parchment paper—lined bottom and loosen the cake—it should pop right off. If you don't have a cheesecake pan, using a springform pan and the graduated baking method is an acceptable alternative.

The most common cause of cheesecake cracking (regardless of which type of pan you use) is overbaking. Cheesecakes are done when they are set around the edges and just barely jiggly in the center. Some other key precautions to avoiding the dreaded cracked surface include the following:

- Have all the ingredients for the filling at room temperature. This may necessitate removing the cream cheese from the refrigerator several hours ahead of time.

- Combine the filling ingredients with a minimal amount of beating. This will reduce the amount of air incorporated into the batter. Additional air causes the cake to expand and subsequently contract, increasing the likelihood of cracks. The cheese-sugar base should be completely smooth before you start to add any liquid or eggs to the batter. To ensure this, scrape down the mixing bowl several times with a rubber spatula during the mixing process. Once the eggs are added, mix the batter until they are just combined—do not overbeat!
- Don't forget to line the sides (and bottom) of the baking pan with lightly buttered parchment paper. As cheesecakes cool they tend to shrink in from the sides of the pan. Parchment paper will prevent the cake from clinging to the pan as the cake contracts, thereby eliminating the possibility of cracking. I find it worth the extra step.
- Allow the cake to cool completely before storing it in the refrigerator.
- If, despite all your best efforts, your cheesecake still cracks, don't despair—it will still taste delicious, and remember that artfully arranged garnishes can cover any irregularities!

Cousin Steve's Cheesecake

SERVES 10 PEOPLE

When I was a child, cheesecake reigned supreme as the most often served "company dessert" in our house. The formula for this delicious cake was developed by my cousin Steve Ganzell. Pure, unadulterated, and simple, it is, to me, the epitome of cheesecake.

INGREDIENTS FOR THE CRUST
   ¾ cup graham cracker crumbs
   2 tablespoons sugar
   3 tablespoons (1½ ounces) butter, melted

INGREDIENTS FOR THE CHEESECAKE

24 ounces cream cheese, at room temperature

1 cup sugar

1 cup sour cream

1 teaspoon vanilla

3 eggs, beaten

PREPARATION FOR THE CRUST

1 Preheat oven to 350°.

2 Butter an 8 × 3-inch cheesecake pan and line both the bottom and sides of the pan with buttered parchment paper. Make sure that the strips lining the sides extend slightly over the top of the pan. Remove from oven and cool.

3 In a mixing bowl, combine the graham cracker crumbs, sugar, and butter. Stir until well combined and press into the bottom and ¼ inch up the sides of the reserved pan. Bake at 350° for 8 to 10 minutes until lightly golden brown. Cool completely.

PREPARATION FOR THE CHEESECAKE

1 Preheat oven to 350°. Using a mixer with a paddle attachment, combine the cream cheese with the sugar. Mix until very smooth, occasionally scraping down the sides and bottom of the mixing bowl. Add the sour cream and vanilla and mix till blended in.

2 Add half the beaten eggs and mix until just combined. Scrape down the bowl and add the remaining eggs, again mixing until just combined.

3 Pour the mixture into the reserved crust. Place the pan in a larger baking pan to create a water bath and pour in enough hot water to reach halfway up the sides of the cheesecake pan.

4 Place on the bottom oven rack and bake at 350° for 60 minutes. Turn the oven to 325° and bake approximately 20 minutes more. When done, the cheesecake should be set around the edges but still a bit jiggly in the center. The top will feel set to the touch. Remove the cake pan from the water bath and allow to cool for 5 minutes. Run a paring knife around the outer perimeter of the pan to loosen the cake. Cool completely. Refrigerate for several hours or up to 2 days before serving.

5 To remove the cake from the pan, begin by dipping the pan in very hot water or passing it over an open gas flame briefly. Gently remove the parchment strips from the sides of the pan. With a sharp, thin-bladed knife, loosen the

cake from the sides of the pan. Cover the top of the cake with a piece of parchment paper and place a plate or cardboard cake circle over the parchment. Invert the cake onto the plate. Remove the parchment paper from the bottom of the cake. Place the service platter over the bottom of the cake and reinvert so the cake is right side up. Cut with a thin-bladed slicing knife, wiping the blade clean and dipping the blade in very hot water between each cut. Serve chilled. The cake can be frozen, in which case it should be defrosted overnight in the refrigerator before serving.

Baker's Note: This recipe can be doubled and baked in a 10 × 3-inch cheesecake pan.

Serving Suggestions: I usually like this cheesecake straight up, but if you are partial to fruit-garnished cheesecake, try serving this cake with cinnamon spiced blueberry sauce (page 45), strawberry crush (page 49), strawberry rhubarb compote (page 148), or sweet and sour cherry compote (page 155).

Brown Sugar Sour Cream Cheesecake

SERVES 12

This is an elegant, satiny smooth cheesecake with a touch of a down-home Southern accent. You will need to bake this cake in a springform pan, using the "turn down" baking method because it has a sour cream topping.

INGREDIENTS FOR THE CRUST
  1½ cups graham cracker crumbs
  ½ cup yellow cornmeal, preferably stoneground
  2 tablespoons sugar
  6 tablespoons (3 ounces) butter, melted

INGREDIENTS FOR THE FILLING
  1½ pounds cream cheese, at room temperature
  8 tablespoons (4 ounces) butter, at room temperature
  1¼ cups brown sugar
  2 tablespoons molasses
  2 teaspoons vanilla
  ½ cup sour cream

¼ cup cream

4 eggs

INGREDIENTS FOR THE TOPPING

1½ cups sour cream

2 tablespoons brown sugar

1½ tablespoons peach brandy, bourbon, or orange juice

PREPARATION FOR THE CRUST

1 Preheat oven to 350°. Butter a 10-inch springform pan, line the bottom and sides with parchment paper, and butter the parchment paper.

2 Combine the graham cracker crumbs, cornmeal, sugar, and melted butter in a bowl. Mix with a fork until the crumbs are evenly moistened. Press the crumbs into the bottom and ½ inch up the sides of the pan. Bake at 350° for about 8 minutes, until the crust just starts to pick up a bit of color around its edges. Remove from oven and cool.

PREPARATION FOR THE FILLING

1 Preheat oven to 350°. Using a mixer with a paddle attachment, combine the cream cheese, butter, and sugar, mixing till very smooth, occasionally scraping down the mixing bowl. Add the molasses and vanilla and blend. Add the sour cream and blend. Add the cream and mix just to blend in. Add the eggs, one at a time, and mix just to incorporate. Scrape the bowl, making sure the filling is well mixed. Pour the filling into the prepared crust.

2 Bake at 350° for 20 minutes and then turn the oven to 300°. Bake for an additional 20 minutes and turn the oven to 250°. Bake for 20 minutes more and turn the oven to low (or 225°). Continue baking until the cake looks set around the edges but just a bit jiggly in the very center. In the meantime, prepare the topping.

PREPARATION FOR THE TOPPING

1 Whisk together the sour cream, brown sugar, and peach brandy (or other liquid). Reserve.

2 As soon as the cake is done, remove it from the oven and turn the oven to 350°.

3 Slowly and evenly pour the sour cream topping over the cake. You can use an offset spatula to help spread the topping.

4 Bake at 350° for 3 minutes, till the topping is just set. Remove and cool thoroughly. Chill several hours or overnight before serving.

Baker's Note: When forming the crumb crust for this cake (or any other dessert) I use a metal ¼-cup dry measuring cup to smooth and tamp down the crumbs, forming an even, compact crust. I always use Breakstone sour cream for the topping on this cake. For some reason certain commercial brands form unpleasant yellowish skins when baked—I think it has something to do with gum additives. Do not use low-fat sour cream!

Serving Suggestions: I usually serve this cake with bourbon poached peaches (page 149) or cinnamon spiced blueberry sauce (page 45).

Black Bottom Gentleman Jack Cheesecake

SERVES 12

The classic two-toned black bottom pie is a vintage recipe that's been around since the early 1900s. This creamy, bourbon-spiked cheesecake version features a fudgey bottom layer and a crunchy pecan crumb crust.

INGREDIENTS
  1 cup graham cracker crumbs
  1 cup finely ground pecans
  1 tablespoon sugar
  6 tablespoons (3 ounces) butter, melted

INGREDIENTS FOR THE BLACK BOTTOM FILLING
  5½ ounces semisweet chocolate
  7 tablespoons (3½ ounces) butter
  2 eggs
  ¼ cup sugar
  2 tablespoons flour
  2 tablespoons Gentleman Jack whiskey or good-quality bourbon

INGREDIENTS FOR THE CREAM CHEESE FILLING
  24 ounces cream cheese, at room temperature
  8 tablespoons (4 ounces) butter, at room temperature

1 cup sugar

1 teaspoon vanilla

¼ cup + 2 tablespoons Gentleman Jack whiskey or good-quality bourbon

¼ cup heavy cream

4 eggs

PREPARATION FOR THE CRUST

1 Preheat oven to 350°. Butter and line a 10-inch springform pan with parchment paper. Lightly butter the parchment paper.

2 Combine the graham cracker crumbs, ground pecans, sugar, and butter and stir until well combined. Press the crumb mixture into the bottom and 1 inch up the sides of the springform pan.

3 Bake for 8 to 10 minutes until lightly golden. Remove from oven and cool.

PREPARATION FOR THE BLACK BOTTOM FILLING

1 Preheat oven to 350°. Combine the chocolate and the butter in the top of a double boiler and melt. Remove from heat and reserve.

2 Combine the eggs and sugar in a mixing bowl and whisk to blend. Whisk in the melted chocolate mixture and the flour. Add the bourbon and whisk to blend. Pour the mixture into the prepared crust and bake for approximately 10 minutes, until the mixture is barely set. Remove from the oven and reserve.

PREPARATION FOR THE CREAM CHEESE FILLING

1 In the bowl of a mixer fitted with a paddle, cream the cream cheese and butter until very smooth. Add the sugar and beat, scraping the bowl once or twice, till well blended. Add the vanilla and the bourbon and mix to combine. Add the cream and mix just to blend. Add the eggs, one at a time, beating and scraping just until each is incorporated. Pour the cream cheese filling over the black bottom filling.

2 Bake at 350° for 20 minutes and then turn the oven to 300°. Bake for an additional 20 minutes and then turn the oven to 250°. Bake for another 20 minutes and then turn the oven to low (or 225°). Bake until the cake is set around the edges and still a bit jiggly in the center. Remove from oven and cool. Chill several hours or overnight before serving. This cake can be made up to 2 days in advance.

Baker's Note: This cake can also be baked in a cheesecake pan (see page 239 for baking instructions). A more traditional gingersnap crumb crust can also be used, and some people might wish to substitute dark rum for the bourbon in this recipe.

Serving Suggestions: This cake is a knockout all on its own, but if you want to add a little "plate interest," you can serve it with a drizzle of cocoa fudge sauce (page 37) and a sprinkle of pecan praline (page 56). To take it over the top, add some butterscotch baked bananas (page 154).

Pumpkin Cognac Cheesecake Brûlée

MAKES 6 PORTIONS

In the quest for a Thanksgiving dessert that was a bit different, I tried baking a pumpkin cheesecake recipe in individual servings. A crunchy, caramelized crust turns this simple recipe into an elegant finale.

INGREDIENTS

16 ounces cream cheese, at room temperature
5 tablespoons (2½ ounces) butter, at room temperature
⅔ cup sugar
½ cup pumpkin purée
½ teaspoon ginger
½ teaspoon cinnamon
½ teaspoon nutmeg
1¾ tablespoons cognac
1 tablespoon + 1 teaspoon cream
2 eggs
1 egg yolk
additional 5 tablespoons sugar for the brûléed tops

PREPARATION

1 Preheat oven to 325°. Butter 6 1-cup ovenproof ramekins, line the bottoms with parchment paper, and butter the paper; coat the ramekins with sugar, tapping to remove the excess.
2 Using a mixer with a paddle attachment, combine the cream cheese and butter. Gradually add the sugar and mix until smooth. Add the pumpkin and mix to blend. Add the ginger, cinnamon, and nutmeg and mix to blend,

occasionally scraping the bottom and sides of the bowl. Add the cognac and the cream and mix in. Add the eggs and egg yolk and mix just until incorporated.

3   Divide the batter among the prepared ramekins, filling each three-quarters full. Place the ramekins in a water bath and bake at 325° about 45 minutes, until the cheesecakes are set. Remove the ramekins from the water bath and allow to cool. Refrigerate for several hours or up to 3 days before serving.

TO BRÛLÉE THE CHEESECAKES

1   Remove the cheesecakes from the ramekins by placing the chilled cakes in a 350° oven for 1 minute or dipping the ramekins in very hot water for 1 minute. Run the tip of a paring knife around the inside of the ramekin. Turn each cake out into the palm of your hand, remove the parchment paper from the bottom, and place upside down in the center of individual dessert plates.

2   Evenly spread about 1½ teaspoons of sugar over the surface of each cake. Caramelize the top of each cake with a blowtorch until the sugar melts and turns golden brown. Sprinkle each cake with an additional 1 teaspoon sugar and repeat the caramelization process. Double brûléeing gives the cakes an extra crunchy caramel top. Allow to cool for a few minutes before serving.

Baker's Note: The ability to produce a great brûlée with ease is reason enough for purchasing a blowtorch (see page 18). If your kitchen has a very efficient top broiler, you can alternatively caramelize the sugar by broiling: turn the cakes out onto a cookie sheet, caramelize them, and then transfer them to service plates. If you lack both a torch and a broiler, try sprinkling the top of each cake liberally with finely chopped nut praline (page 56). This will provide both crunch and caramel in a different guise.

Serving Suggestions: Cranberry orange compote (page 150) or hot buttered rum raisin sauce (page 41) made with cognac in place of rum would complement this cake.

Peanut Butter Cheesecake

SERVES 12 TO 14

It wasn't until I was in the midst of testing this recipe that I realized I already had a number of peanut butter–flavored desserts in the book. At first I considered editing this one out, but as Mae West once said, "Too much of a good thing can be wonderful."

INGREDIENTS FOR THE CRUST

- 1 cup roasted, lightly salted peanuts, finely ground
- 1 cup fine ground graham cracker crumbs
- 2 tablespoons sugar
- 1½ tablespoons cocoa
- 6 tablespoons (3 ounces) butter, melted

INGREDIENTS FOR THE FILLING

- 24 ounces cream cheese, at room temperature
- 1 cup sugar
- ½ cup creamy peanut butter
- 1 teaspoon vanilla
- 3 tablespoons dark rum
- ¼ cup cream
- 4 eggs

INGREDIENTS FOR THE TOPPING

- 6 ounces semisweet chocolate
- ½ cup sour cream

PREPARATION FOR THE CRUST

1 Preheat oven to 350°. Butter a 10- to 10½-inch springform pan, line the bottom and sides with parchment paper, and butter the paper.

2 Combine the ground peanuts, graham cracker crumbs, sugar, and cocoa in a mixing bowl and stir to blend well. Add the melted butter and stir with a fork until the crumb mixture is evenly moistened. Press the crumbs into the bottom and 1 inch up the sides of the prepared springform pan.

3 Bake at 350° for 8 to 10 minutes, until the edges just start to darken slightly. The crust will start to smell fragrant. Remove from the oven and cool.

PREPARATION FOR THE FILLING

1 Preheat oven to 350°. Place the room-temperature cream cheese in the bowl of a mixer fitted with a paddle. Add the sugar and beat, scraping the bowl several times until smooth and creamy. Add the peanut butter and vanilla and mix till well blended. Add the rum and mix till smooth, scraping the bowl again. Add the cream and mix just to blend. Add the eggs, two at a time, and mix just till well combined, again scraping the bowl once or twice. Pour the filling into the prepared crust.

2 Bake at 350° for 20 minutes. Turn the oven to 300° and bake for an additional 20 minutes. Turn the oven to 250° and bake for 20 minutes more. Turn the oven to low (or 225°) and finish the baking process. When done, the cake will appear set around the edges and just barely jiggly in the center. Remove from oven and cool completely.

3 Once the cake is cool, chill it for several hours in the refrigerator before completing the topping.

4 Remove the chilled cake from its pan by passing the bottom briefly over a range burner. Release the springform sides, remove the parchment paper, and pop the cake off the springform bottom by inserting a long, thin slicing knife between the bottom crust and the parchment paper–lined springform bottom. Transfer the cake to a service platter. Lightly blot the surface of the cake with a paper towel if any condensation has formed.

PREPARATION FOR THE TOPPING

Melt the semisweet chocolate in the top of a double boiler. Working quickly, whisk the sour cream into the chocolate and immediately transfer the mixture to the top of the cake. Using a small offset spatula, spread the chocolate evenly over the cake. Lightly bevel the edges. Chill the cake to set the topping before serving. This cake can be made 2 days in advance.

Baker's Note: To grind the peanuts without overprocessing them, I usually combine them with the graham cracker crumbs. Use short pulses to process them until the nuts are finely ground.

   In lieu of adding the topping, you can leave the top of this cake plain and pour cocoa fudge sauce (page 37) over each plated slice.

Serving Suggestions: Creamy peanut butter and honey sauce (page 39), cocoa fudge sauce (page 37), and peanut praline (page 56) can all combine for a dazzling presentation. Another option is to forgo the chocolate topping and serve the cake with Concord grape syrup (page 50).

Goat Cheese Cheesecake in a Hazelnut Crust

SERVES 12 TO 14

The combination of hazelnuts and fresh goat cheese in this cake turns a familiar favorite into an unusual, sophisticated dinner party dessert. I use a fresh, mild goat cheese from our local Celebrity Dairy (where the goats are named after movie stars), but any young Montrachet-style goat cheese can be used.

INGREDIENTS FOR THE CRUST

    1 cup graham cracker crumbs

    1 cup lightly toasted chopped hazelnuts

    2 tablespoons sugar

    6 tablespoons (3 ounces) butter, melted

INGREDIENTS FOR THE CHEESECAKE

    24 ounces cream cheese, at room temperature

    16 ounces goat cheese, at room temperature

    2 cups sugar

    1 cup sour cream

    1 teaspoon vanilla

    2 tablespoons Frangelico

    4 eggs

PREPARATION FOR THE CRUST

1 Preheat oven to 350°. Prepare a 10½-inch cheesecake pan or springform pan by buttering it lightly, lining the bottom and sides with parchment paper, and buttering the paper (see page 239, on using these two types of pans).

2 Combine the graham cracker crumbs and hazelnuts in a processor with a steel blade and pulse till the nuts are very finely ground. Remove the mixture to a bowl and stir in the sugar and about three-quarters of the butter. You may not need all of the butter, depending on the oil content of the nuts and the brand

of graham cracker crumbs you use. The crumb mixture should just come together if pressed but not feel at all greasy. If the mixture seems dry, add the remaining butter.

4 Press the crumbs into the bottom and ½ inch up the sides of the prepared pan.

5 Bake the crust for approximately 8 minutes at 350°, until the edges just start to pick up a bit of color. Remove from oven and cool.

PREPARATION FOR THE CHEESECAKE

1 Preheat oven to 350°. Using a mixer with a paddle, combine the cream cheese, goat cheese, and sugar and mix till very smooth, scraping the bowl once or twice.

2 Add the sour cream, vanilla, and Frangelico and mix just to blend.

3 Add the eggs, two at a time, and mix on low speed, scraping the bowl once or twice, until just blended in.

4 Pour the filling into the prepared crust.

5 If baking in a cheesecake pan, bake in a water bath at 350° for about 45 minutes. Then turn the oven to 325° and bake for approximately 45 minutes more until the cake is set around the edges but still a bit jiggly in the center. The top will feel set to the touch. Remove from oven and cool for 5 minutes. Loosen the sides of the cake by lightly running a paring knife around the top edge of the pan. Cool completely. Chill for several hours or overnight before serving.

   If baking in a springform pan, bake the cake at 350° for 20 minutes. Reduce the oven temperature to 300° and bake for 20 minutes more. Reduce the oven temperature again to 250° and bake an additional 20 minutes. Turn the oven to low (or 225°) and bake until the cake is done.

6 This cake can be made up to 48 hours in advance.

Baker's Note: The baking times of cheesecakes can vary widely. Cheesecakes are like custards, and egg size, the amount of air beaten into the cake, and the exactness of the oven temperature can all modify the baking time. Sometimes I could swear that atmospheric conditions have an effect also. Check your cheesecakes often. If they seem to be baking a bit too quickly, and particularly if you notice them puffing in a soufflé-like manner, turn the oven down.

Serving Suggestions: Raspberry red wine sauce (page 48) was meant for this cake. It would also be delicious with winter fruits poached in red wine syrup (page 157), peppered Bartlett pears in sherry syrup (page 160), or oven roasted red flame grapes or figs and raspberries (page 151).

Skinning Nuts

Hazelnuts also go by the name filberts. Whole hazelnuts, like walnuts, have bitter, tannic skins that should be removed before using the nuts. Shelled hazelnuts are available whole but unskinned and are also available both whole and chopped in skinned form. The process of removing the skins is a bit tedious, so if the skinned variety is available to you, I would suggest you use it. To skin nuts yourself, place them in a single layer on a baking sheet and toast them at 350° for about 8 to 10 minutes, until they smell fragrant and the papery skins start to detach from the nuts. It is best to set a kitchen timer when you do this. Transfer the hot nuts to a large tea towel, gather the corners of the towel, and rub the nuts together, applying a fair amount of pressure. Open the towel up and rub the nuts by hand to remove the remaining skins. This is best done while the nuts are still very warm. You may not be able to remove every bit of skin. If just a bit remains it should not affect your end product.

Creamy Maytag Blue Cheesecakes with Walnuts in Rosemary Honey

SERVES 12

I am resigned to the fact that there are some people out there who just don't love dessert. My husband happens to be one of those folks who will always choose a cheese plate over a sweet finish to a meal. I usually make him order a dessert anyway, and I end up with two. At Magnolia Grill we don't have a formal cheese course, but we always try to have one dessert selection that is cheese-oriented and savory in nature. This unusual pairing is an example of our combo cheese/dessert offerings.

INGREDIENTS FOR THE WALNUTS IN ROSEMARY HONEY
    1½ cups honey
    ½ cup orange juice

2½ tablespoons fresh rosemary, stripped off the stem

1½ cups walnuts, toasted, skinned, and coarsely chopped

INGREDIENTS FOR THE CHEESECAKES

1½ cups (12 ounces) cream cheese, softened

1½ cups (12 ounces) Maytag blue cheese, softened

½ cup sugar

½ cup sour cream

3 eggs

additional sugar for coating molds

PREPARATION FOR THE WALNUTS IN ROSEMARY HONEY

Combine the honey, orange juice, and rosemary in a medium-sized saucepan. Bring to a boil. Turn off the heat and allow the mixture to steep for 30 minutes. Strain through a fine sieve and stir in the chopped walnuts. Cool to room temperature. These can be made several days ahead if refrigerated, but bring back to room temperature before serving.

PREPARATION FOR THE CHEESECAKES

1 Preheat oven to 350°.

2 Thoroughly butter 12 4-ounce utility cups or ovenproof ceramic ramekins. Line the bottoms with parchment paper, butter the paper, and coat the interiors with sugar, shaking out the excess.

3 In the bowl of an electric mixer fitted with a paddle attachment, combine the cream cheese, blue cheese, and sugar and beat until smooth. Add the sour cream and beat until combined. Scrape the bowl with a rubber spatula. Add the eggs, beating until just combined, scraping down the sides of the bowl once or twice.

4 Divide the batter into the prepared molds. Form a water bath by placing the molds into a shallow baking pan and filling with enough water to reach halfway up the sides of the molds.

5 Place on the bottom oven shelf and bake for approximately 40 minutes at a minimum, reversing the pan halfway through the baking process. When done, the cheesecakes will be lightly browned, set around the sides, and just set in the center. Remove from the water bath and cool completely. Chill for several hours before serving. The cakes can be made up to 3 days in advance and kept covered in the refrigerator.

6 When ready to serve, pass the molds over an open flame, place them in a 350° oven for 1 minute, or dip them into very hot water to loosen the cakes. Further loosen the sides with a paring knife run around the edge of the mold and turn each cake out into the palm of your hand (or onto a flat metal spatula); flip the cake so it is right side up and center on an individual dessert plate. Spoon walnuts in rosemary honey around each cheesecake bit and on top as well.

Baker's Note: If you can't find Maytag blue cheese in your local market, a young Gorgonzola or Roquefort is an excellent substitute. If you don't have 4-ounce ramekins or utility cups to bake these in, you can cut disposable muffin tins into individual cups.

Serving Suggestions: I usually embellish this dessert with a garnish of red wine–poached fruits (page 157). It's an extra step, but one well worth taking, I think. An alternative plating consists of the basic cheesecake and honeyed nuts plus a small salad of oranges and peppery watercress dressed with a bit of walnut vinaigrette and accompanied by a couple of walnut shortbread cookies (page 302).

We All Scream for Ice Cream (& Other Frozen Desserts)

Not-Just-Plain-Vanilla Ice Cream

Burnt Orange Caramel Ice Cream

Bourbon Molasses Ice Cream

Cream Cheese Blackberry Swirl Ice Cream

Peanut Butter Ice Cream

Ruby Port Ice Cream

Mocha Velvet Ice Cream

Beat-the-Heat Frozen Mocha Velvet

Lemon Chiffon Ice Cream

Peppermint Stick Ice Cream

Peanut Butter Blondie & Milk Chocolate Malt
  Ice Cream Cake

Huguenot Parfait Sundae

Strawberry Sorbet

Sugar Syrup

Purple Plum Rum Sorbet

Summer Blueberry Sorbet

Orange Coconut Sorbet

Café du Monde Chicory Coffee Granita

Bittersweet Chocolate Sherbet

Icy-Cold Milk Sherbet

Eggnog Snow Cream

Frozen Sourwood Honey Parfait

Simply put, I love ice cream. My long-term ice cream habit was nurtured as a child—our freezer always contained at least two kinds of Breyer's. As a pastry chef I have enjoyed creating a never-ending parade of ice cream flavors, and, truth be known, I'd love to own a drive-up frozen dessert emporium.

Making ice cream at home allows you to control the quality of all the ingredients. Many commercial products include gums, stabilizers, preservatives, and artificial flavors. In my opinion, they also often contain too much sugar. Ice cream—making is an easy process, not at all time consuming, and should be conveniently done in advance. In this chapter I have given you enough recipes for a grand ice cream social (which by the way is a wonderful idea for a Sunday afternoon party). Coming up with your own variations by means of ingredient substitutions and mix-in additions is encouraged. There are several general points that should be noted.

- Always use a heavy-bottomed nonreactive saucepan to make ice cream bases.
- Ice cream bases should be constantly stirred and cooked over low heat until the mixture thickens and coats a spoon. This means that if you dip the bowl of a spoon in the base, pull it out, and draw your finger down the back of it, a clean line will remain.
- Always strain ice cream bases through a fine-mesh strainer.
- Always chill bases thoroughly before freezing. I like to quick chill them over an ice bath and then allow them to sit overnight refrigerated before actually churning them. This allows the flavors to mellow. A very cold base will also freeze more quickly, incorporate less air, and result in a denser ice cream.
- Electric ice cream makers with self-contained freezer mechanisms produce the smoothest ice cream but are also generally the most expensive appliances. I have also had excellent results with old-fashioned White Mountain rock salt and wooden tub machines and with simple insert canister—style models (both hand-turned and electric).
- I freeze ice cream to a frozen custard—like, soft-serve consistency. These bases are high in butterfat, and if overchurned, the butter will separate and turn the base unpleasantly grainy.

- Allowing the ice cream to ripen overnight will improve the flavor. Pack the churned ice cream into storage containers and freeze it overnight before serving.
- If I'm adding a swirl or mix-in to a base, I layer it with the churned ice cream in the storage container and then give the ice cream a quick fold or two with a rubber spatula. This ensures an even distribution of added ingredients.
- I like the mouth feel of rich, premium-style ice creams. You can lighten the recipes by altering the ratio of cream to half-and-half, substituting milk, or cutting back the quantity of egg yolks—but the resulting texture will then be different.
- Sugar and alcohol both inhibit the freezing process, and it's important to reach the proper balance with both of these ingredients. The type of sweetening you use (honey or maple syrup, for example, as opposed to sugar) can affect both the taste and texture. The addition of a small quantity of a complementary alcohol boosts flavor and also prevents the ice cream from freezing too hard.
- As for most desserts, you should add just a bit of salt to the base—it will help accentuate the other flavors and bring them all into alignment.

Sorbets, granitas, and sherbets fall into another category of frozen desserts. These refreshing ices are most often fruit-based but can also be flavored with herbal infusions, chocolate, vanilla bean, and coffee. A *sorbet* is a smooth frozen ice. *Granita* is granular in consistency and is still-frozen as opposed to being churned. *Sherbets* are sorbets that are enriched with a bit of dairy product. Occasionally you will encounter sorbets and sherbets that also incorporate egg whites. I am not an advocate of this addition and never use it in my recipes.

The best fruit sorbets and granitas are intensely flavored and based on sweet, ripe fruit. While the recipes below are accurate, it is extremely important to season each batch of sorbet or granita to taste due to the variability of fruit. A final adjustment of sugar and or acid is almost always necessary. A few other tips for successful sorbets and granitas include the following:

- As I do for ice creams, I always strain my sorbet and granita bases through a fine sieve.
- If using fruits that have a tendency to oxidize, such as peaches, pears, or apples, I always quick cook them in a nonreactive saucepan with a minimum

of liquid, a bit of complementary citrus juice, and a 500 mg. vitamin C tab. This will prevent the fruit from browning.

- Many fruits are best left uncooked when utilized for sorbets. These include melons, strawberries, raspberries, blackberries, mango, and pineapple. I do cook blueberries to facilitate the puréeing and straining process, and also all stone fruits (plums, peaches, apricots, etc.), grapes, and rhubarb.

- If the flavor balance or texture seems off to you after freezing a sherbet, sorbet, or granita, you can allow the base to melt down, correct the flavoring, and refreeze it. Remember that the addition of a bit more acid or sugar syrup can make the fruit flavor seem more intense. Mixes will taste a bit less sweet when fully frozen, so season accordingly. Adding more sugar syrup or alcohol will remedy an icy sorbet. Always give the mix a final taste and readjust the seasoning if necessary.

Not-Just-Plain-Vanilla Ice Cream

MAKES 2 QUARTS

I find it ironic that the term vanilla has come to mean homogenous or "cookie cutter," middle of the road. Highly aromatic vanilla beans produce a long-lasting, complex flavor finish much like that of an exceptional wine. This versatile ice cream can provide a complementary background flavor for other desserts, but is delicious enough to stand on its own.

INGREDIENTS

3½ cups half-and-half
3 cups cream
2 vanilla beans
14 egg yolks
1½ cups sugar
¼ teaspoon kosher salt

PREPARATION

1 Place the half-and-half and cream in a nonreactive saucepan. Slit each vanilla bean in half and scrape the seeds into the egg yolk–sugar mixture (see step 2).

Add the pods to the half-and-half and cream and bring this mixture to just under a boil over medium heat.

2　Combine the egg yolks with the sugar, salt, and vanilla seeds in a mixing bowl. Slowly whisk in a portion of the hot cream to temper the yolks. Transfer this base back into the saucepan and cook, stirring, until the mixture thickens and coats the back of a spoon. Remove from the heat. Strain the mixture through a fine-mesh strainer.

3　Chill thoroughly and freeze in an ice cream machine according to the manufacturer's directions.

Baker's Note: As is, this ice cream delivers a pure vanilla flavor. If you wish, you can vary the recipe by adding ½ cup of any liquor—bourbon, brandy, or dark rum would all be possibilities. Another variation is to add a tablespoon of ground cinnamon or cardamom to the basic vanilla mix. Any spice addition should be whisked into the egg yolks along with the sugar and vanilla seeds to avoid "clumping."

Serving Suggestions: There are few simple cake- or pastry-based desserts that wouldn't benefit from a scoop of this ice cream. I also like to serve scoops of it in beautiful dessert glasses, topped with a fruit sauce or compote, and then pass cookies on the side. Some possible combinations would be strawberry crush (page 49) and lemonade sugar cookies (page 298), bourbon poached peaches (page 149) and pecan shortbreads (page 302), and butterscotch baked bananas (page 154) and peanut butter blondies (page 274) baked in square pan–format and cut into squares.

Burnt Orange Caramel Ice Cream

MAKES ABOUT 2 QUARTS

Caramel is a truly seductive flavor that hardly needs to be embellished. Having said that, I do believe that adding a tangy orange nuance to the smoky dark sugar base makes for a spectacular combination. For the truly adventurous, try adding some black pepper to the mix.

INGREDIENTS

    2½ cups fresh-squeezed orange juice

    3 cups cream

    1 cup half-and-half

    1¼ cups sugar for caramelizing

    9 egg yolks

    ¼ cup + 2 teaspoons sugar

    ¼ teaspoon kosher salt

    2 teaspoons vanilla

    2 teaspoons freshly ground black pepper (optional)

PREPARATION

1 In a nonreactive saucepan, reduce the orange juice by half (to 1¼ cups). Keep hot and reserve.

2 In a large nonreactive saucepot, heat the cream and half-and-half to just under a boil. While the cream is heating, in a separate heavy-bottomed pot, caramelize the sugar to a deep amber color. Carefully add the reserved hot orange juice to stop the caramelization. Slowly add the hot cream mixture and stir over low heat till the caramel is dissolved.

3 Whisk the egg yolks together with the sugar and salt. Add the black pepper if using. Temper the egg yolks with some of the caramel cream. Pour the mixture back into the saucepot and cook, stirring over low heat, until the mixture thickens and coats the back of a spoon. Add the vanilla.

4 Strain the mixture through a fine sieve. Chill over an ice bath and freeze in an ice cream machine according to the manufacturer's directions.

Baker's Note: As a variation, you can substitute pineapple juice for the orange juice in this recipe.

Serving Suggestions: If you already have the grill fired up for dinner, consider serving a scoop of this over a thick round of rum butter–basted and grilled pineapple. This would also top a slice of the browned butter date nut tart (page 101) quite nicely.

Bourbon Molasses Ice Cream

MAKES 2 QUARTS

The distinctive burnt sugar taste of molasses adds a wallop of flavor to this ice cream with a Southern profile. Great on its own, it really shines as a component of many other desserts as well, making it very versatile.

INGREDIENTS

3¾ cups half-and-half

3 cups cream

14 egg yolks

½ cup sugar

¾ cup + 2 tablespoons molasses

¼ teaspoon kosher salt

¼ cup + 3 tablespoons bourbon

1 teaspoon vanilla

PREPARATION

1 In a nonreactive saucepan, bring the half-and-half and cream to just under a boil over medium heat.

2 Combine the egg yolks, sugar, molasses, and salt in a mixing bowl and whisk to combine. Slowly whisk in a portion of the hot cream mixture to temper the egg yolks. Transfer this base back into the saucepan and cook, stirring, until the mixture thickens and coats the back of a spoon. Remove from heat.

3 Add the bourbon and the vanilla and strain the mixture through a fine-mesh strainer. Chill thoroughly and freeze in an ice cream machine according to the manufacturer's directions.

Baker's Note: You can use a more refined light molasses or a richer, slightly more pronounced dark molasses in this recipe. Blackstrap molasses, however, has too strong a flavor and would be overpowering. I have also substituted sorghum syrup for the molasses. Underutilized as a sweetening agent, this grain based–syrup can sometimes be found at farmers' markets or specialty stores (or see the sources listing at the end of the book).

Serving Suggestions: This would be great topped with butterscotch baked bananas (page 154) or bourbon poached peaches (page 149). You can also serve it with banana upside down cakes (page 224), lemon pecan tart (page 95), or bourbon peach cobbler (page 127).

Cream Cheese Blackberry Swirl Ice Cream

MAKES ABOUT 2 QUARTS

I love the addition of swirls and ripples as flavor boosters in frozen desserts. This ice cream tastes like a chilled fruit-accented cheesccake. Rich, creamy, and delectable, it is a wonderful summertime treat.

INGREDIENTS FOR THE SWIRL

3 cups fresh blackberries (or unsweetened frozen berries)
¼ cup corn syrup
3 tablespoons crème de cassis

INGREDIENTS FOR THE ICE CREAM

2¾ cups half-and-half
¾ cup cream
12 ounces cream cheese, softened
1⅛ cups sugar
11 egg yolks
¼ teaspoon kosher salt
1 teaspoon vanilla
¼ cup crème de cassis

PREPARATION FOR THE SWIRL
Combine the ingredients in a medium-sized nonreactive saucepan and cook, stirring, over low heat until the berries soften and give off their juices. Purée the mixture and strain through a fine-mesh strainer to remove the seeds. Chill over an ice bath and reserve. This can be done up to 3 days in advance.

PREPARATION FOR THE ICE CREAM
1 Combine the half-and-half and cream in a nonreactive saucepan and heat to just under a boil.

2   While the cream is heating, combine the cream cheese and sugar in a stainless bowl (or mixer bowl) and cream until well blended. Add the egg yolks in 3 additions, blending well after each addition. Stop and scrape the bowl several times. Blend in the salt and vanilla.

3   Add a portion of the hot cream mixture to the cream cheese base and whisk in. Gradually whisk in the remaining cream. Transfer the mixture back to the saucepan and cook over low heat, stirring, until the mixture thickens slightly and coats the back of a spoon. Strain through a fine-mesh strainer and add the cassis. Chill thoroughly before freezing in an ice cream machine following the manufacturer's directions.

4   To mix in the blackberry swirl, alternate layers of the reserved swirl with the frozen ice cream in a freezer container. After every few inches, gently take a spatula and give the newly layered section a quick fold or two to lightly mix in the swirl—you want the swirl to remain separate and distinct so do not overmix!

Baker's Note: You can substitute strawberries, raspberries, or blueberries for the blackberries in the swirl. Depending on your yield (which depends on the berries and how efficient you are at straining the purée), you may have excess swirl left over. The balance of ice cream to swirl should be a bit of swirl in every bite of ice cream. If you have extra, you can always use it as a plating sauce or enjoy it in a fruit smoothie.

Serving Suggestions: This is a great fruit pie ice cream—try it with blueberry blackberry pie (page 76). It's also deluxe served with a big ol' bowl of plump, sweet-tart fresh berries or on top of sautéed summer berries (page 146).

Peanut Butter Ice Cream

MAKES 2 QUARTS

Actually a legume, peanuts go by the old-timey name of goober peas in some parts of the country. This amazingly rich concoction should be served in small portions. Goober ice cream, anyone?

INGREDIENTS
   3¾ cups half-and-half
   3 cups cream

⅓ cup + 1 tablespoon peanut butter (see Baker's Note)

14 egg yolks

1½ cups sugar

¼ teaspoon kosher salt

¼ cup dark rum

1½ teaspoons vanilla

PREPARATION

1 In a large nonreactive saucepan, bring the half-and-half and cream to just under a boil over medium heat. Add the peanut butter and whisk until dissolved.

2 In a mixing bowl, combine the egg yolks, sugar, and salt and whisk to blend. Slowly whisk in a portion of the hot cream mixture to temper the egg yolks. Transfer this base back into the saucepan and cook, stirring, until the mixture thickens and coats the back of a spoon. Remove from heat.

3 Add the rum and vanilla and strain the mixture through a fine-mesh strainer. Chill thoroughly and freeze in an ice cream machine according to the manufacturer's directions.

Baker's Note: I recommend using creamy-style commercial peanut butter, but since you have to strain the ice cream base, go ahead and use chunky peanut butter if that's what you normally keep in the pantry. Do be careful to not overchurn this ice cream. The addition of peanut butter increases the fat content, and it is essential to allow the base to thicken only to the thickness of soft-serve—if you take it too far, it will taste unpleasantly "buttery."

Serving Suggestions: The serving possibilities for this ice cream are lots of fun: you can drizzle it with Concord grape syrup (page 50) or cocoa fudge sauce (page 37), top it with butterscotch baked bananas (page 154) and peanut praline (page 56), and perhaps finish it off with whipped cream or marshmallow fluff (page 68). I also like this on top of chocolate chip cookie tarts (page 102).

Ruby Port Ice Cream

MAKES ABOUT 2 QUARTS

Imagine a chilly winter evening, sitting beside a crackling fire and having—a bowl of ice cream? Frozen desserts in the wintertime might seem a bit incongruous, but the flavor of this one really is suited for cooler weather. One might not associate port with American desserts, but it did figure into early American cooking of the 1800s via the British.

INGREDIENTS

    2 cups half-and-half
    2 cups cream
    10 egg yolks
    ¾ cup sugar
    ¼ teaspoon kosher salt
    1 teaspoon vanilla
    1 cup ruby port

PREPARATION

1 Combine the half-and-half and cream in a nonreactive saucepan and bring to just under a boil over medium heat.
2 Combine the egg yolks, sugar, and salt in a mixing bowl. Whisk a portion of the hot cream into the yolks to temper. Transfer this mixture back to the saucepan and cook, stirring, over medium low heat until the mixture thickens and coats the back of a spoon. Remove from heat.
3 Strain through a fine-mesh strainer. Stir in the vanilla and port. Chill thoroughly before freezing in an ice cream machine according to the manufacturer's directions.

Baker's Note: For textural variation, I sometimes fold sun-dried cherries or cranberries that have been plumped overnight in a light port-flavored sugar syrup into the churned ice cream.

Serving Suggestions: This is a fabulous ice cream to serve over winter fruits poached in red wine syrup (page 157) or to top with cocoa fudge sauce (page 37) that has been flavored with a bit of additional port. It would also go well with the apple rhubarb cardamom crumb pie (page 78).

Mocha Velvet Ice Cream

MAKES ABOUT 2 QUARTS

Coffee is one of my favorite tastes to pair with chocolate. This mocha ice cream is everything that I look for in a frozen dessert—it's ultracreamy, intensely flavored, and should be savored in small doses. If you're a fan of soft-serve ice creams, try it shortly after it's been churned when it's at its most "velvety."

INGREDIENTS

    4½ ounces unsweetened chocolate, chopped

    4½ ounces semisweet chocolate, chopped

    2⅛ cups half-and-half

    2⅛ cups cream

    8 egg yolks

    1⅛ cups sugar

    ¼ teaspoon kosher salt

    1⅛ cups hot brewed coffee

    3 tablespoons instant coffee

    ½ tablespoon vanilla

    ¼ cup coffee liqueur

PREPARATION

1 Place both kinds of chopped chocolate in the top of a double boiler and melt over low heat. Reserve.

2 Combine the half-and-half with the cream in a nonreactive saucepot and bring to just under a boil. While the cream is heating, combine the egg yolks, sugar, and salt in a stainless bowl and whisk together. Whisk in the melted chocolate. Dissolve the instant coffee in the hot brewed coffee and whisk this into the egg yolk base. Slowly and gradually whisk in the hot cream and half-and-half.

3 Transfer the mixture back into the saucepot and cook over medium low heat, stirring constantly, until the mixture thickens and coats the back of a spoon. Remove from heat and strain through a fine-mesh sieve. Add the vanilla and coffee liqueur and chill over an ice bath. Freeze in an ice cream machine according to the manufacturer's directions.

Baker's Note: For the smoothest texture when working with chocolate-flavored ice creams, melt the chocolate in the top of a double boiler and whisk it into the egg yolk–sugar base. By doing this prior to adding any liquid, you avoid ending up with "chocolate chip ice cream."

Serving Suggestions: This is an integral component of frozen mocha velvet (see the following recipe). You can also combine mocha brownie thins (page 309) with this ice cream to make delicious ice cream sandwiches. A small scoop of this would also be great with milk chocolate chip poundcake (page 215).

Beat-the-Heat Frozen Mocha Velvet

MAKES 1 GENEROUS SHAKE

I came up with this adult milk shake for Magnolia Grill after two weeks of steamy, 95°+ weather one July. We wanted to showcase a frozen dessert that would "beat the heat," which this one certainly does—at least temporarily. The inspiration for it came from Serendipity, a combo boutique and dessert palace that I used to frequent as a teenager. The synthesis of shopping and their famous frozen hot chocolate continues to make this Upper East Side storefront a hotspot.

INGREDIENTS

2 big scoops mocha velvet ice cream (see the preceding recipe)
1 scant cup ice cubes
½ cup milk
3 tablespoons coffee syrup (page 52)
2 tablespoons brandy
2 tablespoons Kahlua or other coffee liqueur
whipped cream for topping (optional—but why not?)

PREPARATION

1 Place all the ingredients in a blender and blend to mix—you may have to stop the machine and redistribute the ingredients once or twice to get it to blend evenly. The finished product should be thick and creamy with no visible chunks of ice.

2 Pour into a frosted glass, top with whipped cream (if desired), and serve with a spoon and a straw.

Baker's Note: This recipe can easily be doubled to serve two. If you don't want to make your own ice cream, substituting premium store-bought ice cream is perfectly acceptable—perhaps a scoop of coffee and a scoop of chocolate?

Serving Suggestion: At the Grill we always top this with a big dollop of whipped cream and serve it in a hurricane glass placed on a doilied plate with 2 mocha brownie thins (page 309).

Lemon Chiffon Ice Cream

MAKES 2 QUARTS

Fluffy chiffon pies bring to mind images of big party dresses and bouffant hairdos. Especially popular during the 1940s and 1950s, these unbaked refrigerator pies were based on generous poufs of beaten sugared egg whites and were flavored in any number of ways. This recipe takes the idea of a chiffon-style dessert and applies it to a refreshing, rich but airy ice cream.

INGREDIENTS
   1⅞ cups half-and-half
   1½ cups cream
   grated zest of 2 lemons
   7 egg yolks
   1¼ cups + 2 tablespoons sugar, divided
   ¼ teaspoon kosher salt
   ½ cup lemon juice, divided
   1½ tablespoons vodka
   7 egg whites
   2 tablespoons water

PREPARATION
1 In a nonreactive saucepan, bring the half-and-half, cream, and lemon zest to just under a boil over medium heat.
2 Combine the egg yolks with ½ cup + 2 tablespoons of the sugar and the salt in a mixing bowl. Slowly whisk in a portion of the hot cream mixture to temper the egg yolks. Transfer this base back into the saucepan and cook, stirring, until the mixture thickens and coats the back of a spoon. Remove from heat.

3 Add ¼ cup of the lemon juice and the vodka. Strain through a fine-mesh strainer.

4 Chill thoroughly and freeze in an ice cream machine, according to the manufacturer's directions, to soft-serve consistency.

5 While the ice cream is churning, combine the remaining ¾ cup of sugar, the remaining ¼ cup of lemon juice, and the 2 tablespoons of water in a small saucepan. Over medium heat dissolve the sugar and cook until the mixture registers 230° on a candy thermometer. While the syrup is cooking, beat the egg whites in the bowl of a mixer till frothy. Turn the mixer speed to low and add the hot syrup to the egg whites in a thin stream, continuing to beat constantly. Beat until the mixture is completely cool.

6 Place the just-churned ice cream in a mixing bowl and quickly but thoroughly fold in half of the beaten egg whites. Fold in the remaining whites and transfer the ice cream to a freezer container. Freeze overnight

Baker's Note: The heat of the added sugar syrup should bring the egg whites to 160°, the temperature at which salmonella is killed. I always use properly stored farm-fresh eggs, but if you are at all concerned with the possibility of food-born infection, you can try seeking out pasteurized egg whites or you can substitute meringue powder (see the Baker's Catalogue in the sources listing at the end of the book).

Serving Suggestions: For an unusual pairing, try this ice cream layered with scoops of bittersweet chocolate sherbet (page 286) or drizzled with cocoa fudge sauce (page 37). You can also use it to top pastry-based desserts such as blueberry blackberry pie (page 76) or rustic raspberry tart (page 113). A straight-up bowl of fresh or sautéed summer berries (page 146) topped with a generous scoop of lemon chiffon ice cream is perhaps the simplest and possibly the best serving suggestion.

Peppermint Stick Ice Cream

MAKES A GENEROUS 2 QUARTS

The combination of ice cream and candy brings out the kid in all of us. While this ice cream is totally delicious in flavor, the thing I like most about it is its slightly kitschy pink color. The fact that it combines really well with anything chocolate is an extra bonus.

INGREDIENTS

3¾ cups half-and-half

3 cups cream

8 ounces finely chopped peppermint sticks or Starlight mint candies, divided

14 egg yolks

1⅓ cups sugar

¼ teaspoon kosher salt

¼ teaspoon pure peppermint extract

¼ cup vodka

PREPARATION

1 Place the half-and-half, cream, and 2 ounces of the chopped peppermint candies in a nonreactive saucepan. Bring this mixture to just under a boil over medium heat, stirring occasionally to prevent the candy from sticking to the bottom of the pot.

2 Combine the egg yolks with the sugar and salt in a mixing bowl. Slowly whisk in a portion of the hot cream to temper the yolks. Transfer this base back into the saucepan and cook, stirring, until the mixture thickens and coats the back of a spoon. Remove from heat. Strain through a fine-mesh strainer. Add the peppermint extract and vodka.

3 Chill thoroughly and freeze in an ice cream machine according to the manufacturer's directions. When the ice cream is frozen, layer it in a storage container with the remaining 6 ounces of finely chopped peppermints. Give the ice cream a fold or two with a spatula to make sure the candies are well distributed. Freeze overnight before serving.

Baker's Note: The best way to chop the peppermints is to place the candy in a heavy-duty zip-lock bag and smash it with a meat pounder or a rolling pin.

Serving Suggestions: Serve with raised cocoa waffles (page 343), topping with cocoa fudge sauce (page 37). This ice cream also makes great profiteroles using the cream puff shell recipe outlined in banana pudding cream puffs (page 168). Generously top with the same cocoa fudge sauce. To make things simpler, serve a peppermint stick ice cream sundae with, yes, that same cocoa fudge sauce and whipped cream.

Peanut Butter Blondie & Milk Chocolate Malt Ice Cream Cake

MAKES 12 TO 14 PORTIONS (BASED ON 2 QUARTS OF ICE CREAM)

During my youth, all family birthdays were celebrated with a festive Carvel ice cream cake. With this particular dessert, you can have your "cake" and your ice cream too. The best part is that it can be made well in advance and it will please children of all ages.

INGREDIENTS FOR THE BLONDIES

6 tablespoons (3 ounces) butter, at room temperature

7 tablespoons peanut butter (chunky or smooth, *not* natural-style)

1½ cups brown sugar

1 egg + 1 egg yolk

2 teaspoons vanilla

1½ cups flour

¾ teaspoon baking powder

¼ + ⅛ teaspoon baking soda

¼ teaspoon kosher salt

INGREDIENTS FOR THE ICE CREAM

8 ounces milk chocolate, finely chopped

2 cups cream

2 cups half-and-half

½ cup malted milk powder (preferably Horlick's)

8 egg yolks

3 tablespoons sugar

¼ teaspoon kosher salt

¼ cup crème de cacao

PREPARATION FOR THE BLONDIES

1 Preheat oven to 350°. Butter a 10-inch springform pan and line the bottom and sides with parchment paper. Lightly butter the bottom parchment round.

2 Using a mixer with a paddle attachment, cream the butter, peanut butter, and brown sugar until well combined. Add the egg, egg yolk, and vanilla and mix

to blend. Add the flour, baking powder, baking soda, and salt and mix to combine, scraping the bowl once or twice.

3 With a small offset spatula, evenly spread the batter into the prepared pan.

4 Bake at 350° for approximately 35 minutes, until the blondie is set and golden. It will test moist but shouldn't be raw. Remove from oven and cool in the pan.

PREPARATION FOR THE ICE CREAM

1 In the top of a double boiler, melt the milk chocolate over very low heat, stirring often. Use caution to see that the water is at a bare simmer—it is very easy to scorch milk chocolate. As the chocolate is melting, bring the cream and half-and-half to just under a boil in a nonreactive saucepot. Dissolve the malted milk powder in the hot liquid and reserve on very low heat.

2 Combine the egg yolks, sugar, and salt in a stainless bowl. Whisk the melted milk chocolate into the egg yolk mixture. Gradually whisk in the hot cream mixture. Return the custard to the stove and cook over low heat, stirring constantly, until the mixture thickens enough to coat the back of a spoon. Remove from heat and add the crème de cacao.

3 Strain the mixture through a fine-mesh strainer and chill over an ice bath. Freeze in an ice cream machine according to the manufacturer's directions. If not assembling the cake right away, place the frozen ice cream in the freezer. If the ice cream is made more than a few hours ahead of time, you may have to soften it slightly before filling the blondie shell.

ASSEMBLY AND SERVICE

1 Place the ice cream on top of the cooled peanut butter blondie base, using an offset spatula to smooth the top. Place back in the freezer and freeze for at least 4 to 5 hours or for up to 2 weeks before serving. If you're freezing the cake for longer than 4 to 5 hours, cover the surface with a round of parchment paper and wrap the top with plastic film.

2 To remove for serving, briefly pass the bottom of the springform pan over a gas burner or preheated electric range burner for a second or two. Remove the sides of the springform pan as well as the parchment paper lining the sides and (if applicable) top. With a long, thin-bladed slicing knife, loosen the blondie base from the parchment lined bottom. The cake should release easily. Transfer the cake to a service platter.

3 I like to leave the top of this cake plain and then plate individual portions with zigzags of both cocoa fudge sauce (page 37) and creamy peanut butter and honey sauce (page 39). If you wish, you can also pipe or spread a layer of whipped cream over the top surface of the cake just before serving.

4 To slice this cake use a heated heavy, long-bladed knife, making sure to clean the blade and reheat the knife between each cut.

Baker's Note: This cake is a perfect example of how you can simplify a recipe to suit your needs. While the homemade milk chocolate malt ice cream is superb, you could substitute a premium brand store-bought ice cream rather than make your own. Using the two sauces as a garnish is ideal; however, making only one will not significantly detract from the dish—in fact using a good store-bought chocolate sauce is also an option. You can also bake the peanut butter blondies in a 9-inch square pan and simply serve blondie squares with scoops of ice cream, drizzled with sauce.

Serving Suggestions: If you wanted to garnish this dessert to the max you can also prepare some peanut praline—follow the recipe for pecan praline (page 56), substituting lightly salted peanuts for the pecans—to scatter on the plate. When coarsely chopped, it makes a wonderful, crunchy textural contrast to the cake. My son, however, suggests halved chocolate-coated malt ball candies.

Huguenot Parfait Sundae

SERVES 8, WITH LEFTOVER CRUMBLES FOR THE COOK

This dessert is loosely based on a very light apple and nut cake that is often thought to have a Charleston, South Carolina, pedigree. In his fascinating book, *Hoppin' John's Low Country Cooking*, John Martin Taylor actually traces the origins of so-called Huguenot torte to the Ozarks and claims it is not even remotely Huguenot (or a torte, for that matter). In any event, this variation comes from Michelle Gilland Laskey, my first baking assistant at Magnolia Grill. It was her mother's recipe, and rather than in a cake, it results in chewy, crunchy fruit nut crumbles that are fabulous layered with ice cream.

INGREDIENTS FOR THE CRUMBLES

  1½ cups sugar

  4 tablespoons flour

  2½ tablespoons baking powder

  ¼ teaspoon kosher salt

  1 cup coarsely chopped pecan pieces

  1½ cups peeled, small-diced Granny Smith apples

  2 eggs, beaten

ADDITIONAL INGREDIENTS FOR THE SUNDAE

  1 recipe not-just-plain-vanilla ice cream (page 261), made with brandy

  ½ cup ruby port

PREPARATION

1 Preheat oven to 350°. If you own a nonstick silpat sheet, line a baking pan
   with it—it will make cleanup much easier! If not, use an unlined, unbuttered,
   shallow-rimmed baking sheet—do not use parchment paper.

2 In a medium-sized bowl, combine the sugar, flour, baking powder, salt, and
   pecans. Mix to blend. Add the apples and eggs. Mix until evenly moistened
   and turn out onto the baking sheet. Spread to a medium thickness with an
   offset spatula.

3 Bake until the mixture starts to take on an even brown color. It will spread
   significantly and bubble—this is normal. With a lightly oiled spatula or wooden
   spoon, stir to break up the top crust—it will be quite moist underneath.
   Return the baking sheet to the oven. Repeat this procedure several times: the
   object is to gradually dry out the mixture, at which point "crumbles" will begin
   to form. This process takes approximately 35 to 45 minutes. If the crumbles
   seem to be browning too quickly, turn the oven down to 325°. Remove from
   oven when evenly deep golden brown and baked through. They will harden
   somewhat as they cool. If you are using an unlined baking sheet, scrape up
   the crumbles to loosen them from the pan while they are still warm. If you
   are using a silpat-lined pan, there's no need to do this other than to perhaps
   break up any large chunks. Cool and store airtight. The crumbles can be made
   up to 3 days in advance.

ASSEMBLY

Place a layer of crumbles in a parfait or sundae glass. Top with a scoop of
ice cream and drizzle with ½ tablespoon of ruby port. Repeat layering with

crumbles, ice cream, and port. Finish with a few additional crumbles. Serve immediately.

Baker's Note: You can substitute walnuts for the pecans and pears for the apples in this recipe. If you used an unlined baking sheet to bake these, and the sheet has turned into a crusty mess, just submerge it in very hot water and give it a long soak. If it still doesn't come clean, you can fill it with a film of water and place it in a 350° oven for about 5 minutes to loosen any residue. (But, again, if you use a silpat sheet, cleanup is a snap.)

Serving Suggestions: If you are a port lover, you can substitute ruby port ice cream (page 268) for the brandy vanilla. If you want to break out of the parfait glass mold, you can also place a scoop of crumble-topped ice cream on top of a puddle of applesauce (page 47) and drizzle the whole plate with cider caramel (page 46).

Strawberry Sorbet

MAKES 2 QUARTS

Strawberry sorbet should reflect the essence of the fruit. For all intents and purposes, it should taste like a giant frozen berry. If you're in an area where strawberries are grown, please try to prepare this recipe with locally produced berries at their seasonal peak.

INGREDIENTS

    8 cups hulled, thick sliced strawberries
    ⅛ teaspoon kosher salt
    1 tablespoon Grand Marnier
    1 tablespoon Kirsch
    1½ tablespoons orange juice
    1½ tablespoons lemon juice
    1 scant cup sugar syrup (page 281) or to taste

PREPARATION

1 Purée the berries until smooth. This can be done in a food processor, in a blender, or with a wand-style handheld blender (see Baker's Note). Strain the

purée through a fine-mesh strainer and discard the seeds. You should have about 5 to 6 cups of strained strawberry purée.

2 Combine the purée, salt, Grand Marnier, Kirsch, orange juice, and lemon juice. Add almost all of the sugar syrup and taste for seasoning. Depending on your fruit and your own personal taste, you may wish to add all of the sugar syrup and/or a bit more citrus juice.

3 Freeze in an ice cream maker according to the manufacturer's directions. Pack the frozen sorbet into a storage container, cover, and freeze several hours, overnight, or up to several days.

Baker's Note: I often rely on a wand-style handheld blender for puréeing fruit. It's compact enough to be stored in a drawer, inexpensive, and easy to clean.

Serving Suggestions: I would serve this topped with a perfect whole strawberry in a pretty dessert glass with cookies on the side. My Milanos (page 305), lemonade sugar cookies (page 298), or cornmeal vanilla bean shortbreads (page 300) would go well with this sorbet.

Another option would be to plate this with sautéed summer berries (page 146) and crème fraîche (page 67). Strawberry sorbet would also be delicious paired with bittersweet chocolate sherbet (page 286) or orange coconut sorbet (page 284).

A refreshing strawberry dreamsickle float can also be made by alternating scoops of this sorbet and not-just-plain-vanilla ice cream (page 261) and adding a bit of natural strawberry soda.

Sugar Syrup

I make sugar syrup in a 1:1 ratio, which means that for every cup of water I use 1 cup of sugar. It's something that I always keep around for sweetening sorbet mixes. It's also great for sweetening lemonade or iced tea or for moistening sponge cakes. To make sugar syrup, combine equal quantities of sugar and water (I usually use 3 cups of each) in a saucepan and bring to a boil, stirring occasionally. Simmer over medium heat until the sugar is completely dissolved. Cool, transfer to a clean container, and store in the refrigerator, where it will keep for months.

Purple Plum Rum Sorbet

MAKES ABOUT 1½ QUARTS

Originally I paired rum with plums because I liked the way it sounded phonetically and read on a menu. What started as a nonculinary decision resulted in a natural blending of flavors. I think cooking intensifies the flavor of plums, as does a hint of spice.

INGREDIENTS

2 pounds plums
½ cup orange juice
¼ teaspoon cinnamon
½ teaspoon ginger
¼ teaspoon cloves
¼ teaspoon kosher salt
1 cup sugar syrup (page 281) or to taste
½ teaspoon vanilla
3 tablespoons dark rum

PREPARATION

1 Pit and slice the plums and combine them in a medium-sized nonreactive saucepan with the orange juice, cinnamon, ginger, cloves, and salt. Add ½ cup of the sugar syrup and cook, stirring occasionally, until the plums have released their juices. Remove from heat.

2 Cool slightly and purée till the mixture is smooth. Strain the mixture through a fine-mesh strainer. Cool over an ice bath.

3 Add the rum and vanilla. Add the remaining ½ cup of sugar syrup and taste. Adjust seasonings if necessary.

4 Freeze in an ice cream machine according to the manufacturer's directions. Pack the frozen sorbet into a storage container and freeze for several hours, overnight, or up to several days.

Baker's Note: Try using small, dusky-skinned Italian prune plums if you can get them. Although they are green-fleshed when raw, if they are cooked the resulting purée is a gorgeous deep purple color. Castelmann or Santa Rosa plums also work well for this sorbet. Brandy can be substituted for the rum if you wish.

Serving Suggestions: Serve this in tandem with eggnog snow cream (page 288) or not-just-plain-vanilla ice cream (page 261). Almond butter cookies (page 308) or cornmeal vanilla bean shortbreads (page 300) would be an excellent accompaniment.

Summer Blueberry Sorbet

MAKES 2 QUARTS

In North Carolina we are fortunate to have bumper crops of fabulous blueberries virtually every summer. Turning this fruit into a refreshing sorbet is a nice change from the usual pies, cobblers, and muffins.

INGREDIENTS

4 pints blueberries
¼ teaspoon cloves
1 cup sugar syrup (page 281) or to taste
3 tablespoons crème de cassis
2 tablespoons lemon juice
1 tablespoon lime juice
¼ teaspoon kosher salt

PREPARATION

1 Place the blueberries and ground cloves in a large nonreactive saucepan with ½ cup of the sugar syrup. Over medium heat, bring the mixture to a boil, then turn the heat to low and simmer for about 15 minutes, until the berries have completely popped and released all their juices. Remove from heat and cool completely.

2 Purée the berry mixture until smooth. This can be done in a food processor or blender or with a wand-style handheld blender. You should have 5 to 6 cups of strained blueberry purée.

3 Add the cassis, lemon juice, lime juice, salt, and almost all of the remaining ½ cup of sugar syrup. Mix to blend and taste the mixture for seasoning. Depending on your fruit and your personal taste, you may wish to add more sugar syrup or a bit more citrus juice.

4 Freeze in an ice cream maker according to the manufacturer's directions.

Pack the frozen sorbet into a storage container, cover, and freeze several hours, overnight, or up to several days.

Baker's Note: Be careful working with blueberry purée—it stains like crazy! When seasoning sorbet mixes, always remember that, once frozen, the base will taste a bit less intense. You generally need a bit more sugar syrup than you might think to compensate for this. If the finished frozen base doesn't come out the way you want it to, most textural and flavor problems can be corrected. Just melt the base down and make adjustments. If the sorbet is too icy, try adding more sugar syrup or a bit of alcohol. If it doesn't taste sweet enough, add more sugar syrup. If it's too sweet, adjust with citrus juice or add more of the base purée.

Serving Suggestions: Serve as part of a red, white, and blue trio with strawberry sorbet (page 279) and orange coconut sorbet (directly below). A simple dish of sorbet garnished with a few fresh blueberries is also nice with a side of cornmeal vanilla bean shortbreads (page 300).

Orange Coconut Sorbet

MAKES 2 QUARTS

There are few recipes that are this easy to make and produce such delicious results. I must thank Anne Clark, co-author of the *Frog Commissary Cookbook*, for the inspiration. Sweetened coconut cream (I use the Coco López brand) can usually be found in the cocktail mixer aisle.

INGREDIENTS

2 15-ounce cans sweetened coconut cream
½ teaspoon vanilla
2 cups water
2 cups orange juice
¼ teaspoon salt
2 tablespoons dark rum

1   Make sure the coconut cream is smooth and emulsified before measuring. It has a tendency to separate. Blend it in a processor, with a handheld wand-style mixer, or with a whisk if necessary.

2   Combine all the ingredients and whisk till well blended. Strain through a fine-mesh strainer. Do not refrigerate before freezing—if chilled, the coconut cream will separate and solidify.

3   Freeze in an ice cream machine according to the manufacturer's directions. Pack into a storage container and freeze several hours, overnight, or for several days.

Baker's Note: I have had good results substituting lemon, lime, passion fruit, or pineapple juice for the orange juice in this recipe.

Serving Suggestions: This is wonderful with jumbo molasses spice cookies (page 315) served on the side. For a complexly flavored but light and refreshing dessert, serve this with golden pineapple soup (page 162).

Café du Monde Chicory Coffee Granita

MAKES 1½ QUARTS

This recipe transforms a steaming cup of New Orleans–style chicory coffee into a refreshing frozen granita. Beignets remain the perfect accompaniment.

INGREDIENTS

   3 cups hot brewed chicory coffee (see Baker's Note)
   ¾ cup sugar
   a few grains kosher salt
   ½ cup water
   2 tablespoons coffee liqueur

PREPARATION

1 Combine the hot coffee, sugar, and salt. Stir till the sugar dissolves. Add the water and coffee liqueur. Taste and adjust the sugar if necessary. Chill the mixture over an ice bath.

2 Transfer the mixture to a metal or plastic pan or bowl and place it in the freezer. It will start to freeze around the edges first. Once ice crystals start to form, stir the ice with a wooden spoon to break the crystals up. Continue to stir the ice every 15 minutes or so, until the entire mixture is granular and icy. This can be made several days ahead of time. Stir lightly before serving.

Baker's Note: Café du Monde brand coffee can be found in many supermarkets and specialty stores (also see the sources listing at the end of the book). You can substitute another strong brewed coffee or espresso, but you may have to adjust the sugar amounts to suit your taste.

Serving Suggestions: I like to layer this granita with lightly whipped, lightly sweetened cream and serve it with powdered sugar—coated black pepper beignets (page 347). It's also delicious paired with bittersweet chocolate sherbet (directly below).

Bittersweet Chocolate Sherbet

MAKES 1½ QUARTS

As a kid, I was always a big fan of Good Humor Fudgsicles, which probably explains why I love the intense, simple purity of this ice. It's a delicious finish to any meal, and if there's such a thing as a sinful yet almost guilt-free chocolate dessert, this is it.

INGREDIENTS

1¼ cups sugar

⅔ cup cocoa

¼ teaspoon kosher salt

1½ cups milk

3 cups water

¼ cup corn syrup

10 ounces bittersweet chocolate, finely chopped

PREPARATION

1 Place the sugar, cocoa, and salt in a medium-sized nonreactive saucepan and whisk to combine. Gradually whisk in the milk. Gradually whisk in the water. Add the corn syrup. Place over medium heat and bring to a simmer, whisking frequently. Allow to simmer for 2 minutes. Remove from heat and add the chopped chocolate. Whisk till the chocolate has melted.

2 Strain through a fine-mesh strainer. Chill over an ice bath, stirring occasionally, till completely cool. If you make this base ahead of time and refrigerate it, the chocolate in the mix will set up and you will have to reheat it just until the chocolate remelts before churning.

3 Freeze in an ice cream machine according to the manufacturer's directions.

Baker's Note: You may substitute semisweet chocolate for the bittersweet if you prefer.

Serving Suggestions: Serve in tandem with icy-cold milk sherbet (directly below), Café du Monde chicory coffee granita (page 285), or strawberry sorbet (page 279). It's also elegantly enticing all on its own, garnished with a few fresh raspberries and accompanied by a plate of my Milanos (page 305).

Icy-Cold Milk Sherbet

MAKES 2 QUARTS

This incredibly refreshing sherbet is different from, but no less delicious than, the richest vanilla ice cream. The absence of eggs and cream really allows the flavor of the vanilla beans to shine.

INGREDIENTS

   3 vanilla beans
   2 cups sugar
   8 cups milk
   ¼ teaspoon kosher salt
   ½ cup liqueur of your choice (I am rather partial to Frangelico)

1 Split the vanilla beans and scrape out the seeds. Reserve the pods. Combine the seeds with the sugar in a saucepan and stir to blend well. Gradually whisk in the milk. Add the reserved pods and the salt. Cook this mixture over medium heat, stirring, until the sugar has totally dissolved. Do not allow the milk to boil. Remove and strain the mixture through a fine-mesh strainer. Add the liqueur and chill over an ice bath.

2 Freeze in an ice cream machine according to the manufacturer's directions. Pack into a storage container, cover, and freeze for several hours, overnight, or up to several days.

Baker's Note: I like to use full-throttle whole milk for this recipe for the best taste and texture. If you would like to make a tangy, reduced-fat version of this sherbet, dissolve the vanilla, sugar, and salt in 4 cups of milk, take it off the heat, and add 4 cups of buttermilk.

Serving Suggestions: For a twist on a familiar theme, serve this sherbet with a side of your favorite chocolate chip cookies or a couple of mocha brownie thins (page 309). It's also wonderful served on top of a mix of fresh summer berries.

Eggnog Snow Cream

MAKES 1½ QUARTS

This is a re-creation of a childhood treat that I consider to be very special. Many people have vivid memories of running outside to gather buckets of freshly fallen fluffy snow. Swiftly transported to the kitchen, the flakes were enriched with cream, sweetened with sugar, and flavored with vanilla. A crowning drizzle of maple syrup can be considered a regional variation. Quickly served and eaten, their moment was as fleeting as the snow itself. This granita-like version is not weather dependent and has been flavored to resemble frozen eggnog.

INGREDIENTS

1 cup sugar
¾ teaspoon freshly grated nutmeg
¼ teaspoon kosher salt
2 cups cream

1 ½ cups water

1 teaspoon vanilla

2 tablespoons + 1 teaspoon brandy

2 tablespoons + 1 teaspoon dark rum

PREPARATION

1 Combine the sugar, nutmeg, and salt in a saucepan and stir to blend.
Gradually whisk in the cream and water over medium heat and, stirring
occasionally, cook the mixture until the sugar is completely dissolved.
Remove from heat and add the vanilla, brandy, and rum.

2 Cool the mixture over an ice bath. Once it is chilled, pour it into a shallow
pan and place it in the freezer. After about 20 to 30 minutes, the very edges of
the mixture should start to freeze. Break up the frozen granules, stir the mix,
and place the pan back in the freezer. Continue to stir the mixture every
20 minutes or so until it has frozen into medium-sized granular crystals.
Break up any large chunks. The mixture should resemble a granita or
Italian water ice. Pack it into freezer containers and freeze for up to 1 week.
Stir briefly before serving.

Baker's Note: You can omit the alcohol if you wish, but the ice will be a bit more
granular. Since the brandy and rum act as flavoring as well, you should punch
up the flavor of the ice if you omit them by adding the seeds of 1 vanilla bean
(mix the seeds with the sugar and nutmeg to prevent "clumping") or increase
the amount of vanilla extract to 1 tablespoon.

Serving Suggestions: You can serve this alongside an arranged citrus salad that has
been lightly sugared and brûléed or use it to accompany cranberry orange
compote (page 150). Pecan shortbreads (page 302), bourbon balls (page 318),
or hazelnut sandies (page 314) could also be served alongside the snow cream.

Frozen Sourwood Honey Parfait

MAKES 1 QUART

A rich parfait is softer and creamier than traditionally churned ice creams. This
still-frozen dessert is an excellent choice for those who don't own an ice cream machine but want to serve a refined, totally satisfying, chilled treat.

INGREDIENTS

1½ cups cream

6 egg yolks

¾ cup sourwood honey

⅓ cup orange juice

⅛ teaspoon kosher salt

PREPARATION

1 Whip the cream to medium soft peaks and reserve, chilled, until needed.

2 Place the egg yolks in the bowl of a mixer fitted with a whip and beat on medium low speed till thickened and light. Meanwhile, combine the honey and orange juice in a medium-sized saucepan and cook until the mixture reaches 235° on a candy thermometer. Be careful as this mixture has a tendency to bubble over if cooked at too high a heat. Once the syrup has reached the proper temperature, remove it from the heat, turn the mixer to low speed, and pour the hot syrup over the egg yolks, trying not to spatter it about the bowl. Add the salt.

3 Whip the egg yolk mixture at medium high speed until it is cool to the touch. It should become very pale and very thick. This should take 8 to 10 minutes.

4 Fold half of the egg yolk mixture into the reserved whipped cream and then fold that mixture back into the remaining egg yolks. Transfer the parfait mix to a freezer container and freeze overnight before serving. This can be made 3 days ahead of time.

Baker's Note: The type of honey you use can really affect the flavor of this parfait, although even a commercially mass-produced brand will give you terrific results. I love sourwood honey, but other varieties can be substituted. Orange blossom honey, acacia honey, and lavender honey are also highly recommended. Herbal honeys might be a viable option depending on how you plan to serve the parfait, but I would shy away from particularly strong, dark varietals such as chestnut or buckwheat honey.

This parfait can be scooped or frozen in molds. Collared individual soufflé dishes can be filled for a frozen soufflé presentation.

Serving Suggestions: This is outstanding served with cocoa fudge sauce (page 37) and my Milanos (page 305). I also like to serve a scoop of this parfait with winter fruits poached in red wine syrup (page 157) or sautéed summer berries (page 146).

The Joy of Cookies

Giant Chocolate Chip Celebration Cookies

Lemonade Sugar Cookies

Cornmeal Vanilla Bean Shortbreads

Pecan Shortbreads

Orange Tarragon Benne Seed Wafers

My Milanos (Made with Brown Edge Wafer Cookies)

Almond Butter Cookies

Mocha Brownie Thins

Salty Peanut Squares

Hazelnut Sandies

Jumbo Molasses Spice Cookies

Maple Walnut Jammies

Bourbon Balls

Meringue Mushrooms

Joel's Oatmeal Cookies

Chocolate Chunky Brownie Bars

Brooklyn Black-&-Whites

Extra Crunchy Peanut Butter Cookies

I contend that the average American's first memorable exposure to the wonderful world of desserts is through a simple cookie (most often chocolate chip). I've come across people who proclaim, "Cheesecake just doesn't do it for me," or "I'm not a big fruit fan," but have you ever heard a single soul say, "I don't like cookies"?

Who can resist the lure of the cookie jar? I think that the most enticing aspect of these delectable sweet bites is that cookies are associated with the home kitchen. In today's world, when many people seem to have neither the time nor the inclination to bake, even nonbakers will venture into the role of cookie maker.

The best cookies are packed with flavor and are texturally interesting to eat—so interesting that it's hard to refrain from eating them in multiples. They might be chewy, crunchy, or crumbly, and they can come in a myriad of shapes and flavors. One overall generalization that can be made, though, is that the very best cookies are always freshly baked and made from great ingredients.

Most cookies take very little time to put together if the ingredients are at the proper temperature. Unless otherwise noted, eggs and butter should be at room temperature—try to think ahead and pull them out of the refrigerator several hours before you plan to bake. Both at work and at home, I make up many cookie doughs ahead of time and either refrigerate or freeze them. This time-saving step means that you can do part of your dessert preparation work several days ahead, that you can use a portion of dough and freeze the rest for later use. It is even possible to make, roll, cut, and freeze the dough for many cookies. Pulled directly from the freezer and baked, they can be served as a freshly made dessert for last-minute company.

I think a selection of cookies constitutes a great dessert on its own, but if you feel the need to be more elaborate, serve cookies with ice cream (your own or store-bought). Add a sauce if you really want to fuss. Alternatively, a seasonal fruit compote accompanied by crisp, buttery cookies is hard to beat. Is a mini—chocolate malt served with chocolate chip cookies overkill? I don't think so.

Each of the recipes in this chapter will give you specific directions for making and storing the dough for the cookie being prepared. Since ovens vary, please pay careful attention to the visual clues given for doneness. The following general tips are based on my baking experiences and can be broadly applied.

- The exact measurement of ingredients is always important, but it is particularly important in making cookies. A tablespoon less flour or a bit of extra liquid can have a noticeable effect on the ultimate texture.
- Avoid using thin, flimsy baking sheets, which have a tendency to overbrown cookie bottoms. My preference is for professional weight, rimmed half sheet pans that measure 12 × 17 inches. They are also great for bar cookies and can double as jellyroll pans.
- Many cookies can be quickly and easily portioned by using a spring-loaded ice cream scoop. These come in a variety of sizes—¼ cup for monster cookies, tablespoon-sized scoops for larger cookies, and teaspoon-sized scoops for smaller cookies.
- Reverse the cookie sheets midway through the baking process to promote even baking—even if well calibrated, most ovens have a minor hot spot.
- Unless otherwise specified, I cool all my cookies on their lined baking sheets, forgoing the often recommended step of transferring cookies to a rack to cool. There's no harm in allowing cookies to cool on a rack, and if you have a limited number of baking sheets, you may wish to do this; however, I've never noticed any detrimental effects from pan cooling. Delicate cookies that become brittle once cooled are an exception, as are cookies that must be shaped while they are still warm, such as tuille cups or brandy snaps.
- Allow cookies to cool completely before storing them. While cookies jars are charming, I think that the best way to store cookies is in relatively shallow, lidded plastic storage boxes. Separate layers of cookies with parchment paper. Pack crisp, crunchy cookies separately from chewy, cakey cookies.
- High–butter content cookie dough can be frozen very successfully. You can roll many doughs into log form for easy slice-and-bake cookies. Drop-cookie dough can be frozen in small containers so that you can have freshly baked cookies with little or no hassle on a regular basis. Dough for rolled cookies should be patted into flattened rounds to facilitate the rolling process. Rolled and cut cookies can also be frozen. Freeze them till firm on a baking sheet; then pack them between layers of parchment paper and return to the freezer. Bake them from a frozen state. Frozen doughs should be well wrapped, dated, and used within 3 months. Ideally, unless precut, frozen doughs should be defrosted overnight in the refrigerator before using; however, you can also defrost them at room temperature and then rechill them briefly if necessary.

- Cookie recipes will double and even triple with great success. Cookies are one of the easiest desserts to bake for a crowd.

Giant Chocolate Chip Celebration Cookies

MAKES 2 HUGE COOKIES

These cookies truly are giant. Each weighs in at close to 1½ pounds, and they are ideal for making a statement. They were originally baked for a last-minute birthday party and are meant to be cut into wedges for serving. The large surface area provides a perfect canvas for piping out celebratory messages. And don't forget the candles!

INGREDIENTS FOR THE COOKIES
    16 tablespoons (8 ounces) butter, at room temperature
    ¾ cup brown sugar
    ¾ cup sugar
    1 teaspoon vanilla
    2 eggs
    ½ teaspoon kosher salt
    1 teaspoon baking soda
    2¾ cups flour
    2¼ cups (11½ ounces) semisweet chocolate chips

INGREDIENTS FOR THE ICING
    1 cup sifted confectioners' sugar
    scant 1½ tablespoons cream, half-and-half, or milk

PREPARATION FOR THE COOKIES
1 Preheat oven to 350°.
2 Using a mixer with a paddle, cream the butter with both the brown and white sugar until well blended. Add the vanilla and mix to blend.
3 Add the eggs and scrape down the bowl.
4 Add the salt and baking soda. Gradually add the flour. Add the chips and mix just to blend. Chill the dough for several hours or up to 2 days.

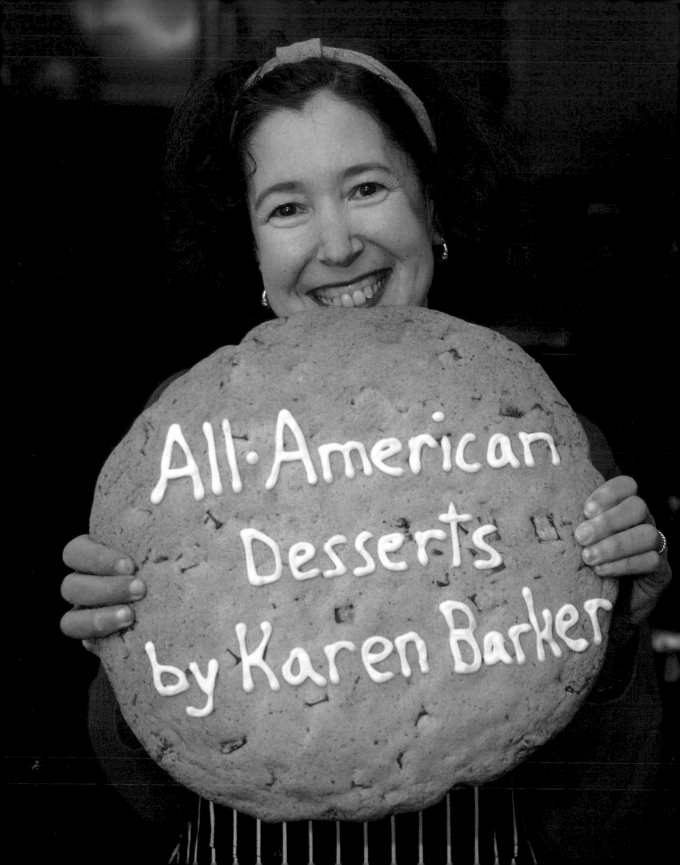

(Chilled cookie dough holds its shape better and has less of a tendency to spread while baking.) It can also be frozen if you wish—defrost overnight in the refrigerator before using.

5 Line 2 baking sheets with parchment paper or silpat sheets. You can also bake these cookies on ungreased cookie sheets. Put half of the dough on each sheet and pat into a circle approximately 7 inches in diameter and ½ inch thick.

6 Bake the cookies at 350° for approximately 25 to 30 minutes, until they are just set and golden brown, reversing and repositioning the baking sheets midway through. Cool the cookies on the pan. When completely cool, prepare the icing.

PREPARATION FOR THE ICING

1 Place the confectioners' sugar in a mixing bowl and gradually add enough milk, half-and-half, or cream to moisten the sugar. The consistency should be smooth and barely fluid—sort of like Elmer's glue. If it seems too thin to pipe, add more sugar; if it's too thick, add a few more drops of liquid.

2 Place the icing in a pastry bag fitted with a small writing tip. Alternatively, place the icing in a small zip lock bag, seal, and move the icing down to one corner of the bag, gathering the bag so that there are no air pockets; snip the corner to form a small makeshift "writing tip." A third option is to make a disposable parchment paper cone (see instructions following recipe). Proceed to pipe your message on top of the cookie.

3 Allow the icing to set for at least 1 hour before serving.

Baker's Note: I usually use homemade chocolate chips (page 54) for these cookies, but good-quality commercial chips also work well. My favorite brand is Ghirardelli double chocolate chips because they're larger in size and more bittersweet in flavor.

I like to slip 12-inch cardboard cake circles under these cookies once they're baked to maneuver them around and protect them against breaking.

If you have an oven that accommodates a full-size sheet pan, you can bake one enormous cookie using this recipe. The dough will just fit on a standard professional-size sheet pan.

Serving Suggestions: You can serve birthday cookies with a scoop of your favorite ice cream on top of each wedge. Another possibility is to form a giant ice cream sandwich by placing one baked and cooled cookie upside down on a baking sheet and topping it with a thick layer of slightly softened ice cream (you'll need about a half gallon). Top with the remaining cookie, pressing down gently to form a sandwich. Wrap in plastic film and return to the freezer until just before serving.

Making a Parchment Paper Cone

Parchment paper cones are terrific for piping fine-lined melted chocolate decorations or inscriptions made with a powdered sugar icing. A parchment cone will give you maximum control and a precise line.

To make one, cut out an 8-inch square of parchment paper and fold it in half diagonally. Make a clean cut along the fold (I use a chef's knife to do this) to form two triangles. Reserve one triangle for future use. Hold the triangle in front of you, with the longest edge at the bottom. Bring the right-hand bottom corner up to the top point, allowing the parchment to curve inward. Wrap the left-hand bottom corner around to the other side so that both corners meet at the top point. Tighten the cone to form a sharp point at the bottom. Fold down the top of the cone to hold the paper in place. Fill the cone with melted chocolate and fold the top down again to secure. Cut the tip of the cone to the desired width.

Lemonade Sugar Cookies

MAKES 3 DOZEN

Every Fourth of July there is a neighborhood celebration at Oval Park, which is located near Magnolia Grill, in Durham. Traffic is cordoned off; and led by the local fire department, children of all ages (often accompanied by festively outfitted canines) march, bike, skate, scoot, and are strolled around the block for a brief but glorious parade. Afterward, patriotic songs are sung and refreshments of frosty lemonade and sugar cookies are served. These plain-to-look-at but delicious-to-eat cookies always make me think of simple summer days.

INGREDIENTS

2½ cups flour

½ teaspoon baking soda

1 teaspoon baking powder

¾ teaspoon kosher salt

grated zest of 2 lemons

8 tablespoons (4 ounces) butter, at room temperature

¼ cup canola or other vegetable oil

1¼ cups sugar

2 eggs, at room temperature

1 teaspoon vanilla

2 tablespoons fresh lemon juice

additional sugar for forming cookies

PREPARATION

1 Sift together the flour, baking soda, baking powder, and salt. Reserve.

2 In the bowl of a mixer with a paddle attachment, combine the grated lemon zest with the butter. Blend until smooth and add the vegetable oil. Add the sugar and mix to blend. Add the eggs and again, occasionally scraping the bowl, mix to blend. Add the vanilla and the lemon juice. Add the reserved dry ingredients and mix just until combined. The dough will be fairly loose.

3 Chill the dough for several hours (or overnight) before forming and baking the cookies.

4 Preheat oven to 350°.

5 Roll tablespoon-sized scoops of dough into round balls, coat with sugar, and place on parchment paper—lined baking sheets. The cookies will spread, so leave several inches between them.

6 Bake at 350° for approximately 20 minutes, until the tops of the cookies feel "just firm" when gently pressed. The bottoms of these cookies will turn a light golden brown, but the tops will remain pale in color.

Baker's Note: This is a very soft dough, and it is easier to work with chilled, so plan ahead. You can certainly substitute orange or lime flavoring for the lemon if you wish.

Serving Suggestion: Fresh fruit and lemonade sugar cookies—the perfect picnic dessert!

Cornmeal Vanilla Bean Shortbreads

MAKES 32 2-INCH CUTOUTS OR 16 WEDGES

Every baker has a favorite recipe for shortbread cookies, and here is mine. The addition of fresh vanilla bean and the slight crunch of cornmeal make these buttery treats irresistible. You can customize their shape, depending upon your mood and the occasion. Try cutout stars for Christmas or the Fourth of July, hearts for Valentine's Day, or Scottish-style wedges for tea.

INGREDIENTS

16 tablespoons (8 ounces) butter, at room temperature
seeds of 1 vanilla bean
¼ teaspoon kosher salt
½ cup + 1 tablespoon sugar
1½ cups flour
¼ cup cornstarch
½ cup stoneground yellow cornmeal

PREPARATION

1 Using a mixer with a paddle, cream the butter with the vanilla bean seeds, salt, and sugar, scraping the sides of the bowl once or twice.

2 Combine the flour, cornstarch, and cornmeal and add to the creamed butter in 3 additions. Scrape the bottom and sides of the bowl to make sure the dough is evenly mixed. Gather the dough together, divide in half, flatten into rounds, and wrap in plastic. Chill for 1 hour or up to 2 days. This dough can be frozen. Defrost overnight in the refrigerator before using.

3 Preheat oven to 350°.

4 A. For shortbread cutouts: On a lightly floured surface, roll the dough out ¼ inch thick. Cut the cookies into desired shapes and place them on a parchment paper—lined baking sheet. Gather the scraps and reroll one time.

B. For shortbread wedges: On a lightly floured surface, roll each piece of dough into a circle 8 inches in diameter and ¼ to ½ inch thick. Use a plate or a cake pan as a guide. Place on a parchment paper—lined baking sheet. Score each round into 8 wedges, being careful not to cut all the way through the dough. Decoratively prick the shortbread with the tines of a fork if desired.

5 Bake at 350° for about 15 to 20 minutes, until the edges just start to brown. Reduce oven to 325° and bake an additional 10 to 20 minutes. Wedges will need a longer baking time than cutouts. Rotate the baking sheet midway through the baking process—you want the shortbreads to remain fairly light in color, but you do want to make sure they're baked through. You can always break a cookie open to test for doneness. No traces of raw dough should exist in the very center. The texture of the cookies will crisp up once they are cool. You'll want to recut the scored shortbread wedges once the cookies are baked.

Baker's Note: You can keep an airtight box of rolled shortbreads on hand in your freezer and bake them as needed.

Serving Suggestions: These are great all on their own or as a side cookie to a scoop of purple plum rum sorbet (page 282) or bourbon molasses ice cream (page 264). I have also fashioned a stacked shortcake-like dessert by layering 2 shortbread cookie wedges with fresh strawberries or bourbon poached peaches (page 149) and whipped cream.

Pecan Shortbreads

MAKES ABOUT 4 DOZEN 1½-INCH COOKIES

The brown sugar and pecans in these cookies emphasize their buttery richness. They are delicious with ice creams and fruit desserts or all by their lonesome.

INGREDIENTS
   16 tablespoons (8 ounces) butter, lightly softened
   ½ cup brown sugar
   ½ teaspoon kosher salt
   ¾ teaspoon vanilla
   1¼ cup + 2 tablespoons flour
   2 tablespoons cornstarch
   ½ cup (2 ounces) lightly toasted, finely ground pecan pieces

PREPARATION
1 In the bowl of a mixer fitted with a paddle, cream the butter with the brown sugar till smooth. Add the salt and vanilla and mix to combine. Combine the

flour, cornstarch, and pecans and add to the creamed butter in 3 additions. Scrape the bottom and sides of the bowl to make sure the dough is evenly mixed.

2   Divide the dough in half, flatten into discs, and wrap with plastic. Chill the dough for about 1 hour, until firm. This can be done up to 2 days ahead of time. The dough can also be frozen—defrost overnight in the refrigerator before using.

3   Preheat oven to 350°.

4   Remove the dough from the refrigerator and allow it to sit at room temperature for a few minutes. On a lightly floured surface, with a lightly floured rolling pin, roll the dough out ¼ inch thick; cut out cookies and place them on a parchment paper— or silpat-lined baking sheet. You can cut these cookies into any simple shape or size you desire. You can gather the scraps and reroll them one time. If at any point the dough gets soft and difficult to roll, briefly place it in the refrigerator or freezer to firm it up quickly.

5   Bake at 350° for approximately 15 to 20 minutes, reversing the baking sheet midway, until the cookies are golden around the edges. Cool completely and store airtight.

Baker's Note: You can also form this dough into a 1½-inch diameter log, chill it, and then slice the dough with a sharp knife to make slice-and-bake cookies. The recipe can also be varied by substituting lightly toasted, skinned, and finely ground walnuts, hazelnuts, or almonds for the pecans.

Pecan shortbreads can also be dressed up by dipping half of each baked and cooled cookie in melted semisweet chocolate. Place the dipped cookies on a parchment paper—lined baking sheet and chill briefly until the chocolate is set.

Remember, you can make cookie dough like this up to several months ahead of time if it's wrapped well and kept in the freezer. Defrost it overnight in the refrigerator before using.

Serving Suggestions: Serve with bourbon poached peaches (page 149), eggnog snow cream (page 288), summer blueberry sorbet (page 283), or bourbon molasses ice cream (page 264).

Orange Tarragon Benne Seed Wafers

MAKES ABOUT 5½ DOZEN SMALL COOKIES

"Benne seeds" is another name for "sesame seeds," an ingredient that has found its way from Africa into low country Southern cooking. The savory combination of orange, tarragon, and benne seeds is totally unexpected in a delicate cookie. I classify these as "nibblers"—small, buttery, flavorful crisps that are often eaten in multiples.

INGREDIENTS

½ cup sesame seeds
8 tablespoons (4 ounces) butter, at room temperature
1 cup sugar
grated zest of 1 orange
½ teaspoon kosher salt
1 egg
½ teaspoon vanilla
½ teaspoon orange oil or extract (optional)
2 tablespoons finely chopped tarragon
¾ cup flour

PREPARATION

1 Preheat oven to 375°.
2 In a small, dry sauté pan, lightly toast the sesame seeds over medium heat, tossing them occasionally, till they turn a light golden brown. Cool and reserve.
3 In the bowl of a mixer with paddle attachment, combine the butter with the sugar, grated orange zest, and salt.
4 Add the egg, vanilla, and optional orange oil. Mix to combine, scraping the bowl once or twice. Add the reserved sesame seeds, tarragon, and flour and mix just to combine.
5 Put the dough into a pastry bag fitted with a ½-inch open tip. Pipe the dough out onto a silpat-lined baking sheet, leaving about 1½ inches of space between cookies (they spread a fair amount!). If you don't own silpat sheets, pipe the cookies onto a lightly buttered baking sheet—parchment paper does not work as well for this recipe.

6 Dip your finger in water and lightly press down any points that may have formed in the piping process—your cookies should look like small buttons.

7 Bake at 375° for approximately 12 minutes, reversing the baking sheet midway through. Bake until just the outer perimeter of the cookies is golden brown; the centers should remain lighter in color.

8 If baking on silpat, you can cool the cookies on the baking sheet if you wish. If baking on buttered baking sheets, remove the cookies from the sheet and transfer them to cooling racks with a thin offset spatula. They are harder to get off buttered sheets once cool.

Baker's Note: Check these cookies frequently during the final few minutes of baking. They go from underbaked to burnt in no time.

Serving Suggestions: For a simple, elegant dessert serve these cookies with Grand Marnier—macerated strawberries and a scoop of not-just-plain-vanilla ice cream (page 261) or burnt orange caramel ice cream (page 262). These would also go well with orange coconut sorbet (page 284) or with frozen sourwood honey parfait (page 289) and some sliced fresh figs.

My Milanos (Made with Brown Edge Wafer Cookies)

MAKES 2½ DOZEN SANDWICH COOKIES

By far, my favorite commercially produced cookie is a crisp, buttery, chocolate-filled Pepperidge Farm Milano (the original, please). In *Not Afraid of Flavor*, I included a recipe for a delicate brown edge wafer cookie. If you sandwich semisweet chocolate with two of these, you wind up with a cookie that is remarkably similar to my beloved Milano.

INGREDIENTS

8 tablespoons (4 ounces) butter, at room temperature
½ cup sugar
⅛ cup (2 tablespoons) egg whites, at room temperature
⅛ teaspoon salt
¾ cup flour

½ teaspoon vanilla

3½ ounces semisweet chocolate, chopped into small pieces

PREPARATION

1 Preheat oven to 350°. Line baking sheets with silpats or lightly butter the sheets. Do not bake these cookies on parchment paper.

2 Using a mixer with a paddle, cream the butter with the sugar. Add the egg whites and mix till well combined. Add the salt, flour, and vanilla and mix just until blended, scraping the bowl once or twice. This dough can be made ahead—if refrigerated, bring to room temperature and stir lightly before forming into cookies.

3 Place the dough in a pastry bag fitted with a plain, large open tip. Pipe small discs out onto the baking sheet, making each cookie about ¾ inch in diameter. Lightly flatten any Hershey's Kisses–shaped points that might have formed with a damp fingertip. Space the cookies 1½ inches apart, as they will spread.

4 Bake the cookies at 350° for 7 to 10 minutes, reverse the baking sheets, and bake for an additional 7 to 10 minutes. When done, the outer perimeter of the cookies will be golden brown. Immediately remove the cookies from their baking sheets with a spatula, placing them on a rack to cool.

5 Melt the chocolate in the top of a double boiler. Pair the cookies, trying to match shapes and sizes as much as possible. Turn one cookie from each pair over so it is bottom side up and place about ½ teaspoon of melted chocolate in the center. Take the corresponding tops and lightly press down to form chocolate-filled sandwiches.

6 You should have some melted chocolate left. For a pretty presentation, I place this in a pastry bag with a fine writing tip (or you can make your own parchment paper cone or simply use a plastic zip lock bag and snip off a corner). Line the filled sandwiches up in rows on a parchment lined sheet and, using a zigzag motion, pipe fine lines of chocolate back and forth across the cookies. Chill the cookies briefly just to set the chocolate. These are best served within 2 days of when they are made. Store in an airtight container at room temperature, separating layers of cookies with parchment paper.

Baker's Note: Once they are baked, these cookies are placed on a rack to cool. If left on the hot baking sheet, they have a tendency to overbrown.

Serving Suggestions: These are delicious with an array of fruits, sorbets, and ice creams. I love them at the very end of a meal, with a cup of coffee.

Almond Butter Cookies

MAKES 3½ DOZEN

At Christmas, I go into cookie elf mode and turn out dozens for a holiday assortment. There's always a mix of tried-and-true favorites with an occasional innovation. My mother-in-law, Jeanette Barker, is a big fan of anything made with marzipan or almond paste, and one year I created these cookies for her.

INGREDIENTS

¾ cup almond paste, at room temperature

¾ cup + 1 tablespoon sugar

8 tablespoons (4 ounces) butter, at room temperature

1 tablespoon vegetable oil

1 egg

¼ teaspoon kosher salt

¼ teaspoon almond extract

½ teaspoon vanilla

1 teaspoon baking soda

1 tablespoon cornstarch

1½ cups flour

1 cup blanched, sliced almonds, crushed

additional sugar for shaping cookies

PREPARATION

1 Preheat oven to 350°.

2 Combine the almond paste with the sugar and mix well. Add the butter and vegetable oil and beat till smooth. Add the egg. Add the salt, almond extract, and vanilla. Scrape down the bowl. Add the baking soda, cornstarch, and flour and mix to combine.

3 Form the dough into walnut-sized balls and roll in crushed almonds. Place 2½ inches apart on a parchment paper–lined baking sheet. Dip the bottom of a glass or small measuring cup in sugar and press down on each cookie to flatten.

4 Bake at 350° for approximately 18 to 20 minutes, reversing the pan midway through, until the cookies are lightly golden.

Baker's Note: I try to bake these cookies within a day or two of serving them, but you can make the dough several days ahead and refrigerate it. Or you can make it even further ahead and freeze it, in which case defrost it in the refrigerator overnight before you use it.

Serving Suggestion: Try serving these with lightly sugared strawberries that have been tossed with a bit of Amaretto and topped with a dollop of whipped cream or crème fraîche (page 67).

Mocha Brownie Thins

MAKES 2½ TO 3 DOZEN BROWNIES,

DEPENDING ON HOW YOU CUT THEM

The "thin" moniker refers to these cookies' svelte silhouette (at least as far as most brownies go). While I make no dietary claims, I do believe that one of these slim treats will at least temporarily satisfy even a die-hard chocoholic's craving.

INGREDIENTS

4 ounces unsweetened chocolate

10½ tablespoons (5¼ ounces) butter

1⅓ cup flour

1 teaspoon baking powder

½ teaspoon kosher salt

2 tablespoons instant espresso or coffee

4 eggs

2 cups sugar

2 teaspoons vanilla

PREPARATION

1 Preheat oven to 350°. Butter a half sheet pan or an 11 × 17-inch jellyroll pan, line the bottom with parchment paper, and butter the parchment paper.

2 Combine the chocolate and butter in the top of a double boiler. Melt over low heat, stirring occasionally, till smooth. Reserve.

3 Sift together the flour, baking powder, salt, and instant espresso. Reserve.

4 In a bowl, whisk the eggs with the sugar till thickened and light. Add the vanilla. Beat in the reserved chocolate mixture. Add the reserved flour mixture and mix in just until thoroughly combined.

5 Transfer the batter to the prepared pan. Using an offset spatula, smooth the batter so that it is of even thickness.

6 Bake at 350° for about 7 minutes. Rotate the pan and bake an additional 7 to 8 minutes. The brownies are done when they feel just set in the center and they *just* start to pull away from the sides.

7 Cool completely before cutting. To remove from the pan, run a paring knife along all the edges. Cover brownies with a sheet of parchment paper and a flat cookie sheet. Holding the cookie sheet in place, invert the brownie pan. Reinvert brownies so they are right side up on a cutting surface. You can cut brownies into any desired shape. I like to use a 1½-inch plain round cutter to punch out rounds, but you may prefer squares or rectangles.

8 These can be made up to 1 day in advance. Store airtight in a covered container, separating layers with parchment paper. They can also be well wrapped and frozen.

Baker's Note: I often use this recipe to make ice cream sandwiches because even when the thins are frozen they maintain a fudgey, creamy texture. To form sandwiches, cut the pan of brownies in half widthwise. Working quickly, scoop a generous, tightly packed layer of slightly softened ice cream (flavor of your choice) on top of one of the brownie layers. The ice cream should be at least 1 inch thick. Use a palette knife to smooth the ice cream. Top with the second brownie layer, pushing down lightly to eliminate gaps. Place in the freezer for several hours or overnight. Trim the edges and cut into individual bars.

Serving Suggestions: I like to serve these alongside a goblet of beat-the-heat frozen mocha velvet (page 270). They're also nice as part of a platter featuring assorted brownies and bar cookies, such as peanut butter blondies (page 274), chocolate Chunky brownie bars (page 323), and cornmeal vanilla bean shortbreads (page 300).

Salty Peanut Squares

MAKES A LARGE BATCH OF 88 COOKIES—SHARE WITH FRIENDS

One of my all-time favorite cookies, these nut-packed squares are based on Pecan Diamonds—a sweet that I learned to make at the Culinary Institute of America. Imagine the best peanut brittle combined with chewy caramel and an exceptional brown sugar shortbread. Do not be shy about the salt component—it is a necessary foil to the sweet caramel filling and creates an ideal yin-yang balance.

INGREDIENTS FOR THE CRUST

   3⅛ cups flour
   1 cup brown sugar
   1 teaspoon kosher salt
   22 tablespoons (11 ounces) butter, chilled and cut into pieces

INGREDIENTS FOR THE FILLING

   16 tablespoons (8 ounces) butter
   ¼ cup sugar
   1½ cups + 2 tablespoons brown sugar
   ½ cup honey
   ¼ cup + 1 tablespoon cream
   ¼ teaspoon kosher salt
   1 teaspoon vanilla
   3½ cups (18½ ounces) roasted salted peanuts

PREPARATION FOR THE CRUST

1 Form a foil liner for a half sheet pan or jelly roll pan by inverting the pan and molding a sheet of aluminum foil over the bottom of the pan. The foil should extend over the edges of the pan. Reinvert the pan, butter it, and fit the foil liner into the pan. Butter the foil. Reserve. This will make it much easier to remove the baked cookies from the pan.

2 Place the flour, sugar, and salt in a food processor with a steel blade and pulse to blend. Add the butter and process until the dough just starts to come together—do not let the dough form a ball. Evenly press the dough into the bottom and up the sides of the prepared pan. Chill the dough until firm (about 30 minutes). The crust can be prepared to this point up to 2 days ahead of time.

3   Preheat oven to 350°.

4   Bake the chilled crust until lightly browned (about 25 to 30 minutes). Check the crust periodically, and if it's puffing up at all, press it down gently with a fork. You will want to reverse the pan midway through the baking process. Reserve the baked crust while you make the filling.

PREPARATION FOR THE FILLING

1   Combine the butter, sugar, brown sugar, and honey in a saucepan and cook, whisking, over medium heat until the butter is melted and the mixture is smooth. Bring to a boil and boil for 3 minutes, whisking several times. Remove from heat and add the cream, salt, vanilla, and peanuts. Stir to blend.

2   Pour the filling over the baked crust, spreading evenly with an offset spatula. Make sure the nuts are well distributed.

3   Bake at 350° for about 30 minutes, until the filling is evenly bubbling and golden brown. The filling will appear fairly set when the pan is shaken. Remove from the oven and allow to cool completely.

4   To remove the cookies from the pan, briefly pass the pan over a range burner to barely heat the bottom of the pan. This will loosen the crust if the butter has solidified. Grasp the foil liner and pull up to loosen the foil from the pan. Cover the cookies with a baking sheet and invert. Peel the foil liner off the crust. Cover the cookies with a second baking sheet and reinvert onto a cutting surface.

5   With a long, heavy knife, cut cookies into 1¼-inch squares. These can be made up to 3 days ahead of time.

Baker's Note: Baking to proper doneness is critical with these cookies. If underbaked, the filling will not set up properly; and if overbaked, they will be unpleasantly hard. Although the filling will start to bubble after about 15 minutes, the bubbles will become more numerous and appear larger as the end of the baking time nears. Color is your best indicator—the filling should appear nicely caramelized but should not even approach dark brown.

Coarsely chopped macadamia nuts can be substituted for the peanuts.

Serving Suggestions: I like to serve these alongside not-just-plain-vanilla ice cream (page 261) that has been drizzled with Concord grape syrup (page 50). They also pair well with milk chocolate malt ice cream (page 274) or deep dark chocolate pudding (page 184).

Hazelnut Sandies

MAKES 2½ DOZEN

I have seen this type of cookie called a variety of names. In addition to sandies, they often are designated as tea cookies, wedding cakes, or butterballs. Regardless of what you call them, the end result is a melt-in-your-mouth, nut-packed butter cookie that is extremely easy to make. A mainstay in many Christmas cookie assortments, these are so good they deserve to be showcased year round.

INGREDIENTS

16 tablespoons (8 ounces) butter, at room temperature
¾ cup confectioners' sugar, sifted,
   plus an additional 1½ cups for finishing
½ teaspoon kosher salt
1 teaspoon vanilla
2 cups flour
1 cup lightly toasted, skinned, finely chopped hazelnuts

PREPARATION

1 Using a mixer with a paddle, cream the butter, sugar, and salt. Add the vanilla and scrape down the bowl. Add the flour and nuts and beat just until the mixture is combined—make sure to scrape the bottom of the bowl as well as the sides.

2 Chill the dough till fairly firm but still malleable (about 45 minutes). This dough can be made ahead and kept frozen or refrigerated but make sure to bring it back to a chilled/malleable consistency before proceeding.

3 Preheat oven to 350°.

4 Form the dough into 1-inch diameter balls (a 1-inch ice cream scoop is the perfect tool for shaping these). Place the cookies on a parchment paper– or silpat-lined baking sheet.

5 Bake at 350° for about 18 to 20 minutes, reversing the baking sheet midway through the baking process. When done, the cookies will pick up little color on their tops but feel set to the touch. The bottoms of the cookies will be golden brown.

6 Remove the cookies from the oven, and while they are still hot, dust them heavily with a portion of the additional sugar. Allow the cookies to cool and

place them in a mixing bowl with the remaining powdered sugar and toss
gently to coat completely. Store these cookies airtight for up to 3 days.
Re-coat with powdered sugar just before serving if necessary.

Baker's Note: You can substitute lightly toasted pecans, walnuts, or almonds for the
hazelnuts. For the best texture, I like to chop the nuts by hand. If you do use a
food processor, be sure to pulse them, to achieve a finely chopped as opposed
to ground texture.

Serving Suggestions: Try these with a combo of eggnog snow cream (page 288) and
purple plum rum sorbet (page 282). They're also nice alongside winter fruits
poached in red wine syrup (page 157) topped with crème fraîche (page 67).

Jumbo Molasses Spice Cookies

MAKES 1 ½ DOZEN

It's the spicing on these extra large, extra delicious cookies that sets them apart.
Crispy on the outside, with a chewy interior, their flavor just keeps coming at you.

INGREDIENTS

2 ⅓ cups flour
1 teaspoon baking soda
1 teaspoon ground ginger
½ teaspoon cinnamon
¼ teaspoon nutmeg
¼ teaspoon cloves
¼ teaspoon freshly ground black pepper
½ teaspoon kosher salt
1 teaspoon instant coffee or espresso powder
8 tablespoons (4 ounces) butter, at room temperature
¼ cup + 1 tablespoon (a total of 2 ounces) vegetable shortening
grated zest of 1 orange
2 teaspoons very finely chopped peeled fresh ginger
½ cup sugar
½ cup brown sugar
1 egg

¼ cup molasses

additional ½ cup sugar for forming cookies

PREPARATION

1 Preheat oven to 350°.

2 Sift together the flour, baking soda, ground ginger, cinnamon, nutmeg, and cloves. Add the black pepper, salt and instant coffee. Reserve.

3 In the bowl of a mixer, with a paddle, combine the butter, vegetable shortening, orange zest, and chopped ginger. Add both kinds of sugar and mix until lightly creamed. Add the egg and mix to blend. Add the molasses. Add the reserved dry ingredients and mix, scraping the bowl once or twice, till just combined.

4 Form the dough into generously heaped tablespoonsful and roll into balls. Dredge each in the additional ½ cup sugar and place on a parchment paper–lined baking sheet, spacing the cookies several inches apart.

5 Bake at 350° for about 18 minutes, reversing the sheet midway through the baking process. The cookies will puff and then flatten slightly. When done, they will be barely set to the touch and just picking up color on their bottoms. Do not overbake them, or the cookies will be crispy instead of chewy.

Baker's Note: This dough can be made ahead and then refrigerated or frozen. The cookies can also be made smaller if you wish, in which case the baking time will be a minute or two shorter.

Serving Suggestions: These make excellent ice cream sandwiches when filled with lemon chiffon ice cream (page 271) or not-just-plain-vanilla ice cream (page 261). In small-size format they also can be served alongside purple plum rum sorbet (page 282).

Maple Walnut Jammies

MAKES 2½ DOZEN SANDWICH COOKIES

The mellowness of maple syrup combined with toasty walnuts and plenty of butter makes a very special cookie. If you have access to black walnuts, use them—they make a special cookie spectacular! The fruity filling may seem like overkill, and the cookies are great on their own; but the jam lends them a contrasting flavor and texture.

INGREDIENTS

16 tablespoons (8 ounces) butter, at room temperature

¾ cup sugar

1 egg yolk

¼ cup maple syrup

½ teaspoon vanilla

¼ teaspoon kosher salt

2 cups flour

1 cup lightly toasted, skinned walnuts, finely chopped

⅜ cup good-quality jam (I like American Spoon strawberry rhubarb)

PREPARATION

1 Using a mixer with a paddle, lightly cream the butter with the sugar. Add
the egg yolk and mix to blend. Add the maple syrup and vanilla and mix till
incorporated. Add the salt and flour and mix till just blended, scraping the
bowl. Add the walnuts.

2 Remove the dough from the mixer bowl, divide in half, and pat into a
flattened round. Wrap in plastic and chill till the dough is firm (usually about
1½ hours) or for up to 3 days. The dough can be frozen at this point—defrost
overnight in the refrigerator before using.

3 Preheat oven to 350°. If the dough is very hard, you may want to leave it at
room temperature for 5 to 10 minutes before rolling.

4 Pound the dough with a rolling pin to soften it slightly and then roll it out
to between ⅛ and ¼ inch thick. Use a 1½-inch cutter to cut out rounds and
place cookies on a parchment paper– or silpat-lined baking sheet. To form a
"peekaboo" top for the sandwich, take a ½-inch cutter or a small round open
pastry tip and remove the center portion of half the cookies. Gather the dough
scraps, chill briefly if necessary, and reroll one time.

5 Bake the cookies at 350° for approximately 18 to 20 minutes, reversing the pan
halfway through, until the edges are lightly browned. Cool them completely
before filling.

6 To fill, place about ½ teaspoon of jam in the center of the solid round cookies
and spread the jam slightly. Cover with a cutout top and lightly press together.
These are best served within 24 hours of being filled, but you can leave the
baked cookies unfilled for up to 3 days.

Baker's Note: You can cut out alternative shapes and/or leave the cookies unfilled. Pecans or hazelnuts can be substituted for the walnuts. Experiment by using different flavored jams—peach, seedless blackberry, and strawberry rhubarb are my favorites.

Serving Suggestions: This is a great cookie to serve with a simple scoop of ice cream or sorbet. Try a fig jam–filled one with ruby port ice cream (page 268) or strawberry rhubarb jammies with strawberry sorbet (page 279).

Bourbon Balls

MAKES 2 DOZEN

A Southern holiday favorite, this spirited confection should be made at least a week or two in advance. The requisite aging period will allow the rather pronounced bourbon flavor to mellow a bit.

INGREDIENTS

2 ounces semisweet chocolate, chopped into small pieces

1⅛ cups (5 ounces) ground vanilla wafer crumbs (see brown edge wafer cookies, page 305, or use commercial Nilla Wafers)

2 tablespoons cocoa

2 tablespoons corn syrup

⅓ cup lightly toasted, finely chopped pecans

¼ cup good-quality bourbon

2 cups confectioners' sugar

PREPARATION

1 Place the semisweet chocolate in the top of a double boiler and melt over low heat, stirring, till smooth. Reserve.

2 In a bowl, stir together the cookie crumbs, cocoa, corn syrup, pecans, reserved chocolate, and bourbon. The mixture should appear fairly moist. Don't worry if it appears very buttery—it will set up when chilled. If it seems dry, add a touch more bourbon. Place the mixture in the refrigerator and chill for 1 hour, stirring once or twice.

3 Place the confectioners' sugar in a bowl and remove the chilled bourbon mixture from the refrigerator. Form generous, well-rounded, teaspoon-sized bourbon balls. Roll the balls in the confectioners' sugar to coat completely.

4 When all the bourbon balls have been formed, place them and the remaining confectioners' sugar in a covered storage container. Store covered at room temperature for up to 3 weeks. Every few days (and the night before serving) give the container a good shake to redistribute the sugar and recoat the bourbon balls.

Baker's Note: You can substitute dark rum for the bourbon and walnuts for the pecans in this recipe. If you look in almost any Junior League or community cookbook from the South, you will find a recipe for bourbon balls. Most call for store-bought Nilla Wafers and do not include semisweet chocolate. I'm not entirely convinced that using homemade cookies is a great improvement; however, the addition of a touch of great chocolate is definitely worth the extra step.

Serving Suggestions: I like to serve these post-dessert, with coffee. They're also an excellent addition to a festive dessert buffet. By no means, however, are they only a holiday item—try them in the summertime served with not-just-plain-vanilla ice cream (page 261) that has been sauced with mint syrup (page 51).

Meringue Mushrooms

MAKES 3 DOZEN

I attended the Culinary Institute of America before the school instituted a formal baking program. I was, however, incredibly lucky in that, while I was there, Master Pastry Chef Albert Kumin occasionally taught enrichment classes that focused on specialty cakes, candy, and chocolate-making. The first time I witnessed the production of these faux mushrooms, I was amazed at how realistic the little baked meringues looked. Since then, I have come across recipes almost identical to the one in my CIA notes in several French cookbooks, as well as one by Maida Heatter. Traditionally used as a garnish for Bûche de Noël, these wonderful confections are great on their own.

INGREDIENTS

½ cup egg whites (about 4 whites), at room temperature

½ teaspoon cream of tartar

¼ teaspoon kosher salt

1 cup sugar

1 teaspoon vanilla

3½ ounces semisweet chocolate, chopped into small pieces

cocoa for garnish

PREPARATION

1 Preheat oven to 250°. Line a baking sheet with parchment paper or a silpat.

2 Place the egg whites in the bowl of a mixer with a whip and beat till frothy. Add the cream of tartar and salt and beat till soft peaks form. Very gradually add half the sugar and beat till stiff peaks form. Add the vanilla and gradually add the remaining sugar. Continue to beat until the meringue is very stiff and glossy.

3 Place the meringue in a large pastry bag fitted with a plain open tip. Pipe the mushroom caps by forming rounds that are approximately 1 to 1½ inches in diameter. Separately form the mushroom stems by piping out ½ to 1 inch high bases. Visualize that you will eventually be attaching the mushroom caps to the stems—some variation in size and shape is fine. I like to pipe out a row of caps followed by a row of stems to ensure that I wind up with the same quantity of each.

4 You can take a damp (not wet) finger and lightly tamp down any points that may have formed—remember, you want rounded caps, not Hershey's Kisses.

5 Bake at 250° for 40 minutes. Turn the oven to 200° and bake an additional 2 hours or until the meringues are dry and crisp. You want them to maintain their white color. Cool the meringues and store airtight if not assembling right away.

6 To assemble, melt the semisweet chocolate in the top of a double boiler. To form a mushroom you will need to have an empty egg carton or a trough formed from a double thickness of aluminum foil to cradle the finished mushrooms. Place ¼ to ½ teaspoon of melted chocolate in the center of the flat bottom of the mushroom cap. Do not allow the chocolate to drip over the sides of the cap. Attach a stem to the cap by placing it in the chocolate. Place the mushroom cap down into the egg carton. After forming enough

mushrooms to fill the carton, place them in the refrigerator or freezer briefly, just long enough to set the chocolate. Remove the mushrooms to a plate and place them right side up. Assemble the remaining mushrooms.

7 Place a small amount of cocoa in a strainer and lightly dust the caps of the assembled mushrooms. Store loosely covered at room temperature in a dry spot. Do not refrigerate or store airtight. These are best served within a day or two.

Baker's Note: As with all baked meringues, you will have greater success with these if you bake them on a cool, dry day.

Serving Suggestions: Use these as a garnish for chocolate chestnut cream roll (page 212). They're also great served alongside peppermint stick ice cream (page 272) drizzled with cocoa fudge sauce (page 37). My favorite way to present them is heaped in a straw basket, which can be put on a buffet or passed at the table.

Joel's Oatmeal Cookies

MAKES 2 DOZEN

Ben and I consider ourselves exceptionally lucky to be part of Joel Fleishman's worldwide circle of friends. He is one of the wisest and most thoughtful individuals we know, and it is totally in character that these humble, unassuming cookies are his favorite. Every December I make a note to myself to bake Joel a batch of these—he prefers his with sun-dried cranberries, but you can also use sun-dried blueberries or cherries if you'd like.

INGREDIENTS

12 tablespoons (6 ounces) butter, at room temperature
1 cup brown sugar
2 tablespoons sugar
1 egg
¼ cup water
1 teaspoon vanilla
½ teaspoon kosher salt
½ teaspoon baking soda

1 cup flour

3 cups old-fashioned oats

1 cup sun-dried cranberries, blueberries, or cherries

PREPARATION

1 In the bowl of a mixer fitted with a paddle, cream the butter with the sugars. Add the egg and mix to blend. Add the water and the vanilla. Add the salt, baking soda, and flour and mix to blend, scraping down the bowl. Add the oats. Add the dried fruit and mix just till distributed.

2 You can bake these right after making the dough, but I prefer to chill the dough before forming the cookies. The dough can be made up to 3 days ahead of time or frozen. If frozen, defrost overnight in the refrigerator before using.

3 Preheat oven to 350°.

4 Using a rounded tablespoon of dough per cookie, place cookies on a parchment paper— or silpat-lined baking sheet, leaving about 2 inches between the cookies. Flatten each cookie slightly.

5 Bake at 350° for approximately 18 minutes, reversing the sheet halfway through the baking time, until the cookies are lightly browned and just set to the touch. I think these are best served freshly baked and slightly warm. But they will keep, stored airtight, for up to 2 days.

Baker's Note: You can use raisins in these, but I like the contrast of a tarter fruit. Adding nuts is optional.

Serving Suggestion: Serve with a large glass of cold milk.

Chocolate Chunky Brownie Bars

MAKES 3 DOZEN

This brownie variation is an ode to the Chunky—that vintage candy bar containing copious quantities of fruit, nuts, and chocolate. If I'm serving an all-adult audience, I sometimes plump the raisins in bourbon or scotch.

INGREDIENTS

    8 ounces unsweetened chocolate, chopped

    16 tablespoons (8 ounces) butter

    5 eggs

    1 cup sugar

    1 cup brown sugar

    1 teaspoon vanilla

    ½ teaspoon kosher salt

    1¼ cups flour

    1½ cups raisins

    1½ cups lightly toasted Brazil nuts, chopped into medium-sized pieces

    1 cup semisweet chocolate chips (homemade [page 54] or store-bought)

PREPARATION

1 Preheat oven to 375°. Butter a 9 × 12 × 2-inch brownie pan (one close in size is fine), line the bottom with parchment paper, and butter the paper.

2 Melt the unsweetened chocolate and butter in the top of a double boiler and reserve.

3 Combine the eggs with the sugars in the bowl of a mixer with a whip attachment and beat until the mixture is very thick, light, and fluffy (about 4 to 5 minutes). Add the vanilla and the salt and mix to blend. Add the reserved chocolate-butter mixture and mix to blend. Add the flour and mix just till combined, scraping the bowl. Add the raisins, Brazil nuts, and chocolate chips and mix just till distributed. Transfer the batter to the prepared pan and use an offset spatula to spread it evenly.

4 Bake at 375° for about 30 minutes, until the brownies are just barely set. The top will appear slightly puffed and will just start to develop a few hairline cracks. Do not overbake—if you test them, they will appear underdone.

5 Cool the brownies and place them in the refrigerator to chill for several hours. To remove them from the pan, briefly heat the bottom of the brownie pan over a range burner, loosen the edges of the brownies with a paring knife, and turn the brownies out onto a parchment paper–lined baking sheet. Peel off the parchment liner and reinvert the brownies onto a cutting surface. Using a sturdy slicing knife and wiping the blade between each cut, portion the brownies into 3 × 1-inch bars. The brownies can be made 1 day ahead.

Baker's Note: If you have trouble finding Brazil nuts, you may substitute pecans. I think these brownies are best served chilled, straight from the refrigerator.

Serving Suggestion: These have brownie sundae written all over them—top with a scoop of not-just-plain-vanilla ice cream (page 261), cocoa fudge sauce (page 37), and whipped cream.

Brooklyn Black-&-Whites

MAKES 8 LARGE COOKIES

This recipe resulted from my efforts to re-create an old childhood favorite. When I was growing up in Brooklyn, every neighborhood seemed to have a corner bakery that turned out an amazing array of danishes, babkas, cakes, and pastries. One of my preferred treats was this saucer-sized "cakey" cookie lavished with both chocolate and vanilla icings. A black-and-white with a large glass of milk still makes me very happy.

INGREDIENTS FOR THE COOKIES
   1½ cups flour
   ¼ teaspoon kosher salt
   ⅛ teaspoon baking soda
   ½ cup + 2 tablespoons sugar
   5 tablespoons (2½ ounces) butter, at room temperature
   ¼ cup (1½ ounces) vegetable shortening
   1 egg
   1 teaspoon vanilla
   2 tablespoons buttermilk

INGREDIENTS FOR THE FONDANT ICING
   2½ cups confectioners' sugar, sifted
   ⅔ tablespoon corn syrup
   3 tablespoons hot water (plus additional hot water as necessary)
   ½ teaspoon vanilla
   ⅔ tablespoon cocoa
   1 ounce unsweetened chocolate, melted

PREPARATION FOR THE COOKIES

1   Preheat oven to 350°.

2   Sift together the flour, salt, and baking soda and reserve.

3   In the bowl of an electric mixer with a paddle attachment, cream together the sugar, butter, and shortening. Add the egg, vanilla, and buttermilk. Add the dry ingredients, mixing until just blended.

4   Line a large cookie sheet with parchment paper and portion the dough into 8 rounded mounds (about 2 generous tablespoons per cookie). Flatten slightly.

5   Bake at 350° for approximately 15 to 20 minutes, until the edges of the cookies just start to turn a light golden brown. Remove from oven and cool completely.

PREPARATION FOR THE FONDANT ICING AND ASSEMBLY

1   In a mixing bowl, whisk together the confectioners' sugar, corn syrup, hot water, and vanilla. Remove half of this mixture to a separate bowl and whisk in the cocoa and melted chocolate until smooth. If necessary, place the chocolate fondant in the top of a double boiler to completely incorporate the chocolate.

2   Both fondants should be of thick but still somewhat fluid consistency—you should be able to spread a thin, even layer of icing. If necessary, you can adjust the consistency by thinning with a bit more hot water (add by the teaspoonful) or by adding body with a bit more confectioners' sugar. Turn each cookie over and ice half the flat bottom side with the vanilla fondant. Repeat by icing the remaining half of each cookie with the chocolate fondant. Allow to set up at room temperature for several hours before serving.

Baker's Note: The only really tricky part of this recipe is getting the fondants to the proper consistency. If the icings start to set up before you finish spreading them, you can place them in the top of a double boiler to restore the fondant to correct viscosity. A small offset spatula is the best tool to use in the icing process. While these cookies are traditionally oversized, you can make them smaller—mini versions look great as part of a cookie assortment.

Extra Crunchy Peanut Butter Cookies

MAKES 2 DOZEN

These crumbly, crunchy cookies are loaded with honey roasted peanuts. They are dedicated to my husband, whose biggest junk food vice is eating generous spoonsful of chunky-style Skippy straight from the jar. Our son is a purist, though, and prefers these "plain"—made with smooth peanut butter and no added nuts. Either way, this cookie is a satisfying example of comfort food at its best.

INGREDIENTS

¼ cup + 1 tablespoon (2 ounces) vegetable shortening

4 tablespoons (2 ounces) butter, at room temperature

½ cup sugar

½ cup brown sugar

½ cup chunky-style peanut butter

1 egg

½ teaspoon vanilla

1 teaspoon baking soda

¼ teaspoon kosher salt

1½ cups flour

¾ cup honey roasted peanuts, chopped into medium-sized pieces

PREPARATION

1 Preheat oven to 350°.

2 Using a mixer with a paddle, cream the vegetable shortening, butter, and both sugars. Add the peanut butter and mix to blend. Add the egg and vanilla and mix, scraping the bowl, till combined. Mix in the baking soda and salt. Scrape down the bowl. Add the flour and mix just to blend. Add the peanuts and mix just till distributed.

3 Portion the dough into generously rounded tablespoon mounds and place them on a parchment paper–lined baking sheet, leaving several inches between cookies. Flatten them slightly with the heel of your hand. With a fork, press lightly and form a crosshatch pattern on top of each cookie. Dip the fork in sugar if sticking is a problem.

4 Bake the cookies at 350° for about 15 minutes. They should be just set and just starting to pick up a bit of color. Remove from the oven and cool.

Baker's Note: This dough can be made ahead of time if kept refrigerated or frozen. Be careful not to overbake these—the tops will remain quite pale but the bottoms will be a light golden brown when done.

Serving Suggestions: There are few accompaniments to these better than a glass of milk (or a couple of scoops of icy-cold milk sherbet [see page 287]). If chocolate and peanut butter is a pleasing combination to you, serve these alongside deep dark chocolate pudding (page 184) and top the pudding with whipped cream and chopped honey roasted peanuts.

Pancakes, Waffles, Fritters, & Other Breakfast-Like Desserts

Celebrity Dairy Blintzes with Raspberries & Honey Cream

Double Pecan Crepes with Butterscotch Baked Bananas

Giant Apricot Popover Pancake

Cinnamon Ricotta Shortstack

Raised Cocoa Waffles à la Mode

Black Pepper Beignets

Maytag Blue Cheese Fritters

Pineapple Fritters

American moms have long championed the importance of breakfast—and I am one of them! Nutritional issues aside, I like the psychological benefits of "morning food," and I also firmly believe that dishes that are traditionally served before noon should be enjoyed at all mealtimes. I think that breakfast is indulgent—not because the dishes themselves are extravagant, but because it represents the luxury of time. Breakfast-style desserts are comforting, familiar, and very easy to execute. While they may initially seem more appropriate for casual family dinners, they can certainly be dressed up to suit even the grandest special occasion. One general rule to follow is that, although the preparation work for most of the recipes that follow can be done in advance, these desserts need to be served hot and fresh from the oven, griddle, or fryer to be successful. Here are some tips that will help you turn out wonderful breakfast treats any time of day.

- I find that most waffles take longer to cook than most irons' automatic indicators suggest. Just as with cakes, smell is an excellent sign of doneness for waffles. After you use it a few times, you will get to know your waffle iron—each brand and type performs differently.
- Avoid overmixing pancake, waffle, and crepe batters. Overstirring can develop flour glutens, which will result in a tougher end product.
- Crepe pans, waffle irons, and griddles should all be lightly regreased during the cooking process, even if they have a nonstick surface.
- Pancakes cook best on a griddle or large, wide, heavy sauté pan with sloping sides. Allow yourself plenty of room to successfully flip the pancakes.
- Keep batches of finished waffles, crepes, fritters, etc., warm in a preheated 250° oven while you complete the cooking process.

And here are a few pointers for fabulous frying.

- Use clean, fresh vegetable oil to fry dessert items. I use canola oil.
- A deep fat frying/candy thermometer is a useful tool for accurately judging frying temperatures. Even electric fry pans or deep fat fryers are occasionally slightly off from their thermostat setting.
- Make sure your nonreactive frying vessel is heavy-bottomed and has plenty of head space—the hot oil will bubble up when food is added. Oil should be at a depth of at least 3 inches.

- Allow the oil to preheat gradually. Do not overcrowd the fryer and always allow the oil to come back to temperature between batches.
- Skim the oil and remove any stray crumbs between batches.
- Drain fried fritters on several layers of lightly crumpled paper toweling. This increases surface absorption area and facilitates excess oil absorption. Replenish if the toweling becomes saturated with oil.
- Oil can be cooled, strained, and stored in a cool place. It can usually be reused one time if it is still clear, light in color, and without "off" odors.

Celebrity Dairy Blintzes with Raspberries & Honey Cream

SERVES 8; MAKES 16 BLINTZES

This dessert is a blast from my palate memory past, as it's very similar to the blintzes my grandmother used to fix. A blintz is essentially a cheese-filled crepe. Traditionally farmer cheese is used for the filling, but I thought that this dessert would be the perfect showcase for the artisanal goat cheese produced in our part of North Carolina by Celebrity Dairy. I'd encourage you to use your own locally produced cheese or else one made by Coach Farms or Laura Chenel, both of which are widely available. A French Montrachet can also be substituted.

INGREDIENTS FOR THE CREPES
   1 cup flour
   2 tablespoons sugar
   ⅛ teaspoon kosher salt
   ¼ teaspoon cinnamon
   3 eggs
   1¼ cup milk
   1 teaspoon vanilla
   6 tablespoons (3 ounces) butter, melted

INGREDIENTS FOR THE FILLING
   8 ounces young, fresh goat cheese, at room temperature
   4 ounces cream cheese, at room temperature

5 tablespoons sugar

2 egg yolks

¼ teaspoon cinnamon

INGREDIENTS FOR ASSEMBLY AND GARNISH

3 tablespoons (1½ ounces) butter, melted

½ cup sugar

¾ cup sour cream

2 tablespoons honey

1½ pints raspberries

confectioners' sugar for garnishing

PREPARATION FOR THE CREPES

1 Combine the flour, sugar, salt, and cinnamon in a mixing bowl. Make a well in the center and reserve.

2 In a separate bowl, whisk together the eggs, milk, vanilla, and melted butter. Gradually whisk the wet ingredients into the well of the reserved dry ingredients, mixing just to blend smoothly.

3 Using a heated, very lightly buttered, 8-inch nonstick skillet, working over medium heat, put about 3 tablespoons of the batter in the skillet, tilting the skillet to completely film the bottom. Allow the crepe to brown lightly (small bubbles will usually start to appear on the surface), then loosen and flip the crepe. Cook the other side for just a few seconds. Turn the crepe out on a plate or tea towel to cool briefly. Repeat, using the remaining batter, lightly rebuttering the pan if necessary. The crepes can be made 1 day ahead, stacked, wrapped with plastic, and refrigerated. Bring to room temperature before filling.

PREPARATION FOR THE FILLING AND ASSEMBLY

1 Combine all the filling ingredients and beat until smooth.

2 Place the cheese mixture in a pastry bag. I use a medium-sized open pastry tip, but if you don't have one you can pipe the cheese directly from the bag, sans tip. Alternatively, you can spoon the filling onto the crepes.

3 Lay the crepes out "nice side" down and pipe a 4-inch-long strip of cheese filling, centered, across the bottom third of each crepe. Fold the bottom edge of the crepe over the filling. Fold the right side of the crepe over the filling to form a right angle. Fold the left side of the crepe over the filling in the same

manner. Roll the crepe snugly shut. The process is the same as forming spring rolls or burritos. Brush the top and bottom of the formed blintz with melted butter and place seam side down on a lightly buttered jellyroll pan. Form only one layer of blintzes as you place them on the pan. These can be filled 24 hours in advance if kept covered in the refrigerator. Bring to room temperature before baking.

4   Preheat oven to 375°. Sprinkle the top of each crepe with about a teaspoon of sugar and bake approximately 10 minutes, until the blintzes are heated through and starting to crisp on the outside.

5   Meanwhile, gently swirl the honey into the sour cream. Serve 2 blintzes per portion. Sprinkle the blintzes with confectioners' sugar and serve topped with some raspberries and a small dollop of the honey cream.

Baker's Note: This recipe gives you ample batter for a few practice crepes. I use a paper towel dipped in soft butter to grease my crepe pan very lightly. Do not let the pan sit too long over the heat without any batter being added to it—it will make the nonstick finish break down. To flip the crepes, I just pick them up with my fingers, but you may use a heat-resistant plastic spatula to aid in the turning process if you wish. Remember that you are in control of this process and you can always raise or lower the heat under your pans.

Serving Suggestions: If I have it on hand, I often add a zigzag of raspberry sauce to the plate. You can definitely vary the fruit garnish on this recipe. Strawberry rhubarb compote (page 148), cinnamon spiced blueberry sauce (page 45), or a combination of fresh figs and blackberries would be wonderful with the blintzes. While fabulous for dessert, this dish can also be served as part of a brunch buffet.

Double Pecan Crepes with Butterscotch Baked Bananas

SERVES 6

For a brief time, while I was in culinary school, I worked at a small creperie. I became adept at turning out massive quantities of the delicate pancakes, but it was quite a while before I even considered putting them on a dessert menu—it is entirely possible to overdose on crepes. Now that I don't have to make them day in and day out, I do occasionally offer them at Magnolia Grill, where they have proven to be a consistent best-seller.

INGREDIENTS FOR THE CREPES
¾ cup + 2 tablespoons flour

¼ cup lightly toasted, finely ground pecans

½ teaspoon kosher salt

3 tablespoons sugar

3 eggs

1½ cups milk

2 tablespoons bourbon

4 tablespoons (2 ounces) butter, melted

INGREDIENTS FOR THE FILLING
½ cup milk

¾ cup sugar

1 tablespoon (½ ounce) butter

2 cups lightly toasted, coarsely ground pecans

½ teaspoon cinnamon

1 tablespoon bourbon

¾ cup fine, dry, unseasoned breadcrumbs

INGREDIENTS FOR FINISHING
1 recipe butterscotch baked bananas (page 154)

whipped cream or ice cream of your choice

PREPARATION FOR THE CREPES
1 Combine the flour, pecans, salt, and sugar in a large mixing bowl.

2 Combine the eggs, milk, and bourbon in a separate mixing bowl and whisk to combine.

3 Form a well in the center of the dry ingredients and add the wet ingredients, whisking until smooth. Whisk in the melted butter and allow the batter to sit for 1 hour.

4 Using an 8-inch nonstick skillet, make the crepes. Brush the skillet very lightly with melted butter, film the bottom with enough batter to lightly coat the pan, tilting the pan to ensure even coverage. Allow the crepe to set and lightly

brown on one side, then flip it over and cook it briefly on the other. Turn the crepe out of the pan and repeat the process using all the batter. Cool the crepes and then place them in small stacks until you are ready to fill them. They can be made 1 day in advance. Wrap the crepe stacks in plastic film and refrigerate. Bring to room temperature before filling.

PREPARATION FOR THE FILLING

1 In a medium-sized saucepan, heat the milk to just under a boil. Add the sugar and butter. When the butter is melted, stir in the pecans, cinnamon, bourbon, and breadcrumbs.

2 To fill the crepes, lay them out "nice" side down. With a small offset spatula, lightly spread the surface of each crepe with the pecan filling. Fold the crepes in half and then in half again. The crepes can be filled 1 day in advance. Lay them out on a baking sheet, cover with plastic wrap and refrigerate.

TO FINISH THE CREPES

1 Bring the crepes to room temperature before heating.

2 Preheat oven to 425°. Place the crepes in the oven and bake them for about 5 minutes, until they are heated through. Time your preparation of the butterscotch baked bananas so that the bananas can go in the oven at the same time as the crepes. When the crepes are heated through and the bananas are bubbling, remove them from the oven.

3 Place two crepes on each dessert plate. Top them with some bananas and butterscotch "sauce" from the banana pan. Serve warm with whipped cream or ice cream.

Baker's Note: These crepes can also be made with walnuts or hazelnuts. The recipe can easily be doubled if you're serving a larger group.

Serving Suggestions: I'm partial to serving these with ice cream, but then again, I'm partial to serving just about everything with ice cream. Bourbon molasses ice cream (page 264) is the perfect accompaniment. If you'd like to add a little crunch to the dish, sprinkle the ice cream and crepes with some chopped pecan praline (page 56).

Giant Apricot Popover Pancake

SERVES 8

This cross between a fruit pancake and an eggy popover puffs to amazing proportions—it looks huge, but it is extremely light and airy. It's most impressive when pulled straight from the oven, served immediately and presented whole at the table.

INGREDIENTS

    4 tablespoons (2 ounces) butter, divided

    8 medium-sized ripe but firm apricots, each sliced into 6–8 wedges

    3 tablespoons sugar, divided

    ½ teaspoon cardamom

    ¼ teaspoon kosher salt

    seeds of 1 vanilla bean

    ½ cup flour

    ½ cup milk

    4 eggs

    4 tablespoons confectioners' sugar, divided

PREPARATION

1 Preheat oven to 450°.

2 Melt 1 tablespoon of butter in a 12-inch heavy skillet (cast iron works well). Add the apricots and sprinkle them with 2 tablespoons of sugar. Over high heat, sauté them till they cook through and start to caramelize. Remove the apricots and reserve. Clean the skillet and reserve.

3 Place 1 tablespoon of sugar, the cardamom, salt, vanilla bean seeds, and flour in a medium-sized mixing bowl. Gradually whisk in the milk till smooth. Whisk in the eggs and mix till well combined. Melt 2 tablespoons of the remaining butter and whisk into the egg mixture. Reserve.

4 While you are putting the popover pancake batter together, preheat the 12-inch ovenproof skillet by placing it in a 450° oven for several minutes. Carefully remove the skillet from the oven and add the remaining 1 tablespoon of butter, tilting the skillet to coat the bottom evenly. Arrange the reserved sautéed apricots in the skillet and pour the reserved batter over the apricots. Place the pan back in the oven and bake at 450° for 15 minutes. Remove the pancake from the oven and sift 2 tablespoons of confectioners' sugar evenly

over it. Return it to the oven for an additional 10 minutes or until it is well puffed and golden brown. Remove, sift the remaining 2 tablespoons of confectioners' sugar over the pancake, and serve immediately.

Baker's Note: You can substitute apples, pears, or nectarines for the apricots if you wish.

Serving Suggestion: I like to serve this with some sweet and sour cherry compote (page 155) and a dollop of crème fraîche (page 67).

Cinnamon Ricotta Shortstack

SERVES 6

For some people, pancakes are merely carriers for butter and syrup. I think you know you've had a great pancake when you don't mind eating it straight up. These heavenly hots are like griddled cheese soufflés. Delicate in texture and flavor, they are very tasty cakes of the pan.

INGREDIENTS FOR PANCAKES
   1 cup ricotta cheese
   grated zest of 1 lemon
   ½ teaspoon cinnamon
   ¼ teaspoon kosher salt
   ½ teaspoon vanilla
   1 teaspoon baking powder
   ¼ cup + 1 tablespoon sugar
   2 tablespoons (1 ounce) butter, melted
   4 egg yolks
   ¾ cup flour
   ½ cup milk
   4 egg whites

INGREDIENTS FOR SERVICE
   1 recipe strawberry rhubarb compote (page 148)
   1½ cups lightly sweetened whipped cream
   6 beautiful small strawberries
   confectioners' sugar

PREPARATION

1 Preheat oven to 225°. Combine the ricotta cheese, lemon zest, cinnamon, salt, vanilla, baking powder, sugar, melted butter, and egg yolks in a mixing bowl and whisk to combine. Whisk in the flour and then gradually whisk in the milk. Mix just to combine.

2 In a separate bowl, beat the egg whites to medium peaks. Lighten the ricotta mixture by folding in one-third of the egg whites. Fold in the remaining whites. Place the batter in a pitcher.

3 Heat a griddle or large skillet (preferably nonstick), film it with butter, and form pancakes that are about 2½ to 3 inches in diameter, using about 3 tablespoons of batter. Cook over medium heat till the pancakes are set. They will start to form a few surface bubbles, and if you peek at the bottom they will be unevenly golden brown. Flip the pancakes and cook till the second side is browned. Repeat, lightly regreasing the griddle, until all of the batter is used.

4 Hold the finished pancakes in a 225° oven until they are all made.

5 To serve, for each portion, place a pancake on a dessert plate. Top with a generous spoonful of strawberry rhubarb compote. Layer with a second pancake, another spoonful of compote, and a dollop of whipped cream. Place a strawberry on top of each short stack and sprinkle the plate rim with confectioners' sugar.

Baker's Note: These pancakes are fairly fragile. To turn them successfully, use a thin-bladed, wide metal spatula and a quickly executed flip of the wrist. Leave plenty of room between pancakes on the griddle.

Serving Suggestions: You can substitute fresh berries or cinnamon spiced blueberry sauce (page 45) for the strawberry rhubarb compote. Lemon curd/custard (page 59) can be used in place of the whipped cream.

Raised Cocoa Waffles à la Mode

MAKES 6 WAFFLES, OR 12 DESSERT PORTIONS

These lightly yeasted waffles take me back to my Brooklyn days of Greek diners and I-HOPs, where breakfast could be eaten all day long. Waffles and ice cream were a frequent "after the movies" evening dessert treat. Choconut that I am, I

couldn't resist developing a dusky, not-too-sweet chocolate version of this childhood favorite.

INGREDIENTS FOR THE WAFFLES

1¾ cups flour

½ cup cocoa

¼ teaspoon baking soda

1 teaspoon kosher salt

1 package (1 scant tablespoon) dry yeast

½ cup + 2 tablespoons sugar

1½ cups milk

2 eggs

1 teaspoon vanilla

2 tablespoons dark crème de cacao (or other liqueur)

6 tablespoons (3 ounces) butter, melted

INGREDIENTS FOR SERVICE

your favorite ice cream and accompanying sauce

whipped cream, if you wish to get excessive

PREPARATION

1 Sift the flour, cocoa, and baking soda into a medium-sized mixing bowl. Add the salt, yeast, and sugar and stir to blend well.

2 Heat the milk till warm to the touch. Make a well in the center of the dry ingredients and gradually whisk in the warm milk.

3 In a small bowl, whisk together the eggs, vanilla, crème de cacao, and melted butter. Add this mixture to the batter and mix till combined. Cover the mixing bowl with plastic wrap, place it in a warm spot, and allow the batter to rise till bubbly and almost doubled in volume. This should take about 1½ hours.

4 Preheat a waffle iron. Generously spray the grids (even if it's a nonstick iron) with cooking spray. Stir the batter to deflate and bake the waffles one at a time, regreasing the grids in between each waffle.

5 As they finish baking, cool the waffles on a rack. These can be made up to a day in advance. Wrap them in plastic and store in the refrigerator. Bring the waffles to room temperature before toasting and serving.

6 To serve, cut the waffles into quarters, toast them lightly (or reheat at 350° for 4 to 5 minutes), and stack, alternating 2 waffle pieces with 2 scoops of ice

cream for each portion. Drizzle the waffle stack with a complementary sauce. Add a dollop of whipped cream for the ultimate in indulgence.

Baker's Note: These waffles tend to be quite delicate and soft when they come off the iron, but they will firm up as they cool.

A note to those who might be inclined to add chocolate chips to this recipe: I occasionally add 2½ ounces of finely chopped chocolate to the batter right before I start to bake the waffles; but this addition does increase the likelihood of sticking, and the melted chocolate residue is a bit messy to clean up.

Serving Suggestions: My favorite way to serve these is with peppermint stick ice cream (page 272) and cocoa fudge sauce (page 37). They're also delicious when paired with the same sauce, fresh sliced strawberries, and whipped cream or not-just-plain-vanilla ice cream (page 261).

Black Pepper Beignets

MAKES 2½ DOZEN

Every cuisine seems to have its variation of a fried dough pastry, and one of my favorites among these is the beignets served at the legendary Café du Monde in New Orleans. In my version, I've added some black pepper to these puffy crisps of sugar-coated air for a bit of unexpected spice.

INGREDIENTS

1¼ teaspoons yeast
2 tablespoons warm water
¼ cup sugar
1 tablespoon vegetable shortening
½ teaspoon kosher salt
1 teaspoon coarsely ground, freshly ground black pepper
¼ cup boiling water
¼ cup cream
1 egg
2–2¼ cups flour
canola oil for deep frying
powdered sugar for finishing

PREPARATION

1 In a small bowl, combine the yeast with warm water and a pinch of the sugar. Allow to proof and reserve.

2 Combine the remaining sugar with the vegetable shortening, salt, and pepper in a mixing bowl. Add the boiling water and stir to melt the shortening. Allow to cool for 5 minutes.

3 Add the cream, egg, and reserved yeast mixture to the mixing bowl and stir to combine. Stir in about 1½ cups flour. Gradually add in enough of the remaining flour to form a soft dough. On a lightly floured surface, knead the dough for about 5 minutes, until it's smooth and elastic. Cover the dough and allow it to rest for 15 minutes.

4 Roll the dough into a 15 × 12-inch rectangle. Trim the edges and, using a pizza cutter or sharp knife, cut the dough into 3 × 2-inch rectangles.

5 If frying the beignets immediately, preheat the frying oil to 350°. If you wish, you can roll the beignets and store them in an airtight container overnight. Separate the stacked layers of beignets with parchment paper. Made-ahead beignets can be fried directly from their chilled state.

6 For frying, the oil should be at least 3 inches deep. These can be fried in a deep fryer, electric skillet, or steep-sided saucepot. Without crowding them, place the beignets in the preheated oil. You will probably need to fry these in several batches. Fry the beignets on one side till golden brown. Turn and fry on the second side till golden. Remove and drain well on lightly crumpled paper toweling. Allow to cool for a few minutes, sprinkle very liberally with powdered sugar, serve, and enjoy!

Baker's Note: You can certainly omit the black pepper in this recipe, if you like, or substitute ground cardamom, grated orange zest, vanilla bean, cinnamon, or nutmeg. Like all fried foods, beignets should be fried shortly before serving.

Serving Suggestions: I like to serve these as an accompaniment to strawberry sorbet (page 279), Café du Monde chicory coffee granita (page 285), bourbon molasses ice cream (page 264), or winter fruits poached in red wine syrup (page 157).

Maytag Blue Cheese Fritters

SERVES 6 TO 8

The notion of lightly sweetened blue cheese fritters might sound like an odd dessert, but trust me—if you have any liking for blue cheeses, you will enjoy these airy little puffs. When paired with any number of fruit garnishes, they can be served at a rustic winter brunch or as a complex finish to a special wine dinner. An accompanying bottle of good port is optional.

INGREDIENTS
    ½ cup + 2 tablespoons flour
    1 ½ teaspoons baking powder
    ⅛ teaspoon kosher salt
    2 grinds fresh black pepper
    4 ounces Maytag blue cheese, at room temperature

4 ounces whole-milk ricotta cheese

¼ cup + 2 tablespoons sugar

2 eggs

canola oil for deep frying

powdered sugar for finishing

PREPARATION

1 Sift together the flour, baking powder, salt, and pepper. Reserve.

2 In a mixing bowl, whisk the blue cheese and ricotta together with the sugar until fairly smooth. Whisk in the eggs and mix till combined. Stir in the reserved flour mixture.

3 Preheat the frying oil to 340° to 350°. The oil should be at least 3 inches deep. These can be fried in a deep fryer, electric skillet, or steep-sided saucepot. Without crowding them, scoop rounded teaspoons of batter into the preheated oil (a spring-loaded ice cream scoop is great for doing this). You will need to fry these in several batches. Once the fritters have risen to the surface and are golden on one side, turn them and fry on the second side till they are evenly browned (about 2½ minutes per side).

4 Drain the fritters on lightly crumpled paper towels and dust liberally with powdered sugar just before serving.

Baker's Note: This recipe doubles easily. You can keep already fried fritters in a warm oven while you finish frying the rest.

Serving Suggestions: Serve these fritters with oven roasted figs and raspberries (page 151), peppered Bartlett pears in sherry syrup (page 160), winter fruits poached in red wine syrup (page 159), or some fresh strawberries tossed with a bit of sugar, black pepper, and balsamic vinegar. You can also set out a basket of these for a buffet brunch, with Granny Smith applesauce (page 47) or Concord grape syrup (page 50) alongside.

Pineapple Fritters

SERVES 6

Where I live, Krispy Kremes and state fair–style "funnel cakes" are held in very high regard. These pineapple fritters were created when we wanted to put an "upscale" fried item on the dessert menu at the Grill. Crispy on the outside, with a tender cake donut–style interior and a surprise of juicy fruit, they are simply irresistible.

INGREDIENTS

½ tablespoon baking powder
½ teaspoon baking soda
1 cup flour
1 cup cornstarch
¼ cup + 2 tablespoons sugar
1 teaspoon kosher salt
2 egg yolks
⅓ cup buttermilk
⅓ cup milk
3 tablespoons vegetable oil
1 teaspoon vanilla
2 egg whites
1 small fresh pineapple, cut into large ¾-inch cubes
canola oil for deep frying
1 cup sugar for finishing
¼ teaspoon cayenne pepper for finishing

PREPARATION

1 Combine the baking powder, baking soda, flour, cornstarch, sugar, and salt in a mixing bowl. In a separate bowl, whisk together the egg yolks, buttermilk, milk, vegetable oil, and vanilla.

2 Whisk the wet ingredients into the dry ingredients, mixing just to blend. Beat the egg whites to medium peaks and fold into the fritter batter.

3 Heat the vegetable oil to 350°. The oil should be at least 3 inches deep. These can be fried in a deep fryer, electric skillet, or steep-sided pot. Spear individual pineapple cubes with a fork, dip in batter to coat completely, and

carefully place in the preheated oil. You may fry several fritters at once but do not crowd them. Turn the fritters halfway through the frying process. They are done when they are a uniform golden brown. Drain on crumpled or paper toweling.

4　Combine 1 cup sugar with cayenne pepper in a small brown paper bag. While the fritters are still warm, place them in the bag, shaking to coat them evenly. Serve warm.

Baker's Note: This is a great basic sweet fritter recipe, and I've found that other not-too-juicy fruits can be substituted for the pineapple—bananas work particularly well. The fruit can be prepared and the batter can be assembled 2 hours before you plan to actually complete the fritters. They should, however, be fried just before you serve them.

Serving Suggestions: Serve with strawberry rhubarb compote (page 148) and strawberry sorbet (page 279). These would also be an interesting accompaniment to ginger crème brûlée (page 194).

A Baker's Bookshelf

Many young bakers are fortunate enough to work with mentors who share their experiences, techniques, and recipes. As luck would have it, professionally I have always worked in kitchens where I had to fly solo. After I finished culinary school, much of my postgraduate baking experience was gained through voracious reading and a fair amount of trial and error. I admit to being a cookbook junkie. Throughout the years I've continued to go back to certain books for information and inspiration, picking up new favorites along the way. People often ask me for cookbook recommendations, so here's my list—a baker's dozen of personal favorites. Some of these volumes are out of print; however, I have had good success locating older books in secondhand bookshops (and, of course, nowadays amazon.com is an option).

- *Joy of Cooking* by Irma S. Rombauer and Marion Rombauer Becker. The new updated version (revised by Ethan Becker) is swell, but I think I prefer the original. When in doubt, I often consult "the girls."
- Any book written by Maida Heatter. I have often called Maida Heatter my dessert goddess. Every volume she has written is chock-full of fabulous, doable recipes that really work!
- Any book written by Nancy Silverton. An amazing array of artisanal bread recipes, simple rustic pastries, and restaurant-caliber desserts can be found within the pages of Nancy Silverton's books. The real deal from one of the very best bakers in America.
- *Classic Home Desserts* by Richard Sax. One of the most complete and delicious collections of traditional, homey desserts ever assembled—sweets for the soul that will please everyone.
- *Chez Panisse Desserts* by Lindsey Shere. Whenever I need seasonal inspiration, I turn to this book. The straight-up, easy-to-execute recipes really showcase the ingredients and make the most of innate flavors.
- *Jim Fobel's Old-Fashioned Baking Book*. This book epitomizes American-style baking. It's an old favorite that I refer to all the time.

- *In the Sweet Kitchen* by Regan Daley. The recipes in this book are almost an extra bonus. What I really value it for is the plethora of truly useful information it contains. Detailed comments on everything from equipment and ingredients to flavor combinations and plating suggestions are offered in this great big book.
- *How to Bake* by Nick Malgieri. As talented a teacher as he is a baker, Nick Malgieri provides wonderful, concise recipes that cover both sweet and savory baking. His *Perfect Cakes* is also a must-have reference.
- *Biscuits, Spoonbread, and Sweet Potato Pie* by Bill Neal. A treasure chest of traditional Southern baking along with (as the original jacket said) "a generous accompaniment of historical lore."
- *The Last Course* by Claudia Fleming with Melissa Clark. A collection of beautiful, simply elegant restaurant-style desserts formatted for the accomplished home baker.
- *Book of Tarts* by Maury Rubin. If you are in search of the perfect tart, you need to own this book—enough said.
- *The American Century Cookbook* by Jean Anderson. While not strictly a baking book, this tour of twentieth-century culinary America is a definitive winner. The dessert recipes are terrific, and the savory sections are equally appealing.
- *The Baker's Dozen Cookbook* edited by Rick Rodgers. An assemblage of mouthwatering recipes from an outstanding collaborative of talented bakers, along with their priceless baking wisdom.

Sources

There are probably kitchenware shops and gourmet markets in your area where you can obtain specialty ingredients and supplies such as those specified in my recipes. Often, local shops are willing to special order for you as well. If you have trouble locating certain items, the following businesses all make products available through mail order.

All-Clad Metalcrafters
800-255-2523
www.allclad.com
Beautifully crafted professional-grade cookware and bakeware

American Spoon Foods
888-735-6700
www.spoon.com
Black walnuts, dried fruits, and terrific preserves

The Baker's Catalogue
King Arthur Flour Company
800-827-6836
www.kingarthurflour.com
Just about everything you'll need for home baking—an array of specialty flours, dried fruits, flavored oils and extracts, sugars, chocolates, equipment, and more

Blenheim Brothers Ginger Ale
800-270-9344
Amazing artisanal ginger ales in hot, extra hot, and diet versions

Boyajian
800-419-4677
Fax: 781-828-9922
www.boyajianinc.com
Fantastic pure citrus oils, natural flavorings, and flavored oils and vinegars

Bridge Kitchenware
800-274-3435
www.bridgekitchenware.com
A very complete collection of knives, pots, pans, flan rings, small wares, and ovenproof baking dishes and ramekins

Chef's Catalog
800-338-3232
www.chefscatalog.com
A wide selection of reasonably priced large and small equipment

Dean and DeLuca
800-221-7714
www.deananddeluca.com
Specialty honey, spices, etc.

Hoppin' John's
800-828-4412
www.hoppinjohns.com
Stoneground cornmeal and great
   Southern cookbooks

Lee Brothers
843-720-8890
www.boiledpeanuts.com
A down-home, quirky, and highly
   personalized selection of indigenous
   Southern products, including
   sorghum, black walnuts, and
   Blenheim ginger ale

Martha Stewart
800-950-7130
www.marthastewart.com
Terrific for seasonal inspiration and
   supplies—unique molds, cookie
   cutters, stylish kitchenware—and a
   great source for boxes, ribbons,
   etc., for beautiful dessert gift-giving

Melissa's Produce
800-588-0151
www.melissas.com
Specialty produce (Medjool dates,
   quince, Meyer lemons, key limes,
   etc.)

New York Cake Supplies
800-942-2539
www.nycake.com
Specialty pans, other equipment,
   and chocolates

Nielsen-Massey Vanillas
800-525-7873
Fax: 847-578-1570
www.nielsenmassey.com
All things vanilla, including a variety
   of whole beans, extract, and ground
   powder

Penzeys Spices
800-741-7787
Fax: 262-785-7678
www.penzeys.com
One of the best mail-order spice
   sources around—also a source for
   vanilla beans and extract

Sur La Table
800-243-0852
www.surlatable.com
Electric mixers, waffle makers,
   specialty tools, knives, pans,
   and gadgets

Sweet Celebrations
800-328-6722
www.sweetc.com
Cake decorating and pastry supplies,
   chocolates, almond paste, etc.

White Lily
800-264-5459
www.whitelily.com
Soft wheat flour for biscuits and
   shortcakes

Williams-Sonoma

800-541-2233

www.williams-sonoma.com

High-quality kitchenware and supplies,
   including a good, well-chosen
   assortment of small appliances and
   cake and candy boxes

Appendix 1 Equivalent Pan Sizes

The following chart shows equivalent pan shapes and sizes based on the number of cups they will hold. The capacity shown is for a completely full pan. Remember that pan substitutions can affect baking time, which may need to be adjusted for the specific pan used.

Round cake pan	8 × 1½-inch	4 cups
	8 × 2-inch	6 cups
	9 × 1½-inch	6½ cups
	9 × 2-inch	8 cups
	10 × 2-inch	11 cups
Square cake pan	8 × 8 × 2-inch	8 cups
	9 × 9 × 2-inch	10 cups
Springform pan	8 × 3-inch	10 cups
	9 × 3-inch	11 cups
	10 × 3-inch	12 cups
Bundt pan	10-inch	12 cups
Angel food cake tube pan	10-inch	16 cups
Pie plate	9-inch	4½ cups
Deep-dish pie plate	9-inch	7 cups
Rectangular baking pan	7 × 11 × 1½-inch	8 cups
	11¾ × 7½ × 1¾-inch	10 cups
	9 × 13 × 2-inch	12 cups
Square baking dish	8 × 8 × 1½-inch	6 cups
	9 × 9 × 1½-inch	8 cups
Oval ceramic baking dish	11 × 2-inch	7 cups
	13 × 8 × 2¾-inch	11 cups
Mini-loaf pan	5¾ × 3¼ × 2-inch	1¾ cups
Loaf pan	8 × 3¾ × 2-inch	scant 5 cups
	8½ × 4½ × 2½-inch	6 cups
	9 × 5 × 3-inch	8 cups

Appendix 2 Metric & Imperial Conversions

The following table provides conversions between U.S., Imperial, and Metric measures. The American method of measuring by cups (and fractions thereof) makes it difficult to give weight equivalents, since a cup of densely packed butter would, for example, weigh considerably more than a cup of flour. The easiest way, therefore, to convert cup measurements in recipes is by volume rather than weight, following the equation 1 cup - 240 milliliters = 8 fluid ounces.

LIQUID MEASURES

Fluid Ounces	U.S.	Imperial	Milliliters
	1 teaspoon	1 teaspoon	5
¼	2 teaspoons	1 dessertspoon	10
½	1 tablespoon	1 tablespoon	14
1	2 tablespoons	2 tablespoons	28
2	¼ cup	4 tablespoons	56
4	½ cup		110
5		¼ pint or 1 gill	140
6	¾ cup		170
8	1 cup		225
9			250, ¼ liter
10	1¼ cups	½ pint	280
12	1½ cups		340
15		¾ pint	420
16	2 cups		450
18	2¼ cups		500, ½ liter
20	2½ cups	1 pint	560
24	3 cups		675
25		1¼ pints	700
27	3½ cups		750
30	3¾ cups	1½ pints	840
32	4 cups or 1 quart		900

Fluid Ounces	U.S.	Imperial	Milliliters
35		1¾ pints	980
36	4½ cups		1,000, 1 liter
40	5 cups	2 pints or 1 quart	1,120

SOLID MEASURES

U.S. and Imperial Measures		Metric Measures	
Ounces	Pounds	Grams	Kilos
1		28	
2		56	
3½		100	
4	¼	112	
5		140	
6		168	
8	½	225	
9		250	¼
12	¾	340	
16	1	450	
18		500	½
20	1¼	560	
24	1½	675	
27		750	¾
28	1¾	780	
32	2	900	
36	2¼	1,000	1
40	2½	1,100	
48	3	1,350	
54		1,500	1½

OVEN TEMPERATURE EQUIVALENTS

Fahrenheit	Celsius	Gas Mark	Description
225	110	¼	cool
250	130	½	
275	140	1	very slow
300	150	2	
325	170	3	slow

Fahrenheit	Celsius	Gas Mark	Description
350	180	4	moderate
375	190	5	
400	200	6	moderately hot
425	220	7	fairly hot
450	230	8	hot
475	240	9	very hot
500	250	10	extremely hot

Index

Custards
about, 167–68
bourbon crème caramel with brûléed
bananas, 171–74
buttermilk panna cotta, 188–89
coffee anise crème caramel, 174–76
ginger crème brûlée, 194–95
lemon or lime curd/custard, 59–60
Cutters, about, 21

Dairy products, about, 15
Dark chocolate Peppermint Pattie cake, 210–12
Dates
browned butter date nut tart, 101–2
cinnamon apple date babycakes, 234–36
Deep dark chocolate pudding, 184–85
Deep-dish brown sugar plum cobbler, 128–29
Devil's food cake with whipped ganache, 203–4
Double lemon custard cake, 220–22
Double pecan crepes with butterscotch baked
bananas, 337–39
Doughs. *See* Pastry doughs
Dumplings
blackberry slump with sweet potato
dumplings, 144–46
rhubarb cream cheese dumplings, 119–22

Eggnog snow cream, 288–89
Eggs, about, 15
Electric fry pans or deep fryers, about, 17
Equipment, kitchen, about, 16–21
Extra crunchy peanut butter cookies, 328–29
Extracts, about, 12

Fall fruits poached in brandied lemon syrup,
159–60
Figs
Fig Newton Zinfandel tart, 97–98
oven roasted figs with raspberries, 151–53
Flaky puff-style pastry, 29–30
Flour, about, 12
Folding, about, 201, 202
Food mills, about, 18–19

Food processors, about, 17
Frangipane
banana and peanut frangipane tarts,
100–101
peanut frangipane, 57–58
Fritters
Maytag blue cheese fritters, 348–49
pineapple fritters, 350–51
Frozen desserts
about, 260–61
Café du Monde chicory coffee granita,
285–86
eggnog snow cream, 288–89
frozen sourwood honey parfait, 289–90
see also Ice creams; Sherbets; Sorbets
Fruitcake, Big Island, 232–33
Fruits
about, 5–8, 125–26
Big Island fruitcake, 232–33
fall fruits poached in brandied lemon
syrup, 159–60
sautéed summer berries, 146–47
summer cherry berry pudding, 191–93
winter fruits poached in red wine syrup,
157–58
see also specific kinds of fruits
Frying, about, 233–34
Fudge pie, chocolate raspberry, 93–94
Fudge sauce, cocoa, 37–38

Giant apricot popover pancake, 340–42
Giant chocolate chip celebration cookies,
295–98
Ginger
Blenheim ginger ale sabayon, 189–90
ginger crème brûlée, 194–95
gingered maple walnut sauce, 42–43
not-afraid-of-flavor gingerbread, 222–23
Goat cheese
Celebrity Dairy blintzes with raspberries
and honey cream, 334–37
goat cheese cheesecake in a hazelnut crust,
252–53

strawberry rhubarb compote, 148–49

strawberry sorbet, 279–81

Sugar, about, 12

Sugar syrup, about, 281

Summer blueberry sorbet, 283–84

Summer cherry berry pudding, 191–93

Sweet and sour cherry compote, 155–57

Sweet potatoes

blackberry slump with sweet potato
dumplings, 144–46

maple bourbon sweet potato pie, 87–89

Syrups

coffee syrup, 52–53

Concord grape syrup, 50–51

mint syrup, 51–52

sugar syrup, 281

Tarts

about, 73–75

banana and peanut frangipane tarts,
100–101

browned butter date nut tart, 101–2

chocolate chestnut tarts, 104–5

chocolate chip cookie tarts, 102–4

chocolate Grand Marnier truffle tart,
106–8

cranberry Linzer tart, 109–10

dough for (see Pastry doughs)

Fig Newton Zinfandel tart, 97–98

lemon pecan tart, 95–97

lime meringue tart, 110–13

pink grapefruit soufflé tarts, 115–18

rustic raspberry tart, 113–15

Thermometers, about, 19

Timers, about, 19

Turnovers, cherry vanilla, 118–19

Vanilla

about, 11

buttermilk vanilla bean custard pie, 85–87

cherry vanilla turnovers, 118–19

cornmeal vanilla bean shortbreads, 300–302

not-just-plain-vanilla ice cream, 261–62

Vegetable oils, about, 13–15

Vegetable peelers, about, 21

Vitamin C tablets, about, 150

Waffle irons, about, 17–18

Waffles, raised cocoa, à la mode, 343–46

Walnuts

black walnut angel food cake with sorghum
syrup, 226–29

creamy Maytag blue cheesecakes with
walnuts in rosemary honey, 254–56

gingered maple walnut sauce, 42–43

maple walnut jammies, 316–18

walnut pastry dough, 33–34

Water baths, about, 22

Whipped cream, 63–64

Whipping, about, 201, 202

Whisks, about, 20

White chocolate cream, 67

chocolate strawberry shortcakes with,
135–36

Wine

fall fruits poached in brandied lemon
syrup, 159–60

Fig Newton Zinfandel tart, 97–98

peppered Bartlett pears in sherry syrup,
160–62

pumpkin cognac cheesecake brûlée, 247–49

raspberry red wine sauce, 48–49

ruby port ice cream, 268

winter fruits poached in red wine syrup,
157–58

Winter fruits poached in red wine syrup,
157–58

Wire strainers, about, 19

Zesters, about, 21